I0797310

FOREVER PRESIDENT

FOREVER PRESIDENT

A BIOGRAPHY OF KIM IL SUNG

MICHAEL J. SETH

REAKTION BOOKS

Published by
REAKTION BOOKS LTD
2–4 Sebastian Street
London EC1V 0HE, UK
www.reaktionbooks.co.uk

First published 2025

EU GPSR Authorised Representative
Logos Europe, 9 rue Nicolas Poussin, 17000, La Rochelle, France
email: contact@logoseurope.eu

Printed and bound in Great Britain by Bell & Bain, Glasgow

A catalogue record for this book is available from the British Library

ISBN 978 1 83639 104 3

CONTENTS

PREFACE

Kim Il Sung was the leader of North Korea for almost half a century. He emerged as the de facto leader of the Soviet zone of Korea in 1945, and when it became the Democratic People's Republic of Korea in 1948 he served at its helm until his death in 1994, one of the longest dictatorships in modern history. During most of that time he was its unchallenged absolute ruler, and he built a society that reflected his vision. Kim's aim was to unify Korea and make it a modern, industrial, prosperous nation that would be strong enough to protect its independence and able to take its place among the ranks of progressive countries. He mostly failed to achieve this aim. He failed to unify Korea and instead turned North Korea into a strange cult-state that remains among the most isolated and totalitarian in the world, and one that was at the time of his death an international pariah on the brink of a mass famine. However, uniquely among modern dictators he carefully planned for his succession, and the system and cult he created and the family that it centres on still rules unchallenged more than thirty years after his death.

Yet for all his importance, writing about Kim Il Sung is a challenge. The state he did so much to bring about is the most closed, most secretive in the world, and it is especially secretive about the ruling elite. Information about Kim Il Sung and his family is often difficult to obtain. The archives are sealed, and the very isolation of the state meant there were few outside observers who were privy to inside developments during or after his lifetime. A principal source comes from defectors, but few of these were high enough in rank to have much access to information about him or his inner circle. Much of his life, therefore, remains a mystery. We do not know for certain the dates of his marriages, how many children he had or even the year of birth of his eldest son and successor, Kim Jong Il. Therefore, this account of Kim Il Sung's life, rather than detailing his private affairs, focuses on his public life and seeks to put it in the context of the times he lived in.

The North Korea that Kim Il Sung did so much to create and which his family still rules is a bizarre and menacing presence in the world. It has also been one of history's starkest examples of how political leadership and policies can impact a society. Few societies sharing a border offer a greater contrast than the two Koreas. On one side of the Korean Demilitarized Zone (DMZ) that separates them is secretive, isolated, repressive North Korea, where much of the population suffers malnutrition; on the other is South Korea, a vibrant democracy that is among the world's most prosperous nations and a global centre of popular culture. Yet in 1945 they were one people, with the same history and culture, arbitrarily divided by outside powers into two states with two different political systems and geopolitical orientations. There is no historical precedent for such a homogeneous population evolving in less than three generations into such different societies. How this happened and how to understand North Korea are the questions behind this book. Its hope is that a better understanding of Kim Il Sung and who he was, and how he managed to build such an unusual state, will help us to answer them.

This book is based mostly on published scholarship in English and Korean. It is indebted to those who have patiently gone through the vast body of official publications and have scrutinized whatever sources are available to uncover what we know about Kim Il Sung. Some day, when North Korea collapses or perhaps transitions to a more open society, and the archives and other information become more accessible, we may learn a great deal more about Kim Il Sung. Most likely, we will need to revise much that has been written here. It is the hope of this author that, for the sake of both the people of North Korea and the world, that day comes soon. Until then we need to understand Kim Il Sung and the state he built.

A Note on Sources

North Korea is the most secretive society in the world, and reliable information about its leadership is so hard to come by that there is much we cannot be certain of. Reliable information on Kim Il Sung's private life is equally difficult to obtain. So his biography must rely heavily on his public activities. However, these are not well documented for his early years. As a result much of my account of this time relies on his autobiography, *With the Century*, written in his last years. Although eight volumes long, it stops in 1945, when he was 33 years old. He died in 1994 before completing the rest, and the last volumes were published posthumously. Much of its content is self-promoting propaganda; some of it is pure fabrication that is easy to dismiss. But some can be verified by other sources, and it does provide revealing information about his early years that cannot be found elsewhere, even in the many official biographies.

A Note on Romanization

Writing Korean names and terms in the Latin alphabet is a challenge since the Korean language has a very different sound system from English or other European languages. This book mostly follows the Revised Romanization system for writing Korean names and terms. This is the system that was officially adopted by the South Korean government in 2000 and has since become increasingly standard, although many academic works still use the older McCune-Reischauer system. It might be added that neither of these systems are commonly used in North Korea, which has not developed a consistent method of romanization. The exception to following Revised Romanization is for names and terms that have come into common use in English, such as Kim Il Sung (instead of Kim Ilseong).

1
EXILED YOUTH

KIM IL SUNG was born Kim Seongju in the village of Mangyeongdae, outside Pyongyang, on 15 April 1912, the day the *Titanic* sank. Around 1935 he adopted the name Kim Il Sung (Kim Ilseong), which means 'sun-star'. The Korea that Kim was born into was an exceptionally old political and cultural entity. As a unified state Korea dates to the seventh century, when Silla (pronounced *shilla*), one of three kingdoms that competed for supremacy on the peninsula with two rival states, Baekje and Goguryeo, emerged victorious in 676.[1] Thereafter, except for a brief period in the early tenth century, one state governed most or all of the Korean Peninsula. The northern border fluctuated somewhat, but since the early 1400s Korea has looked on the map very much as it does today. When the country was partitioned in 1945 it ended thirteen centuries of unity. Few states in the twentieth century were as old or had such stable boundaries. It was also homogeneous to an unusual degree. A variety of peoples had settled in the peninsula, but they had become a single ethnolinguistic group long before the twentieth century. North Korea today is still arguably the world's most ethnically uniform society.

As a people, Koreans were set apart from their neighbours. While China had a profound influence on their society, Koreans maintained a distinctive culture with their own dress, folk traditions, art and customs, their own unique alphabet developed in the fifteenth century, and their own cultural identity. They spoke a language not closely related to any other. Their houses, with heated paper floors, were different from their neighbours', as was their spicy cuisine. Korea was also unusual in another way. Until the late nineteenth century there were no significant Korean communities outside the boundaries of the state, so that it was, uncommonly, a land where political, linguistic, ethnic and cultural boundaries were nearly the same.

Korean history was also characterized by a high degree of historical continuity. Three dynasties ruled from 676 to 1910 without radical change in the state's basic institutions. In the Silla period it was led by the Kim royal family. In 935 a new dynasty came to power and ruled the state from Kaesong in what is now North Korea. They renamed the state Goryeo (Koryo); it is where the English name of the country 'Korea' is derived. After nearly five hundred years the Yi dynasty came to power in 1392, renaming the state Joseon (the name used for the country by North Korea today), and ruled for another five centuries. The new dynasty moved the capital to Seoul and remained on the throne until the Japanese annexed Korea in 1910. Only the intrusion of foreign imperialism and the Japanese takeover brought a break in history, and even then the old aristocratic lineages controlled much of the countryside until the land reforms after 1945.

Korea in the nineteenth century was not only one of the oldest and most homogeneous societies found anywhere, but one of the most isolated. Except on official missions to China and the rare ones to Japan, Koreans were forbidden to leave the country. Foreigners were totally prohibited from entering. When a Dutch ship was stranded on the coast in the seventeenth century, its crew were given Korean wives and government jobs; however, they were not allowed to leave. When some French priests smuggled themselves into the country in the nineteenth century, they were executed. There were two exceptions to this prohibition of foreign visitors. The imperial court of China sent diplomatic missions to the country. These followed a prescribed route that avoided cities and towns; they were not to have any unauthorized contact with locals, entered Seoul through a special gate and were confined to a walled compound. Japanese merchants were allowed to trade in Busan but were also confined to a special walled compound, where they met with only authorized merchants. In this respect it was very much like Kim Il Sung's North Korean state.

Korea in the Joseon period was a rigidly hierarchical society with a centralized government. It was dominated by a hereditary aristocracy called the *yangban*, whose wealth was derived from ownership of land: not big estates but scattered parcels mostly worked by tenant farmers. Their status was derived from their ancient lineages and secured by serving the state as civil officials. To become an official involved years of study and then success in the state-administered examinations. Once a *yangban* became an official, he could not serve in his home area, thus promoting the centralized nature of the system. The Joseon state promoted and enforced adherence to Neo-Confucianism – a form of Confucianism derived from eleventh- and twelfth-century China but given a strict interpretation that was unique to Korea. Nowhere else did such a conservative, rigid and intolerant form of Confucianism prevail. In this way too the Korean state in the nineteenth century resembled North Korea under Kim: centralized, imposing a strict ideological orthodoxy and very hierarchical. But in some ways it differed from later North Korea. The ruling class were not only administrators and enforcers of orthodoxy but poets, artists, gentlemen of refined culture and taste. And, for all their Confucian orthodoxy, earlier religious practices – Buddhism and shamanism – survived if not flourished. It differed in another way, too: although it was a monarchy, the rulers were in practice constrained by institutions such as the Censorate, which reviewed the conduct of the king and his officials, and by custom. Joseon kings were far short of the all-wise, godlike figure that Kim was to become.

Korea's opening to the modern world of imperialism, nationalism, industrialization and modern science was a shock that it was not prepared for. Although at first it resisted French and American intrusions, it opened itself up to trade and diplomacy in the face of Japanese gunboats in 1876. Relations with the United States began in 1882, and those with other nations soon followed. Many Koreans were quick to grasp the need for reform if the nation was to survive, but efforts were complicated by a three-way struggle for control over the country by the empires that encircled it: a declining Chinese empire seeking to control its periphery, an expanding Russian empire seeking warm-water ports, and a new rising Japanese empire seeking to control the land bridge that connected it with the rest of Asia. The Japanese defeated China in a war over Korea, the Sino-Japanese War in 1894–5. Its key battle was fought in Kim's home town of Pyongyang, where Koreans had a ringside seat to view the spectacle of modern warfare. A decade later the Japanese defeated Russia in the Russo-Japanese War (1904–5), another war for supremacy in the peninsula. After its victory over Russia in 1905, Japan effectively controlled Korea. In 1910 the Japanese forced the last monarch of Korea to abdicate, and the ancient kingdom came to an end.

If there is one thing that almost all Koreans today, North and South, can agree on, it is that Japan's rule was a brutally oppressive national humiliation. The Japanese saw themselves as modernizers, lifting Korea out of centuries of isolation, feudalism and backwardness. But like most imperialists they ruled with their own self-interest foremost and with an arrogant sense of superiority over their subjects. Their occupation was initially met with violent resistance. Tokyo responded by creating a gendarmerie to control the population, carrying out arrests of thousands for political offences and closing most Korean-language schools, publications and organizations. Their colonial rule, headed by an all-powerful governor-general, always a general or admiral, took on the character of a military occupation. This was the Korea that Kim was born into.

All of this, the shock of the country's backwardness and weakness, and its victimization at the hands of grasping imperialist powers made a deep impression on the young Kim. Like most of his generation he was bitterly ashamed of what the ruling *yangban* aristocratic elite and the monarchy let happen. Later he wrote, 'While other people were travelling the world by warship and by train, our country's feudal rulers rode on donkeys and wore horse-hair hats, singing of scenic beauties.'[2]

Kim Il Sung was born on the outskirts of Pyongyang, a city that was undergoing rapid modernization. Pyongyang is located about 110 kilometres (68 mi.) from the mouth of the broad, navigable Daedong river, in the middle of a relatively large, level patch of arable land. The region was the most important agricultural centre in the northern half of Korea, and Pyongyang was the largest city. It was also a very ancient city, with origins that are slightly obscure: it was the capital of the Gojoseon (Old Joseon) state from 194 BCE to its conquest by an invading Chinese army in 108 BCE, and it became the capital of the Goguryeo kingdom in the fifth century. After the unification of Korea in the seventh century it remained an important regional centre, serving as a sort of sub-capital from the tenth to the fourteenth century and was downgraded to a provincial capital after the establishment of the Joseon dynasty in 1392. In the late nineteenth and early twentieth century it was the second largest city in Korea, although much smaller than Seoul. Although political, economic, cultural and intellectual life was concentrated in Seoul, Pyongyang was significant as a centre of education and intellectual activity.

Kim's family were Christians. Pyongyang was the centre of Christianity on the peninsula, sometimes called the 'Jerusalem of the East' owing to its substantial Protestant community and the large number of Christian mission schools. The educated elite in Pyongyang often felt they were discriminated against by southerners, and the city was the site of a short-lived rebellion against the dynasty in the early 1860s. Partly for that reason, when foreign missionaries arrived in Korea in the 1880s they found Pyongyang to be fertile ground for the reception of Christianity. Korea's Christian community, many educated by foreign, mostly American Protestant missionaries, were more open to Western ideas, more active in progressive movements than most Koreans, and often saw themselves as agents for modernization and national renewal. They were influential beyond their modest numbers. Although at the time of Kim's birth Korean Christians made up less than 3 per cent of the country's population, they formed a disproportionate number of nationalist activists as well as members of modernizing reform movements. Most were willing to accept the reality of Japanese rule, at least for the present, and work for reform within the system, but some became involved in anti-Japanese activities.

Kim Il Sung's Family

Kim Il Sung was the eldest of three sons. His father, Kim Hyeongjik (1894–1926), was married to Kang Banseok (1892–1932). Family was always important for Kim. He attributed his own ideals and successes to his parents and other members of this family. Later he built monuments and memorials to them and had their virtues extolled in the history books, and his memoirs written towards the end of his life are filled with praise for them and exaggerated accounts of their deeds. In this respect he was very different from other communist dictators such as Vladimir Lenin, Joseph Stalin or Mao Zedong. In power, he filled key positions with family members and established a family dynasty when he prepared his eldest son to be his successor. Koreans often keep track of their lineage over many generations, and Kim as a young man learned the story of his. It traced its origins back twelve generations to North Jeolla Province, a productive rice-growing region of the southwest. The family came to the north and settled in Mangyeongdae, where Kim's great-grandfather Kim Ungu (Eungu) (1848–1878) became a tenant farmer, growing crops on the fields of a rich landowner, Yi Pyeongtaek, in return for taking care of the man's ancestral graves.

Although Kim wildly inflated their importance and at times fabricated their achievements, his family members were actively involved in the nationalist, anti-imperialist movements. Every North Korean knows the story of Kim's great-grandfather and his role in the *General Sherman* incident. In August 1866 a heavily armed American ship, the *General Sherman*, with a crew of Americans, Chinese, Malays and British, sailed up the Daedong river to Pyongyang seeking to open trade. A local official explained that the country was closed to trade with foreigners, but the ship ignored his request to leave. After tense negotiations led to an exchange of fire between the crew and locals, the Koreans burned the ship, which caught on a sandbar, and killed its crew. North Koreans regard the *General Sherman* incident as the beginning of the modern era of imperialist intervention into their country, part of the larger effort by the West to pry open Korea to foreign trade, investment and missionary activity and ultimately to subjugation. The resistance to the *General Sherman*, they learn, was the very inception of the modern Korean anti-imperialist movement.

There is more to the story. For a while the Americans did not know what had happened to the ship. The government in Seoul informed the Chinese of the incident, and through the Chinese, Washington eventually learned of its fate. In 1871 the U.S. minister to China, Frederick Low, led five ships and 1,200 men under Admiral John Rodgers on a punitive expedition. The Americans attacked the island of Ganghwa and some coastal forts. The Koreans fought to the death, inflicting a few casualties on the Americans. Without authorization to proceed further, and frustrated by the Koreans' refusal to talk, Low and Rodgers withdrew. The government was proud to have driven off the barbarians, especially since they had resisted a French putative expedition five years earlier that had come to avenge the execution of French Catholic missionaries. Daewongun, father and regent to the boy king Gojong (r. 1864–1907), erected stone signs that proclaimed: 'Western barbarians invade our land. If we do not fight, we must then appease them. To urge appeasement is to betray the nation.'[3]

North Koreans learn that Kim's great-grandfather Kim Ungu was involved in the attack on the *General Sherman*. In later accounts his role is described as taking the lead in organizing villagers and destroying the ship. He is also credited with heading a successful effort to drive off a U.S. warship, the *Shenandoah*, two years later. There are contemporary Korean accounts of the *General Sherman* incident, but they make no reference to Kim Ungu. It is possible that he was involved in some way, but hardly as a leader or organizer of the destruction of the ship and its crew. It is more likely that Kim Il Sung invented the story of his great-grandfather so that his family could occupy a leadership role in the very birth of the modern anti-imperialist movement.[4] It made him part of what North Koreans call the 'revolutionary lineage': a line of heroic defenders of the Korean nation. Kim Il Sung, in fighting the Japanese and resisting the U.S. imperialists, claimed to be simply carrying on a family tradition. Curiously, Kim towards the end of his life presented a more modest account of his great-grandfather's role. In his autobiography he simply states, 'I was told that my great-grandfather played a major role in this attack.'[5]

Kim's paternal grandfather was Kim Bohyeon, born in 1871. His father Kim Ungu died when he was seven, and he went to live with an uncle. Some official accounts have him joining his father in attacking the *General Sherman* even though he was not born yet. He is, however, celebrated in official publications as much for his dedication to his three daughters and three sons as for his patriotism. According to Kim Il Sung, he was a poor farmer who supported his sons and daughters by collecting human manure for fertilizer. He got up early while everyone was still sleeping to do so, and he supplemented his meagre income by staying up at night making straw sandals by lamplight.[6] Unlike Kim's parents, his grandfather Kim Bohyeon lived to see his grandson become the leader of North Korea;

he was buried in the Revolutionary Martyrs' Cemetery in Pyongyang following his death in 1955.

Kim Il Sung remembered his grandmother fondly. She was proud of her son, Kim's father, for attending the prestigious Sungsil Middle School, and collected and sold shellfish to help pay his tuition. The school was a long walk from where they lived. They were too poor to afford a clock, so she would wake up before dawn and listen for the clock to strike in a neighbour's house and then rouse her son from sleep, get his lunch and send him off.[7]

What we know of Kim's father, Kim Hyeongjik, who died in 1926 when Kim was only fourteen, is mostly based on his adoring son's accounts written decades later. At the age of seventeen he was admitted to Sungsil Middle School (the term 'middle school' is a bit misleading and might be better translated as 'secondary school'). He was still a student, only eighteen years old, when Kim Il Sung was born.[8] The entire family helped pay his tuition, including one of his younger brothers, who also made straw sandals to sell.[9] Founded in 1897 by American Presbyterian missionaries in Pyongyang, Sungsil had a good reputation as a place where a boy could receive a modern education, and like other reputable Christian missionary schools it produced many active and prominent nationalists and reformers. Kim's father appears to have been a good Christian who as a youth attended church every Sunday. That his father was educated in an American missionary school was a little awkward for the later Kim, who insisted that his father quarrelled with the 'American imperialists' at the school, expressing anger at them for their exploitation of his country. We have no way of knowing if any of this is true.[10] Kim wrote that his father was an excellent student in school and an outstanding athlete; he won many athletic competitions, but lost the high jump when his pigtail was caught in a cross piece.[11] After graduating, Hyeongjik taught at two schools. But, according to his son, his real occupation was being a revolutionary, fighting for Korea's independence.

North Korean histories present Kim Hyeongjik as a major nationalist figure, the founder of the Korean Nationalist Association, a nationwide anti-Japanese independence organization. Since it was the largest nationalist organization at the time, this would indeed make Kim's father a very important nationalist leader. This, we know, is false, since Japanese police records indicate that the Korean Nationalist Association was established by Chang In-hwan (Jang Inhwan), an associate of Hawaii-based nationalist leader Pak Yongman.[12] In any case it was also a less important vehicle for the nationalist movement than is portrayed in North Korean histories. It is not known for certain, but it is very probable that Kim Hyeongjik was at least a member of the association. In contrast to many official histories published in North Korea, in his own autobiography Kim does not depict his father as the leader of the nationalist movement in Korea, but as an important nationalist figure who had contacts throughout Korea and Manchuria. There is no clear evidence, however, to support even this claim. Most likely he was an active but minor figure in the underground nationalist movement. Kim Hyeongjik's importance lies in the influence he had on his son. Kim credited his father with instilling patriotism in him, and with encouraging him to win back his country from the Japanese imperialists.

While Kim greatly inflated their importance, his family's nationalist credentials are in fact verifiable. Kim Hyeongjik had two brothers, Hyeongnok and Hyeonggwon. Hyeongnok was, according to Kim, a patriot beaten by the Japanese for not changing his name to a Japanese one when the colonial regime began to order Koreans to do so.[13] Hyeonggwon, the youngest brother, whose activities appear in Japanese police records, was arrested after being involved in a skirmish in the town of Hongwon. He spent his last days in Seodaemun Prison in Seoul, where he died in 1936. Kim later erected a monument to him outside Hongwon.[14] Kim claimed his uncle's death was caused by torture.[15] If so, he would be one of many

Koreans who died from mistreatment in Japan's notorious colonial prisons.

North Korean histories also praise Kim's maternal family for their great patriotism. A whole cult has been built around his mother, Kang Banseok. She came from a farm family in the village of Chilgol, not far from Mangyeongdae. Official accounts leave out that it was a family of devout Christians. In fact her name means 'rock' and is said to have been derived from St Peter, the 'rock' upon which the early Christian Church was built. Although two years older than her husband, she was nevertheless only twenty years old when her first child, Kim Il Sung, was born and only forty when she died in 1932. The Kang family were prominent members of the Presbyterian Church and served as its clerics and church elders as well as teachers and schoolmasters. It is not known why she was married to a man from a less prominent family, the son of a grave keeper. But marriages were arranged, so her family might have considered marriage into another devout Christian family appropriate.[16] Long after her death her family members played a prominent role in North Korea's power structure and were informally referred to as the 'Chilgol faction'. However, they never reached the top rungs of power as did members of Kim's paternal line.

Kang Banseok was not known to have been active in the independence movement. However, years after her death she was raised to the level of a revolutionary hero. In fact in 1967 she became the first member of Kim's family to have her own cult of personality. State propaganda organs began calling her the 'Mother of Korea', a title she later shared with Kim's first wife, Kim Jong Suk. Kim built a museum dedicated to his mother outside Pyongyang; another was dedicated to his father.

Kim Seongju, to use his birth name, was the eldest of three sons. Cheolju, four years younger, also became an anti-Japanese guerilla fighter. According to Kim, Cheolju wanted to join his older brother as a guerilla fighter when he was only sixteen, but Kim refused to allow it, since he was too young. But Cheolju joined the guerillas anyway and was killed in a clash with the Japanese in 1935. He was only nineteen. Kim later felt some responsibility for his death, believing that if he had let his brother accompany him, he could have protected him.[17] His other younger brother, Yeongju (born in 1920), did not become a guerilla fighter but instead went to Moscow State University, where he graduated with a degree in economics. Yeongju later became a key figure in the North Korean regime. Kim even toyed with the idea of making him his successor.

Kim and Korean Nationalism

The intense anti-Japanese sentiment that Kim displays in his memoirs and which he attributes to his family members was not unusual. The Japanese colonial regime was hated by most Koreans. Of course, not every Korean hated the Japanese; some, including many *yangban* landowners, found benefits in supporting the regime. But Korea was a bit atypical among most colonial societies: modern concepts of nationalism spread from the educated elite to much of the population far more quickly than in most other colonies, the level of hostility to the colonial regime was unusually high, and resentment and hatred towards their former colonizers has remained strong three generations after liberation. There were several reasons for this. Japanese rule was direct and especially harsh, more like a military occupation, with a policeman in every village. Unlike most colonies in Asia and Africa that were ruled by distant foreigners, Koreans were ruled by a next-door neighbour who had invaded them in the past. They already had a history of distrust and resentment towards Japan, and the Japanese rulers compounded this resentment by carrying out a policy of forced assimilation in the 1930s and early 1940s that required Koreans to change their names to Japanese ones, worship at Shinto shrines and speak Japanese. Another factor was that unlike colonies such as Indonesia, India, Nigeria or the Philippines, Korea was a pre-existing state, not one created by the imperialists, and it was an ethnically homogeneous society. Furthermore, historically isolated Koreans had little experience of living with and dealing with foreigners, let alone being ruled by them.

Events of 1919

When he was seven two events exposed the young Kim to the political world. In 1919 his father Kim Hyeongjik was arrested by the Japanese for anti-government activities. This would not have been an unusual occurrence: thousands of Koreans spent time in detention for political reasons in the colonial police state. Graduates of foreign missionary schools were especially troublesome for the Japanese since they were disproportionately represented among nationalist activists. The details of his arrest are not known for certain. While in jail, according to his son, he refused the help of his family to secure a lawyer, declaring instead that he would defend himself. The seven-year-old Kim visited his father in prison with his mother; he later recalled this as being one of the most important events of his youth as it gave him a lesson in the cruelty of the Japanese. He was horrified at his father's appearance: 'His face, neck, hands, feet and all the rest of his body were scarred and wounded.'[18] Fortunately, his father was released after less than a year.

At about the same time, the young Kim experienced another event he credits as having shaped his future as a revolutionary. The March First Movement of 1919 was part of a wave of excitement and anti-colonial activity that spread across the world, from Egypt to China. This wave was sparked by the end of the First World War, the ensuing Paris Peace conference and U.S. President Woodrow Wilson's principle of 'national self-determination' set forth in his Fourteen Points. While Wilson's formulation was intended to apply only to Europeans, like so many non-Western colonial subjects Koreans seized upon this principle of self-determination to call for their own independent nation. A small group of educated Koreans, half of them Christians like Kim's parents, met in Seoul to read a symbolic 'Declaration of Independence' calling for the end of Japanese rule. News of this modest event ignited demonstrations in Seoul that quickly spread across the country. Koreans of all social classes – farmers, workers, middle-class professionals – men and women in every city and province participated. It is estimated that between 500,000 and 1 million people out of a country of 14 million participated in the rallies and protest marches, which continued throughout the spring. Although the protests were peaceful, the Japanese authorities reacted violently, killing hundreds and jailing tens of thousands; some of the detained were tortured to death. Pyongyang in the spring of 1919 saw many of these demonstrations. Kim wrote later that, while his father was still in jail, he participated in marches, accompanied by his mother and other family members. This seems very likely. He also claims to have seen many demonstrators shot or struck down with swords by the Japanese police, although this may be a later embellishment.[19]

The March First Movement was a turning point in modern Korean nationalism. The new ethnolinguistic nationalism symbolized using the indigenous Korean Hangeul script, the writing of national history, and the use of foreign borrowed terms like 'nation' and 'nation-state' fused with the popular resentment of Japanese rule. No longer was modern nationalism limited to discussions among intellectuals and the small minority of Christians educated in mission schools; it was now a popular, shared sentiment that bound the Korean people together. In Tokyo the government was surprised at the extent of the hatred its rule had created and embarrassed by the international publicity Japanese brutality had generated. A new, more liberal, pro-Western administration that came to power that year carried out some reforms of its colonial administration in Korea, allowing for some freedom for Koreans to form cultural organizations and print newspapers in their language, and it created a separate but theoretically equal school system for Koreans that allowed them to advance beyond primary school. Japanese schoolteachers in Korea no longer wore swords, and a governor-general from the more liberal navy was put in charge. These did not change the basic reality of Korea's foreign occupation but allowed some space for Korean nationalists to operate within the country if they did not challenge Japanese rule.

But the young Kim did not participate in this relatively liberal period of colonial rule, which began in about 1920 and ended in the early 1930s. Upon his release from jail in 1919, Kim Hyeongjik moved with his wife and children to Manchuria. He was not alone in making this decision; the number of Koreans crossing into Manchuria or going into exile elsewhere accelerated from 1919. While the colonial administration pursued a more tolerant policy towards moderate Korean nationalists who agreed to work within the narrow range of allowable activities, the Japanese Thought Police continue to arrest and torture more outspoken or militant nationalists.

Manchuria

When Kim's family moved to Manchuria they joined thousands of other Koreans, mostly from the north, who crossed into what was a frontier area. Once a sparsely populated part of the Chinese Empire that was preserved as a homeland for the Manchu ethnic minority, it was opened to massive Chinese settlement only after 1860. Despite its harsh winters Manchuria had ample fertile plains, but most Koreans settled in the hilly or mountainous areas in the southeast, adjacent to Korea. Manchuria loomed large for many Koreans as well as for Japanese as a frontier, a land of great open spaces and opportunities. Japanese nationalists sought to make Manchuria a central part of an expanding empire; gaining control over the area was a high priority. For some Korean nationalists, Manchuria, in particular its southern regions, was part of their ancient homeland. The

Goguryeo kingdom that emerged in the first centuries CE was based there before expanding into the territory of present-day North Korea. However, it was not a nationalist zeal to reclaim their ancient homeland that motivated most Koreans to settle there, but poverty and the desire to escape Japanese rule.

Korean emigration to Manchuria began in the late nineteenth century when a small trickle of Koreans crossed over the Yalu or Tumen rivers that marked the border with Korea and settled there. The number of emigrants began to accelerate after Korea's annexation by Japan in 1910. In 1920 some 400,000 Koreans were living there; in 1931, on the eve of the Japanese takeover of Manchuria, the number had grown to 900,000, and by 1945 it was 2 million.[20] Most, like Kim's family, came from northern Korea. The largest area of Korean settlement in Manchuria was Kando (Jiandao in Chinese) in eastern Manchuria, just north of the Tumen river border with Hamgyeong province of northeast Korea, where Koreans made up the majority of the population. Today this region, known as Yanbian, remains a Korean autonomous prefecture within the People's Republic of China; signs in the main city, Yanji, are in Korean and Chinese. It was fertile ground for recruiting anti-Japanese resistance fighters, and it became an important base for guerilla operations. The large Korean community there was also of concern for the Chinese, since there was always the fear that the Japanese could annex it to Korea.

In 1929–30 the famed Sinologist Owen Lattimore travelled throughout Manchuria on a research grant. Lattimore noted the 'spectacular immigration' of the country, mostly by Chinese but also by some Koreans and a smaller number of Japanese. He frequently commented on the frontier-like nature of Manchuria, which compared to the American West as it was being colonized. Banditry was 'endemic', especially so in the borderlands of Korea.[21] Lattimore admired the Koreans' skill at farming this land; they were adept at growing rice in an area previously considered too cold for it. But he also noted that they contributed to the violent nature of the area. 'A great proportion of the Koreans are revolutionaries and anti-Japanese,' he wrote, 'having for that reason migrated from Korean into Chinese territory.'[22] He also noted, 'Numbers of them were enthusiasts for the Russian type of revolution.'[23]

The southeast region, where Koreans settled and Kim would fight the Japanese, was ideal for banditry as well as for guerilla warfare. It was a hilly, densely forested landscape with many caves and some rugged mountains. Chinese *honghuzi* (red beard) bandits as well as Korean ones kidnapped and held richer residents for ransom.[24] Lattimore calls them 'Robin Hood' bandits, but they preyed on the poor as well, with Korean bandits stealing even food from Korean settlers.[25] The Chinese in Manchuria made little headway in imposing order in much of the region. Before the twentieth century it was considered an 'empty zone', although it was never really empty; traders, tiger hunters, ginseng gatherers and others lived there.[26] The Chinese state never established effective administrative control over it, which meant that local armed groups could operate without much government interference. It was an ideal place for waging guerilla warfare and attracted Korean resistance fighters, who started entering the area after the Japanese annexation in 1910.

Manchuria was nominally part of the Republic of China, established on 1 January 1912, but during the time Kim lived there it was an autonomous region ruled by a warlord, Zhang Zuolin. Zhang Zuolin swore loyalty to the newly established Nationalist (Guomindang) government in 1928, shortly after it established itself in the new capital of Nanjing, but he still controlled the region. That same year he was assassinated, and his son Zhang Xueliang drew closer to the increasingly anti-Japanese Nationalist government in Nanjing, a factor in the Japanese decision to seize control over the region in 1931.

Kim's Life in Manchuria

Kim Hyoengjik and his family did not venture far into Manchuria but like most Koreans settled in a small village near the Korean border. After a short time they moved to another town, Badagou, on the Yalu river across from Korea. There Kim's father worked as a Chinese herbal doctor, although this was far from his experience as a schoolteacher. How and why he chose this profession and where he received his training is not clear. According to one source he got a friend to get him a licence. Kim's own account suggests that his father's herbal medicine business was merely a cover for his political activities. Kim Il Sung attended elementary school in Badagou for four years. Interestingly, it was a Chinese-language school; apparently, there was no Korean-language school available. Our main source from this period is Kim Il Sung's memoirs. In these he writes that his father went to a small church, which was where the revolutionaries met. He states that since his father was an important revolutionary, 'many secret agents and plainclothes policemen were sent' to arrest him, but he would manage somehow to slip away.[27] According to his account, while attending school the young Kim helped his father with his revolutionary activities by running errands for him. Every other day, for example, he was sent to the post office to collect Korean newspapers and magazines.[28]

Kim's Return to Korea

At the age of eleven, Kim Il Sung was sent by his father back to Korea, where he lived for a little less than two years. According to the official biographies and his own autobiography, the purpose of sending him back was so that he could learn about oppression in Korea. This journey is celebrated in North Korea as the 'One Thousand *Ri* Journey for Learning' (*Baeum ui cheolli gil*).[29] More likely, his father sent him there to study in Pyongyang at a school where Kang Donuk, his mother's father, a teacher of Chinese characters and the Bible, was vice principal.[30] There he could be instructed in Korean. According to Kim's later retelling of the story, it was a 400-kilometre (250 mi.) journey to the Pyongyang area. Much of it he made on foot. His father had given him a map and a list of places he could stay, and he was helped along the way by members of his father's network of friends and fellow independence fighters. In fact Kim's story is less about boasting what a brave, resourceful eleven-year-old he was than about memorializing his father. Kim claimed his father had such a high reputation and fame among the underground nationalists that such a journey was made possible through the support of their network. After fourteen days he arrived at his mother's home town of Chilgol, where he stayed with his maternal grandparents and studied at his grandfather's Changdok School.

While studying, Kim received first-hand lessons on the evils of imperialism. He observed the poverty and the subservient status of Koreans in their own country, noting the contrast between the modern neighbourhoods with their fine homes of Japanese and American residents in Pyongyang and the shabbier section where the Koreans lived.[31] Writing sixty years later, in the early 1990s, he states that the younger generation of his society cannot 'imagine the poverty' of that time. He was angered over the mandatory classes in the language of the colonial occupiers. His sense of patriotism grew. His fifth-grade Japanese textbook was titled *Mother Tongue*. He scratched out the title and wrote 'Japanese', defiantly declaring Korean was his mother tongue.[32] To help his fellow compatriots he taught night classes for the poor, or so he claims. He also had another first-hand experience in Japanese oppression. An uncle had been arrested by the Japanese for nationalist activities, and the entire family was under police surveillance.

Towards the end of 1924, after less than two years in Korea, he learned that his father had been arrested again. At this news he went back to Manchuria. This return trek is what North Koreans call the

'One Thousand *Ri* Journey for Liberation' (*Gwangbok ui cheolli gil*). At this point, North Koreans are taught, the young Kim 'knew the reality of his homeland, marched across the snowy mountains, [and] on [his] way back across the Amnok River made a resolve to liberate his country at any cost'.[33] Now fully aware of the situation in his homeland, the standard narrative goes, he began his lifelong quest to liberate it from the Japanese and build a great, independent nation. He was still only twelve.

Back in Manchuria

The crisis that led to his return was resolved when his father was released and returned to his revolutionary activities. Back in Badagou, Kim resumed his elementary education. His memoirs narrate the games he and his childhood friends played; he was always the leader. At one point they were playing in a shed where the revolutionaries were storing arms and accidentally set off an explosion, slightly injuring one of the boys. To avoid arousing suspicion, his father hid the boy for twenty days until the wounds healed.[34]

The family moved to Jilin, a major urban centre. Kim went to Hwaseong Uisuk School, a two-year military and political school founded in 1925 for the purpose of training cadres for the Korean Independence Army. But he dropped out after a while. He explains in his memoirs that its education was 'outmoded': much of his schooling consisted of military drills such as running with sandbags tied to his legs. Furthermore, he wrote, the headmaster was corrupt and used tuition money to finance a private wedding.[35] He ended up at Yuwen Middle School, another Chinese-language institution in the city.

North Korean biographies omit the fact that Kim mainly went to Chinese-language schools, but his own autobiography is more open about it. When the eighty-year-old dictator wrote his memoirs, it was the first time this was ever publicly acknowledged. He writes that he went to a Chinese elementary school because there was not a Korean one available and took private Korean lessons at night from his father.[36] Later his fluency in Chinese was an asset as a revolutionary working with the Chinese and as a leader seeking aid from Beijing.

Jilin was an important city, a crossroads that was the centre of political activity in the 1920s. In 1927 Kim had an opportunity to hear a lecture by the visiting Korean nationalist An Changho. An was one of the best-known figures in the independence movement. Based in Hawaii, he travelled to the scattered Korean exile communities with his message of non-violent resistance to the Japanese and of the need for Koreans to educate and modernize themselves for the day that they received their independence. His gradual approach to independence had no appeal to the young Kim, however; rather, it only reaffirmed his belief that his country's liberation could only be achieved by armed struggle, not cultivation of the self.[37]

It was in Jilin that Kim got his first exposure to communism. He claims to have become interested in Marxism-Leninism not long after entering middle school, borrowing books from a library and educating himself in the ideology.[38] He writes in his autobiography that at the age of fourteen he was already giving lectures to his fellow students on *Das Kapital*, and at that time, in 1926, he organized the Down-With Imperialism League, an anti-imperialist student organization. Both assertions are likely fabrications, but his political activism while a student is attested from police documents.[39] In 1928 he was involved in a student strike against 'reactionary teachers'.[40] In October that year he probably participated in an anti-Japanese demonstration set off by the announcement of a Japanese plan to build a highway to connect the city with the southern areas of Manchuria controlled by Tokyo.[41] What is less clear is how well he understood Marxism-Leninism, then or even later. What rings truer is his anti-Japanese sentiments, which he would have shared with most of those around him. A curious story provided in his autobiography deals with matches. The Manchuria he grew up with was flooded with Japanese-manufactured goods. But there was a popular Korean-made 'Monkey' brand of matches that competed successfully with Japanese ones. The Japanese got hold of shipments of these matches and soaked them in water, then repacked them. When customers found they would not light, they stopped buying them, and so, having 'monkeyed around' with them, the imperialists undermined the reputation of Monkey matches.[42] To Kim the story symbolized the Japanese effort to block the Korean people from making progress and keep them forever in a subservient, dependent state.

Not long after the family moved to Jilin, Kim's father Kim Hyeongjik died aged only 31. Kim Hyeongjik was only seventeen and a half years older than the future North Korean leader, and his memories of him were of a young man in his twenties or barely in his thirties. Kim appears to have been extremely close to his father, who was his mentor and model. Hyeongjik's motto was 'aim high', and he instilled a sense of mission in his son. Kim praised his father throughout his life, built monuments and a museum dedicated to him, and promoted him as a paragon of virtue, patriotism and determination. The loss of his father when he was only fourteen must have been a powerful blow to Kim. His death also meant that at a very young age, Kim Il Sung became the male head of the family.

Kim first appears in Japanese police records in May 1929. A report refers to Kim Seonggye, probably a misspelling, as a member of a communist student group.[43] This group was a secret branch of the South Manchurian Communist Youth Association that had been organized at Yuwen Middle School. Later that year, the local Chinese authorities expelled 129 students when they discovered the organization. About a dozen of these were arrested, including Kim. This is one of the few documented incidents in his early life, since the Japanese consulate in Jilin filed a report on the incident including Kim among those arrested. Decades later the report was put on display at the Korean Revolution Museum in Pyongyang.[44] He spent five months in jail before being released on the testimony of several people who vouched for his innocence.[45] His expulsion meant the end of his formal education. He was seventeen.

Kim's Christianity

As ruler of North Korea, Kim Il Sung presided over an atheist state in which organized religious activities were forbidden. Yet he came from a Christian background. This background and the fact that both his mother's and father's families were devout and active church members is excluded in official accounts of his life and not well known among North Koreans. Yet, oddly, Kim Il Sung's own autobiography does not hide this at all. He does, however, go out of his way to explain that his parents ceased being believers. His father stopped attending church and became an atheist. 'You must believe in your own people, rather than in Jesus Christ,' he told him.[46] In fact North Korean histories have Kim's father leading students in a protest against the American missionaries for requiring religious studies as part of the curriculum. Yet Sungsil was a religious school that only admitted those boys who demonstrated their religious devotion, and theology and chapel were part of the curriculum.[47] His mother remained a regular churchgoer, Kim later wrote, but she told him she went to church not out of belief but to 'relax'.[48] However, all other evidence suggests that she was a pious Christian.

Kim himself attended services for a while, but he reportedly found them 'tedious' and the preaching 'monotonous'. He asserts that as a young revolutionary he had shaken off whatever Christian beliefs he had. He also insists he was not influenced by Christianity, 'but I received a great deal of humanitarian assistance from Christians, and in return had an ideological influence on them.'[49] Instead of an apostle for Christianity he became a proselytizer for nationalism, Marxist-Leninism and atheism. His problem with Christianity was that 'some miserable people thought they would go to "Heaven" after death if they believed in Jesus Christ.'[50] Instead of seeking solace in religion, they needed to realize that the hard lives they led were the product of political and social repression. And they needed to understand that this could be challenged and changed. Kim in fact depicts himself as dissuading his fellow young comrades from Christianity.[51]

Nonetheless, he maintained a respect for Christian ministers. In particular, he held a high regard for a Reverend Sohn (Son Jeongdo), whom he calls in his memoirs 'Dr Sohn'. He served as a mentor to Kim in the years immediately after his father died. But although Kim expresses his admiration and gratitude for the reverend, he comments that his religious beliefs were only a 'disguise', that he was instead a patriot.[52] The Reverend Sohn was a prominent Methodist minister in Jilin and in fact active in the nationalist movement. His son, Dr Won T. Sohn, who lived in the United States, recalled Kim Seongju, as he was known then, coming to his father's church regularly with his mother in the late 1920s.[53] The information seems quite credible since the interview took place years before Kim himself confirmed some of the details in his memoirs. He might, of course, have accompanied his mother to church to be a good son, rather than from religious conviction. A Korean American who knew Kim's father, Reverend Shungnok 'Luke' Kim, originally from Pyongyang, returned to his home town for a visit in 1981. While there he got a surprise invitation to dine with Kim Il Sung. According to Reverend Kim, the North Korean leader suggested he say grace. When the reverend finished, Kim Il Sung responded with an 'amen'.[54] Some have been a little sceptical about this story, but in view of the respect Kim shows for some Protestant ministers in his own autobiography, it seems plausible.

Kim was released from prison in the spring of 1930, after five months.[55] The next two years are a rather dark hole in his history. In some accounts he joined the guerillas in Manchuria shortly after his release, but if he did, we have no record of his activities; in other accounts he did not join them until 1932.[56] In 1932 Kim's mother died. Upon the death of his father in 1926 he became the senior male in the family. By 1930, at eighteen, he would have been considered an adult and become head of the household, which consisted of his mother and his two younger brothers, who were sixteen and ten years old. Evidence suggests that Kim took his family responsibilities seriously and would likely have stayed at home to look after his mother and younger siblings. Two years later, with her death and with his brother Cheolju now eighteen, he would have been freer to join the liberation fighters. And it is in 1932 that the young Kim appears in the historical records as an anti-Japanese guerilla fighter.

2

THE GUERILLA FIGHTER

KIM IL SUNG began his days as a guerilla fighter in an area near the border town of Antu in eastern Manchuria. His decision to join the armed resistance to the Japanese is easy to understand. In part he was following in the footsteps of his father, and he was always, even as a child, linked to the anti-Japanese movement. His decision to join a communist party also is not surprising since as a teenager he, along with many of his classmates, was involved in communist-affiliated organizations, and the communists were the best organized and most effective resistance fighters. It is likely the timing of his decision in 1932 reflected the change in his family situation. With the death of his mother, and with his younger brothers now old enough to take care of themselves, he was able to leave home. It also reflects the changing situation in Manchuria. On 18 September 1931 the Kwantung Army of the Empire of Japan began its invasion of Manchuria. By the end of February 1932 it had succeeded in gaining control over the region and set up the puppet state of Manchukuo. Officially Manchuria was now an independent state, but in fact it was now part of the Japanese Empire and under the rule of the Japanese Imperial Army. Koreans like Kim's family, who came to Manchuria to flee Japanese rule, found that the Japanese Empire had followed them. This takeover of Manchuria caused thousands of Chinese and Koreans living there to take up arms against the Japanese.

The young Kim became a member of the Chinese Communist Party (CCP), fought under Chinese communist commanders and from 1936 was part of the CCP-directed Northeast Anti-Japanese

United Army. North Koreans, however, know Kim Il Sung not as a member of the CCP, a fighter who served under Chinese superiors, but as the founder and leader of the Korean People's Revolutionary Army (KPRA). North Korean official accounts have Kim establishing the KPRA on 25 April 1932, a date still celebrated. Yet there is no record of such an organization, which was a later fabrication to disguise the fact that he fought under Chinese communists. In fact at that time there was no independent Korean communist guerilla organization in Manchuria. The KPRA was first mentioned in the late 1940s. The historian Andrei Lankov points out that in the first edition of the first official biography of Kim Il Sung, written by Han Jaedeok in 1947, there is no mention of the KPRA. The second edition, in 1948, contains a footnote correcting this. It states, 'The word the "United Anti-Japanese North-Eastern Army" must be read correctly as the "Korean People's Revolutionary Army"'.[1] By the late 1950s the KPRA was no longer a footnote but the driving force in liberating the country.

The Korean Communist Movement

Kim's attraction to communism was one shared by many younger Koreans, those who, like him, were exposed in the 1920s to a modern education and looked to the West as a model to follow to build a modern, progressive society. They were highly critical of Korea's cultural backwardness, which they saw as responsible for the fall of their country to the Japanese. Some Korean nationalists sought to gradually modernize their society by working within the limitations of the colonial framework. Many others, like Kim, were impatient with the gradualism of these more moderate nationalists and rejected the idea of cooperating with the colonial regime. Furthermore, they were suspicious of both the old 'feudal' *yangban* landowning class and the newly emerging Korean entrepreneurial class and saw the overthrow of both the colonial regime and the indigenous elite as their aim.

A wide range of new ideas flooded Korea at the start of the twentieth century – liberalism, nationalism, democracy, anarchism, anti-imperialism, Pan-Asianism and socialism – but Marxism was little known until the Bolshevik Revolution of 1917. That event fascinated many, mostly young, Koreans. In 1922 hundreds somehow made their way to Moscow to attend the Congress of the Toilers of the East. However, there was never a single, centrally organized communist movement but various geographically dispersed groups that almost never cooperated and often were not even in communication with one another.

The first communist organizations appeared in Siberia, home to several hundred thousand Koreans who emigrated there after 1860. But, by and large, this population of Soviet Koreans was not directly involved in the Korean nationalist movement. They had their own tragic history when in the late 1930s Stalin, fearing the loyalty of so many Koreans living near the border of the expanding Japanese Empire, relocated the entire population to Central Asia. Perhaps one-third of all Soviet Koreans perished in the clumsy and ruthless resettlement. This was accompanied by purges of Koreans in the Bolshevik Party and in the military. As a result the Soviet Koreans in 1945 were isolated from Korea, and Moscow lost a potential cadre of Korean-speaking personnel that could have assisted them in their post-war occupation of northern Korea.

Another communist movement emerged within Korea in the early 1920s, when small organizations of students and intellectuals explored Marxism. Two of these groups, the Tuesday Society and the North Wind Society, came together in April 1925 to form the Korean Communist Party (Joseon Gongsandang).[2] But their efforts to maintain an organized movement under the repressive and efficient Japanese government was extremely difficult. Within months almost all the members were arrested, and the party ceased to exist. A second Korean Communist Party was organized in 1926, but its leaders were soon arrested. Undeterred, a third party was organized in December 1926; most of its members too were arrested in January 1928. Still another, fourth attempt to create a party in February 1928 led to another wave of arrests in August.[3] Yet despite these setbacks, some communists continued to operate underground, organizing labour unions in the cities and peasant unions in the countryside. A few made it to Moscow for training and returned to Korea.[4] But in the 1930s, as the Japanese tightened their grip on colonial Korea even further, it became very difficult for communists to operate within the country. The movement survived only as an isolated, underground one, so much so that it was mostly cut off from communists outside the country.

In the 1930s, with the purges in the Soviet Union and the Japanese repression within Korea, China became the most active area for Korean communists. They were divided by geography into two groups, those on the Chinese mainland and those in Manchuria. Those on the mainland of China were larger in number and better organized. They were made up of Koreans in exile for the purpose of resisting the Japanese. Initially, Shanghai was their base, but after the Guomindang repression of communists there in 1927 they dispersed. Most joined the CCP, and some made the Long March (1934–5) with Mao and the other Chinese communists to their new base at Yanan. These later became known as the Yanan faction. When war broke out between China and Japan in 1937, thousands of Koreans joined the CCP's People's Liberation Army (PLA). Besides working within the CCP and the PLA, Yanan Koreans formed their own Korean Independence League in 1942, headed by Kim Dubong and Choe Changik. Kim Dubong, a distinguished linguist and scholar, became the most prominent Korean communist leader in China. The Independence League had a military wing, the Korean Voluntary Army, headed by Mu Jeong, with Pak Ilu, another prominent leader, as his deputy. Choe Changik, Kim Dubong, Pak Ilu and many other Yanan communists played an important role in the first years of the North Korean state and became political rivals to Kim Il Sung.

Eventually, Koreans working for and fighting with the CCP numbered tens of thousands.[5]

The Manchurian Korean communist guerillas were a somewhat different group, consisting of local ethnic Korean residents who had settled in the region. They were less educated, less ideological, more rough-hewn rural young men and women united by their hatred of the Japanese. Most initially belonged to local communist groups. In 1928 the Comintern ruled that there could be only one Communist Party per country. So, following this directive, all Korean communist fighters in Manchuria became members of the CCP. After being absorbed into the CCP they remained a separate group; most spoke little or no Chinese and saw the struggle as part of the liberation of their homeland.

The Chinese Community Party was weak in this area and mainly focused on appropriating land from Chinese landlords. With the Japanese takeover over of the region, the CCP refocused on organizing anti-Japanese resistance. In 1931, when the Japanese army began its occupation of Manchuria, most communist resistance fighters there were Koreans operating in small independent units with little supervision or control.[6] But then more Chinese in the region entered the guerilla ranks, and the CCP began to place all the bands of communist-affiliated fighters under tighter central command. In 1933 the CCP reorganized the various groups of guerillas into the Northeast People's Revolutionary Army following party directives in 1935 to form united fronts with non-communists; it was reorganized again in February 1936 as the Northeast Anti-Japanese United Army with Yang Jingyou as commander.

Early Years as a Guerilla Fighter

Kim Il Sung was a typical Korean immigrant to Manchuria who joined the communist-led anti-Japanese resistance movement. What distinguished him from most was that, although possessing only a secondary education, he was fluent in Chinese and came from a family of independence activists. He soon became unusual, but not unique, in rising to positions of leadership within the movement at a very young age. Kim's first assignment as a member of the CCP was to head up a special detachment of Koreans in Antu to fight alongside anti-Japanese guerilla leader Wang Delin and his group, the National Salvation Army. Wang had become affiliated with the Guomindang.[7] With the Japanese occupation of Manchuria, the CCP reversed earlier policies and cooperated with all anti-Japanese guerilla units, including those of the anti-communist Guomindang. Kim's assignment was to work with Wang and persuade him to join the CCP. It was a large responsibility for a young new member, but Kim must have impressed his new supervisors, and his fluency in Chinese was helpful. His unit and Wang's group carried out a joint operation against the small city of Dongning, which failed. But it earned Kim a reputation as an able fighter. Still, he was very young, only twenty; one guerilla who met him at the time later recalled he still wore his school clothes.[8] It is ironic for the future communist leader that his first distinction in battle was working with anti-communists. During the operation he managed to save the life of a Guomindang commander, Shi Zhongheng, who, a couple of years later, returned the favour.[9]

Kim also acquired a little bit of administrative responsibility in the base camps. In the winter of 1932–3 the Chinese communists established People's Revolutionary Governments (PRGs).[10] In the next two years more were established in areas with Korean populations. Official North Korean histories give great importance to both these PRGs and Kim's role in creating and directing them. 'The guerilla bases set up and consolidated by Comrade Kim Il Sung played a great role,' reads one history, 'as mighty rear bases giving material support and manpower to the Anti-Japanese Guerilla Army and as revolutionary bases instilling in the masses of the people a firm conviction of victory in the revolution, inspiring and encouraging them to the anti-Japanese struggle.' They represented, apparently, 'the broad section of patriotic people in our country including workers and peasants.'[11] In reality, the bases were quite small, most containing only 2,000 to 3,000 men, women and children, and in total perhaps 20,000 lived under the control of the partisans.[12]

Later, official histories would have Kim carrying out reforms in these experimental, Soviet-style communities. It is not clear, however, how involved he was. He may have overseen one People's Revolutionary Government for a short time.[13] If so it was his only administrative experience before emerging as a leader of North Korea. Nor did Kim organize them; they were organized by the Chinese communists.[14] The emphasis of the guerilla armies was land redistribution. Land was expropriated from landlords and 'Japanese puppets' and redistributed to poor peasants, including women. Left-over land belonged to the revolutionary government. Yet despite the Robin Hood redistribution of wealth, it is not clear that the guerillas in Manchuria won over many of the hearts and minds of the ordinary people. They often resorted to forcing young Koreans into serving in the resistance armies, levied unwelcome taxes on local peasants and raised money by kidnapping wealthy farmers for ransom.[15] These were hardly measures to win popular support. After 1935 the CCP was no longer willing to support these PRGs, even though they were modelled on the ones Mao Zedong and others had established in mainland China. The focus was on armed conflict with the Japanese.

Around this time Kim Seongju changed his name to Kim Il Sung.[16] It was common for partisans and revolutionaries to adopt a *nom de guerre*. He was not the first to adopt this name, which meant 'sun-star'. One guerilla fighter who was born in 1888 and died in 1926 had used it, and there was another resistance fighter named Kim Il Sung, who left Korea for Russia after 1919 and joined the Bolsheviks. A victim of the Stalinist purges, he was arrested in 1939 and died in a concentration camp.[17] Later, the fact that the name Kim Il Sung was used by at least three prominent guerilla fighters caused some confusion, perpetuated and compounded by a South Korean misinformation campaign that insisted that Kim Il Sung the North Korean leader was not the 'real guerilla fighter' but an impostor. Kim never took credit for the other guerillas who shared his name. He didn't have to, since soon after taking on this new name his achievements as a warrior for independence began to greatly outshine those of his namesakes.

Minsaengdan Incident

Although Kim began his career as a guerilla fighter with some impressive achievements, it was nearly cut short not long after it started, not by the Japanese but by the regional CCP. In response to the Japanese takeover of Manchuria, some Korean residents formed a pro-Japanese organization called the Minsaengdan (People's Livelihood Corps) in February 1932. The group sought the protection of Japan from communist and Chinese authorities and the creation of an autonomous Korean region in the Kando region while remaining under Japanese rule. Tokyo ignored them. Their request for autonomy ran counter to the Japanese plan for a multiethnic Manchuria under Japanese control, and it was opposed by the Governor-General of Korea, who feared it would undermine Japanese rule in the rest of the region. Chinese communists were even more opposed to the idea and carried out attacks, including arson and murder, on suspected Minsaengdan members or sympathizers. Facing this response in October 1932, the Koreans who formed the organization disbanded it.

However, the short-lived organization triggered suspicions among many CCP leaders that the Korean minority was untrustworthy, secretly cooperating with the Japanese, and seeking to dismember Manchuria and subvert the communist movement there. This suspicion extended to Korean members of the CCP. There was a widespread belief, born in part of prejudice, that Koreans, even those who called themselves communists, had their own agenda. It is true that Korean communist guerillas such as Kim Il Sung were nationalists first and communists second. But the CCP leadership underestimated their intense hatred of the Japanese and the commitment they had made to unite with their Chinese comrades to defeat them. The Eastern Manchurian Special Committee of the CCP (EMSC), the main CCP arm in the area, began conducting purges in 1933 of Korean party members. In the autumn of 1934 these purges were escalated, led by two CCP members, Zhong Ziyun and Cao Yafan, who claimed 70 per cent of Koreans in the base area and 80–90 per cent of the Korean revolutionary fighters were Minsaengdan members.[18] This was a pure paranoid fantasy since there was no secret Minsaengdan organization; it existed only in the minds of some CCP members who disliked the Korean migrants and saw them as potentially disloyal.

In the early stages some Korean party members participated in the purges, only to find themselves, in turn, purged and executed. By the end of 1934 it was clear that almost all ethnic Koreans were being removed. Kim later recalled the insanity of the purges. People became suspects for minor mistakes such as undercooking rice.[19] Kim himself became a suspect in 1934 and was arrested. He was spared, however, no doubt for a number of reasons: he was fluent in Chinese, unlike most Koreans;[20] he had friends in the EMSC leadership; and he was still very young. Many were betrayed by fellow Koreans who were rivals in the faction-ridden Korean communist movement, but the 22-year-old Kim was not linked to any faction. He also had the support of the Guomindang commander Shi Zhongfeng, now allied with the CCP, who protested his arrest to the EMSC. Shi's protests may have been what saved his life. Additionally, the Chinese needed competent guerilla commanders. So, at the end of 1934, he was reinstated and put in charge of a unit in Jidong, where the communist leader Zhou Baozhong was sympathetic to the Koreans. Kim then led a three-month campaign with this small band of men.

In February 1935 Kim attended a party meeting where he argued for an end to the purges. He made the same argument at a meeting the following month. At this time most of the Korean guerillas were either under arrest, condemned to execution or at least under suspicion. Kim became their outspoken champion. The purges slowed in 1935 and came to an end in March 1936 under instructions from the Comintern.

Kim Il Sung and the Northeast Anti-Japanese United Army

In February 1936 the CCP created the Northeast Anti-Japanese United Army (NEAJUA) under Chinese commander Yang Jingyu. In Jidong, Zhou Baozhong ignored the directives from the EMSC and placed Kim in charge of the Third Division of the Second Army of the newly formed NEAJUA. Zhou also appointed other Koreans to positions of responsibility. The NEAJUA, based primarily in southern and eastern Manchuria, was divided into three Route Armies, which were subdivided into small units or corps confusingly also sometimes labelled 'armies'. Yang Jingyu directly served as commander-in-chief of the First Route Army. Its second corps consisted mainly of Koreans, including the Third Division, commanded by Kim Il Sung. Other prominent commanders in the NEAJUA included Choe Hyeon, Choe Yonggeon and Kim Chaek, who all later held prominent positions in the DPRK.[21] Although working under the CCP leadership, ethnic Koreans made up the majority of fighters in the border area of Jilin province, where Kim Il Sung was active.[22] The label 'armies' was rather grandiose for what were modest-sized units rarely numbering more than several hundred fighters. Although more than half the CCP guerilla fighters in eastern Manchuria were ethnic Koreans, they served under the Chinese and Chinese was the operational language.[23]

Kim Il Sung then took steps that revealed some of his leadership skills and his personal boldness, and by doing so cemented the loyalty of many of his Korean guerilla comrades. After the purges were formally ended in 1936, he burned all the investigation records of those Koreans still under suspicion. Then he appointed many of them to the new Third Division, where they formed the core of his unit. When the Third Division, renamed the Sixth Division, carried out successful attacks on the Japanese, it vindicated his decision. One other action he took was to take twenty orphans of executed comrades and form what was informally called the 'Minsaengdan kids'. These young people became his orderlies and even bodyguards. By most accounts he made special efforts to treat them like his own children. A young guerilla fighter, Kim Jong Suk, was placed in charge of caring for them. She later became Kim's second wife.

The Minsaengdan Incident was a tragic blow to the Korean communist guerillas. At least five hundred Koreans were executed, including some of the most experienced guerilla fighters and anti-Japanese organizers. Some estimates put the figure much higher – up to 2,000.[24] Minsaengdan embittered relations between the Chinese and Korean communists. The Kando region, with the largest concentration of ethnic Koreans, could no longer serve as the most important base of support for the Korean guerillas since fear and resentment of the CCP was strong. Kim lamented that this region – so important as a recruiting ground for revolutionaries – had become completely 'terrorized'.[25] Koreans had long seen themselves as victims, a small country at the mercy of larger powers, and the purge and CCP attacks on falsely accused civilians reinforced this. For Kim and his fellow guerillas the incident made it clear that the Chinese would always put their own interests first.

But while the Minsaengdan Incident weakened the Korean anti-Japanese resistance fight in Manchuria, it strengthened the role of Kim Il Sung as a leader. It demonstrated his courage and leadership skills and made Kim a hero among his guerilla comrades, forging a bond of loyalty to him. In his memoirs Kim makes clear his pride at his achievements during Minsaengdan.[26] Between 1959 and 1969 the North Korean government published twelve volumes of memoirs by the Manchurian guerillas in which they praised Kim's leadership at this crucial point.[27] These were written after he had consolidated power and can be easily dismissed as propaganda, which of course they were. However, the loyalty shown to him and his comrades' confidence in his leadership was demonstrated in other ways that suggest that, exaggeration aside, this was indeed the real turning point in his rise as a leader of the Korean Manchurian guerillas. And these guerilla loyalists eventually formed the core of the North Korean power structure and Kim's loyal base of support.

Bocheonbo and the Arduous March

Now a commander of a small division of Korean fighters, Kim worked closely with his compatriots on the other side of the border. There the Korean Fatherland Restoration Association (Hanin Joguk Gwangbokhoe), an anti-Japanese group, was active. Due to the intensive and efficient colonial police their activities were restricted; there were no armed bands within Korea at the time. But the association was able to provide logistical support as well as intelligence information. This was done through the Gapsan (Kapsan) Operations Committee (Gapsangkongjak wiwonhoe), named after the Gapsan border area. It proved to be short-lived. Pak Geumcheol, its leader, was arrested in October 1937 and a year later the Gapsan Operations Committee was destroyed by counter-insurgency forces. Yet during that short period they were crucial to Kim's most prominent military successes. The veterans of this organization, known as the Gapsan group, for a while held many high-ranking posts in North Korea, although they never enjoyed quite the prestige or power of the actual guerilla fighters.[28] The coordination between Kim's fighters and the Gapsan group made possible the most important military victory of his career, the taking of the small Korean town of Bocheonbo. The town was strategically located and chosen for the publicity its capture would receive.[29]

After six months of careful planning, Kim launched his raid on 4 June 1937. This amounted to no more than killing seven Japanese policemen, destroying the police post and other Japanese buildings, and then occupying the town for several hours. Kim Il Sung made a speech, handed out some leaflets and left. According to Japanese police reports, only about eighty guerillas were involved. Although it was a rather minor affair, it was one of the few successful raids across the heavily patrolled border at that time and was reported in the Japanese and Korean press.[30] Kim himself called it 'an ordinary raid' that 'produced few casualties'. Caught by surprise, the Japanese were quickly defeated. In fact the capture went so smoothly that some of his men found it disappointing.[31] It was not the exciting, heroic battle they had expected.

Even before that incident the Japanese-controlled press in Korea had reported on Kim Il Sung's 'banditry', but it was the 'battle' of Bocheonbo that received the most publicity and laid the foundation for his later reputation. North Koreans would later celebrate this as a great turning point in the anti-Japanese struggle. According to an official account, 'the significance was not in the fact that we killed a few Japanese but in the fact that the Pochonbo [Bocheonbo] battle threw revolutionary rays of hope, inspiring confidence in the Korean people that they were alive and could beat Japanese imperialism if they fought against it.'[32] Kim said it was important because it showed that the national independence movement was still alive and the communists were 'spearheading' it.[33] In reality it was far less significant.

Still, the attack on Bocheonbo was a rare example of partisans crossing into Korea. Aided by the natural barrier of the Yalu and Tumen rivers and rugged Baekdusan (Paektusan), the highest mountain in Korea, the colonial regime had created an almost impenetrable border. The raid was a shock. It was followed up shortly after when Kim, teaming up with fellow guerilla commander Choe Hyeon, attacked a well-defended Japanese timber camp, killing ten policemen, taking nine hostages and capturing weapons and ammunition.[34] In another raid, Kim's division joined forces with a band led by Chinese partisan Cao Guoan, attacking a Japanese expeditionary force sent to hunt him and his partisans. Fighting on Baekdusan just after a heavy snowfall and camouflaged in white sheets, they surprised the Japanese, forcing them to retreat, killing thirteen and taking seventeen prisoners.[35]

News of the raid on Bocheonbo featured prominently in the Korean press on 6 June 1937.[36] The *Chosun ilbo*, one of the two leading Korean-language newspapers, reported Kim's exploits, describing him as a bandit plundering Korean farmers in Manchuria. This of course was how the Japanese authorities labelled the partisans: bandits preying on poor villagers. Korean newspapers described how he and his comrades raided villages, collecting 'taxes' in the way of cash, food and supplies and paying with promissory notes. They also recruited new fighters by kidnapping young men. All of this was likely true, although of course omitted from later North Korean accounts.[37]

Kim Il Sung was becoming a person of concern to the Japanese authorities. Police reports made frequent reference to 'Kim Il Sung bandits' carrying out raids. It is from one of these reports in 1938 that we have the first biography of Kim Il Sung. In contrast to the voluminous official biographies or his own eight-volume autobiography, this is extremely brief. 'Kim Il-song: Age 30. Origin – Korea. Family whereabouts unknown. Background – farmer. He was engaged in farming before turning to banditry as a result of Communist propaganda.'[38] The Japanese appear to have known little about him; what they thought they knew was mostly wrong. He was only 26 at the time; he was never a farmer. Nonetheless, they made great efforts to kill or capture him, creating a special unit for that purpose.

For 110 days in the winter of 1938–9, Kim and his little band was forced to flee from his pursuers. They barely evaded capture. It was 'the bitterest trial in the anti-Japanese struggle', Kim recalled.[39] They could not even light a campfire for fear of being spotted by a search plane.[40] But he evaded capture. This whole incident was later heralded as the 'Arduous March' (*Gonan ui haenggun*).[41] This became an important part of the official legend of Kim Il Sung in North Korea. Every citizen knows the story, depicted in endless posters and films, taught to every schoolchild: how Kim and his men marched through the forest in deep snow, hungry and cold, eluding their pursuers. They were, the account goes, chronically short of food and unable to cook what they had.[42] Later embellishments aside, the story is essentially true. Kim and his men were not caught, and the Japanese expedition was a failure. Interestingly, the Japanese unit hunting Kim included several Koreans who later held important positions in the South Korean military during the Korean War, including Baek Seonyeop, who later was the South Korean army chief of staff during the Korean War.[43]

Kim continued a series of raids and attacks throughout 1938 and 1939, becoming the most troublesome of the partisans for the Japanese. The most successful raid was the brief capture of the Korean city of Musan in 1939. The following year colonial authorities sent another Japanese special police force, led by Maeda Takeshi, to hunt him down. This time they managed to find him, but then Kim suddenly attacked, killing Maeda and 58 Japanese officers.[44] By that time Kim was now ranked with the NEAJUA leader Yang Jingyu as the highest priority target for the Japanese counter-insurgency forces in eastern Manchuria.

In 1937 the Japanese had begun their invasion of China proper. After initial successes they encountered unexpected resistance from the Guomindang government and found themselves bogged down in a major conflict. Meanwhile, to meet the needs of wartime, Japan expanded its industrial development in Korea and in the puppet state of Manchukuo it had created in Manchuria. The Chinese and Korean partisans in Manchuria were only a minor annoyance and did little to impede this expansion of the Japanese Empire. Still, fighting them diverted resources needed for the greater war effort, so at the close of the 1930s the Japanese forces made a determined effort to put these guerilla raids to an end. The Japanese expanded a collective hamlet system they created in 1934, moving millions of peasants to secure locations. And in October 1939 the Japanese police and the Manchukuo Army launched a massive and very effective counterinsurgency campaign. Almost all the partisan leaders were killed or forced to flee. One, Lim Woo Sung, went over to the Japanese, and on 23 February 1940, Yang Jingyu was killed.[45] Kim was now the last important guerilla leader still in the field. But the cause was lost, and the Comintern advised that the remaining guerillas retreat across the Soviet border.

While fighting the Japanese Kim Il Sung fell in love with one of the members of his partisan group, Kim Jong Suk. The daughter of a farmer, she joined the partisans at age sixteen and later looked after the 'Minsaengdan kids'. They were married, probably in 1940 before Kim fled to Siberia. Kim Jong Suk was the mother of Kim's first son, Kim Jong Il, who succeeded him as the leader of North Korea. As such she later became the centre of her own personality cult, referred to as the 'mother of Korea'. She is portrayed in official propaganda as a tough, heroic partisan fighting in battles, a model revolutionary. In a questionnaire Kim Il Sung completed at the request of the Soviets in 1941, he more modestly described her as a 'dressmaker for the partisans' and a member of the CCP.[46] Russian historian Andrei Lankov interviewed a Soviet commander who met her in the late 1940s and described her as a 'small, quiet woman, not particularly well educated, but friendly and life-loving'.[47] She died giving birth to a child in 1949.

Kim Jong Suk is generally referred to as Kim's first wife. In fact she was his second. He was first married to Kim Hyosun, another guerilla. In contrast with the praise and many stories surrounding the memory of his second wife, there is an official silence about Kim Hyosun. She is believed to have been captured by the Japanese in 1940. Later she held many mid-level positions in North Korea, but it was never publicly acknowledged that she had been married to Kim.[48]

On 23 October 1940 Kim crossed into the Soviet Union with about a dozen other partisans. After the better part of a decade as an anti-Japanese fighter in Manchuria, his efforts had ended in failure. In 1942 he wrote a report for the Communist Party, in Chinese; it analysed the failures of the guerilla movement. The report is clear-sighted, frank and makes no excuses for the failure of the guerillas. The partisans failed to work effectively with other anti-Japanese groups. They carried out military attacks on the Japanese prematurely, without taking the time to build up their forces. The guerillas were simply too few and too poorly equipped to take on their enemy.[49] It was a realistic appraisal by a young but experienced fighter.

In North Korea the experience of Kim Il Sung and his fellow Manchurian guerillas in their conflict with the Japanese has provided the main background for plays, films, songs, operas, children's stories and every conceivable form of entertainment. It provides examples and metaphors for all forms of economic, political and social activity. People are constantly being taught to learn from the examples of their great leader and his heroic comrades. Perhaps more importantly, it has shaped the way the country's leadership interpret and understand the world. Yet, as large as it looms in North Korea, and for all its importance in understanding that state's history, the Manchurian partisan campaign was a rather small-scale one. As Kim's report clearly shows, he was fully aware of this. The Korean guerillas were tiny in number, and their area of activity was largely confined to remote peripheral areas in the mountainous countryside just north of the Korean border. Despite their aim of liberating Korea, they rarely penetrated the well-protected border of the colony. Overall, the guerilla attacks on the Japanese imperialists were little more than a nuisance.

Officer in the Red Army

For the next five years Kim Il Sung lived in Siberia. This is another part of his life that is left out in official accounts. Instead, they have him spending these years directing guerilla operations against the Japanese from his secret mountain headquarters on Baekdusan. The symbolism of this is important. Mountain worship or veneration has long been a part of Korean culture. Nearly every Buddhist temple has a shrine to Sansin, the mountain spirit. And no mountain is more sacred than Baekdusan, the home of the mythical progenitor of the Korean people. It is mentioned in the national anthems of both North and South Korea and remains one of the most important symbols of Korea and Korean-ness. In official North Korean accounts, Kim was on that sacred mountain on the Korean side, not the Chinese, actively fighting the Japanese as the head of the KPRA. Countless paintings depict Kim Il Sung directing the fighting from this mountain. It is all pure fiction, invented and elaborated on while Kim ruled North Korea. He spent the rest of the Second World War living in the Soviet Union, wearing the uniform of the Soviet Red Army, and never saw any combat. It is unlikely this was where he wanted to be; he was a man of action, a fierce patriot and without question a courageous guerilla.

When crossing into the USSR, he was arrested by the always suspicious Soviets, interrogated and then released. The partisans fleeing the Japanese were divided into two groups; some, including Kim, were put in Camp A in Vyatskoye, near the Soviet Far Eastern city of Khabarovsk, and others in Camp V near Ururiysk, then called Voroshilov. They were trained in intelligence-gathering and sabotage. Kim, who is referred to in Russian records by his Chinese name,

Jin Richeng, was sent with his family to Vyatskoye, where he had his training and studied Russian. Some accounts suggest he went to Moscow for training, but there is no confirmation of this. He was sent on a mission back to Manchuria in April 1941 to bring back partisan commander Wei Zhengmin. Accompanied by a friend, An Kil, and a small team, he spent four months there, only to report back that Wei had been killed.[50]

In the summer of 1942 the Soviets formed a special unit: the 88th Special Reconnaissance Brigade of the Soviet 25th Army, made up of Chinese and Korean ex-Manchurian guerilla fighters. The 88th Reconnaissance Brigade was a curious creation. It was the only unit of the vast Soviet Red Army in the Second World War primarily made up of foreigners. It was commanded by a prominent Chinese guerilla leader, Zhou Baozhong, who had sided with the Koreans, including Kim, during the Minsaengdan Incident. The brigade had four battalions, with Kim, now a captain in the Red Army, commanding the first battalion. All totalled, there were between 1,000 and 1,700 men in the brigade, including 200 to 300 Soviets attached. About 140 to 180 Koreans served in the battalion under the command of Kim Il Sung, most of whom had previously served with him in the 1930s.[51] The brigade was to carry out intelligence and sabotage work, and some members did so. Except for the mission to search for Wei Zhengmin, there is no evidence that Kim Il Sung participated in these.

Kim was now an officer in the Red Army, the second foreign military force he had served in. He made every effort to learn Russian, which set him apart from most of his comrades and attracted the attention of his Soviet superiors. He even named his son Yura (although Jong Il was his Korean name), perhaps, it has been suggested, after the Russian general and Second World War hero Georgy 'Yuri' Zhukov. Zhukov had commanded the forces that defeated the Japanese at the Battle of Nomonhan in 1939. This little-known but militarily important clash had a world-changing impact.

Outmatched by Soviet tanks and heavy weaponry, the Japanese decided to avoid conflict with Moscow and never came to Germany's assistance when it went to war with the Soviets in 1941. For Kim, Zhukov was a man he could admire – he had inflicted a crushing defeat on the Japanese. This was in sharp contrast to the efforts by Korean fighters. Kim became a believer in the need for modern equipped armies and the industrial capacity to support them.

Kim had learned to win the good graces of the Chinese, helped by his mastery of their language; this served him well and helps account for his meteoric rise as a partisan leader. He now learned how to win the support of the Russians, working hard to learn their language and impress his superiors with his loyalty and competence. His efforts at becoming competent in Russian set him apart from most of his comrades, who had little interest in learning it since they had no intention of remaining in the Soviet Union. Kim, however, was interested in cultivating good relations with his hosts and was always good at impressing his superiors, which he took pains to do. Yet life there was not easy for him. The Soviets kept a close watch on the Koreans. This was Stalinist Russia, the same regime that had deported almost the entire Korean population from Siberia to Central Asia for fear that they might cooperate with the Japanese. Those whom the Soviet secret police found suspicious were relocated to northern camps, never to be heard from again.[52] In July 1944 Kim himself came under suspicion. At a meeting of the CCP an official made an accusation that the NEAJUA had killed communists. Furthermore, it was alleged that a unit that Kim Il Sung headed was responsible for doing so. Kim defended himself by saying that only some Trotskyites were killed. Apparently, that was enough to spare him.[53] Yet despite these tensions there were some pleasant times at Vyatskoye, too, such as fishing in the Amur river. He also had time to spend with his family, which expanded with the birth of a second son, Shura. His Russian name was in honour of General Aleksandr Vasilevsky, the hero of the Battle of Stalingrad.[54] Compared with the years before and after, the five years Kim lived in Siberia were quiet, uneventful ones. Moscow seems to have forgotten about the 88th Reconnaissance, which had little to do.

Kim Jong Il

It was in Siberia that Kim's son and future heir, Kim Jong Il, was born. Officially he was born on 16 February 1942, in a cabin on Baekdusan. A rainbow appeared in the sky, and although it was in the bitter cold of winter, flowers bloomed. No part of this official picture is true. He was born outside Khabarovsk in Siberia, no miraculous events are known to have accompanied this event, and he was born not on 16 February 1942 but a year earlier. The evidence for the last point is circumstantial but convincing. According to Soviet records, his father was in Manchuria from April to 28 August 1941, and there are no records of Kim Jong Suk being with him. It would be hardly likely that he would take his wife with him on a dangerous mission. More likely, his wife was pregnant in 1940, which would have been a reason for Kim to have left Manchuria at that time. Of course, all the remaining partisans were leaving, but it would have been in keeping with his character for him to stay as long as was possible. He was still young in 1940, only 28, and had continually defied the odds, always to survive. But having a wife whom he deeply loved – and by all accounts he did – who was carrying their first child may well have persuaded him to flee to safety.

There are other reasons to believe that his son was born on 16 February 1941. In the 1970s South Korean intelligence reported that officials had been required to write letters of congratulation to Kim Jong Il on his 33rd birthday in 1974. This was before Kim Jong Il's emergence as his father's successor and before any official information about him, including his age, was published. In fact his birth date was publicly announced only on his supposed 40th birthday in 1982. It is not clear why Kim changed his son's birthday, but other parts of the fabricated story are easier to understand. He did not want his son born in Russia, and he did not want to be known as a man who had fled the battlefield and who wore the uniform of a foreign country's military.

The War Ends

The end of the conflict with Japan came faster than most had anticipated. It is likely that Kim was as taken by surprise by the swift flow of events in the summer of 1945 as nearly everyone else was. On 6 August 1945 the Americans dropped the atomic bomb on Hiroshima. Two days later the Soviet Union declared war on Japan and began an offensive along the border of Manchuria, along the tiny border with Korea and on the Japanese half of Sakhalin. On 15 August Japan surrendered.

When the Second World War came to this sudden end with the surrender of Japan, the Korean communist movement consisted of several thousand personnel fighting and serving with Mao Zedong in the interior of China; the remnants of the Manchuria-based guerillas now mostly living in the Soviet Far East, some serving in the Red Army; and a barely surviving underground movement within Korea. There were also ex-Communist Party members and communist-leaning leftists in Korea who were in jail or no longer active. Many of the latter had been 'turned' and were at least ostensibly supporting the Japanese war effort. A few Comintern members were in the Soviet Union. These groups had little contact with one another or, in many cases, may not even have been aware of one another's existence. There was no coordinated communist movement and no obvious leadership. In this they resembled the other Korean non-communist nationalist groups: small, isolated exile groups in China and the USA who also lacked any effective organization or widely recognized leadership. Thus, with the collapse of imperial Japan, Korea was a political vacuum.

On 15 August Kim was in the Khabarovsk area with his wife and two sons. The liberation of his country, to which he had dedicated his still short life, was about to happen. Yet this would be due not to the efforts of liberation fighters like himself but to the intervention of outside powers as he and his comrades stood on the sidelines, a fact that must have been humiliating to him. With the American forces hundreds of miles away on Pacific islands while the Red Army was already crossing the border into the peninsula, it appeared to most Koreans at the time that their country was soon to be occupied by the Soviet Union. Kim's goal now was to join that occupation.

3
THE CHOSEN ONE

When Japan surrendered and the liberation of his country was about to begin, Kim Il Sung was far away, in Siberia, a helpless onlooker in the moment he and his father before him had dreamed about. We do not know Kim's initial reaction to Tokyo's formal announcement of surrender, but we do know that it was greeted with jubilation by Koreans almost everywhere. People danced in the streets of Seoul, Pyongyang and other cities and towns. They hung home-made Korean flags from their houses, and crowds set fire to Shinto shrines, hated symbols of Japan's forced assimilation policy; witnesses reported that one could see the glow from the fires in almost every direction.

What Kim and other Koreans could not know, however, was that Moscow and Washington had secretly agreed to the partition of their country. The Soviets had declared war on Japan on 8 August and made immediate progress against the hollowed-out Japanese border forces. The next day reports arrived in Washington of the Red Army's crossing into the Korean Peninsula. With the surrender of Japan imminent, Americans quickly began seeing Korea much as Tokyo had, as a strategic bridgehead into Japan. While Soviet forces were already entering the northeast of Korea, the closest American forces were 1,000 kilometres (620 mi.) away in Okinawa and would not be able to reach Korea for several weeks. It was therefore urgent that the USA work out an agreement to prevent the entire peninsula from falling into Soviet hands. On the night of 10 August U.S. officials drew up a proposal to divide the peninsula into two occupation zones. They chose the 38th parallel as the boundary since it split the country into roughly equal halves. There would be a southern, American half and a northern, Soviet one. Although similar in area, the southern occupation zone contained Seoul and was more populous. The area north of the 38th parallel contained only 9.3 million people of Korea's total population of 28 million. Eight million of these were rural and 1.3 million urban.[1] With President Truman's approval, the proposal was sent to Moscow, and Stalin sent back his agreement the next day. It is not clear why he did so when his forces could have easily marched all the way to Busan in the far south. Stalin may have hoped that, by agreeing to a joint military occupation, the door would be left open for a Soviet role in the occupation of Japan. He was also concerned to avoid a potential conflict with the USA in Korea.[2] No Koreans were consulted or even knew of these decisions until days after their implementation had begun. It is unlikely that many Koreans, not least Kim, would have approved of them.

The choice of the 38th parallel was not based on any historical or geographical boundaries; it cut across the two provinces, Gyeonggi and Gangwon, splitting counties and valleys. It simply divided the country into two zones of roughly equal size. It became a central axiom of North Koreans – indeed of all Koreans – that the division of their country was unnatural and unacceptable. But Koreans had little say in the matter. As had been the case in the late nineteenth and early twentieth centuries, Korea was a pawn in the hands of great powers.

Two days after declaring war on Japan the Soviet Union's 25th Red Army under General Ivan Chistiakov crossed the border into northeast Korea. On 26 August the Red Army entered Pyongyang. Kim and his 88th Reconnaissance Brigade were not involved; they could only look on as the Red Army quickly occupied all the territory north of the 38th parallel. Kim must have been puzzled when the Soviets stopped and did not go on to occupy Seoul. But it must have soon become obvious that some sort of arrangement had been made, since the U.S. forces did not begin to land in the south until 8 September 1945.

Kim Il Sung made attempts to join the new Soviet occupation. At one time he and his comrades made it to the border but were turned back. It took several weeks before they could arrange a return to Korea, on 9 September. By that time the Soviets were in complete control of their zone north of the 38th parallel. He had no part in the liberation of Korea, and when he returned, his success in emerging as a leader was totally dependent on his ability to gain the support of the Soviet occupiers.

The Soviet military had come to fight the Japanese, not to govern the Koreans, and were surprisingly unprepared for the occupation. They arrived in North Korea with no clear policy or blueprint for what to do next and had little knowledge of the internal affairs of the country.[3] They did not bring Korean experts to help them – in fact they did not even have interpreters.[4] Nor did they have contacts within the peninsula. This situation was mirrored in the south, where American forces found themselves equally unprepared. For the Soviets this lack of expertise was in part due to the purge of ethnic Korean military and intelligence officers during 1936–8. It was also a result of the isolation of the domestic communists in Korea, who under intensive and effective Japanese repression were unable to establish regular contact with Moscow. Other Korean communists were in remote regions of China working with the Chinese Communist Party and had virtually no communication with the USSR.

The Soviets initially sent military officers, untrained in civil administration, to oversee Korea's local districts, but in early October they set up the Civil Administration. This worked closely with the people's committees that Koreans had organized all over the peninsula after 15 August. Despite their communist-sounding name, people's committees were ad hoc groups of prominent Koreans, of all political views, formed to deal with issues such as food administration and public order that were brought about by the collapse of Japanese authority. By November there were committees in all seven provinces in the Soviet occupation zone, in nine cities, seventy counties and twenty townships.[5] In the south the U.S. forces ignored them, but the Soviets worked with them. In November the Soviets created the beginning of a state structure in the north, the Five Provinces Administrative Bureau (Odo haengjeongguk), with ten departments to carry out much of the administration, each headed by a Korean but with a Soviet adviser to assist. They utilized members of the people's committees to serve in them. Cho Mansik, the head of the Pyongyang People's Committee, was appointed to head the Five Provinces Administrative Bureau. Although to a considerable extent they directed the events in North Korea, the Soviets preferred to give the appearance that Koreans were initiating change. And to some extent this was the case, since when the Soviets found Korean communists with whom they were comfortable working, they let them implement policies. The problem for the Soviets was finding those Koreans.

General Chistiakov, the Red Army commander, left the civil administration to Major General Andrei Alekseevich Romanenko. But the most important figure during the three-year occupation was Colonel General Terentii Shtykov. Shtykov, the Political Commissar, was a party functionary, not a military man. He played a key role in shaping the occupation from 1945 to 1948 and continued to serve as the first Soviet ambassador to the new state after 1948.

Finding Suitable Partners

Kim's arrival in Korea came at a time when the Soviets were still searching for reliable Korean partners. As in Eastern Europe, Moscow's method was to form broad coalitions between communist and non-communist nationalists before gradually giving greater control over to the communists and removing uncooperative elements.

The Soviets, however, had to deal with the fact that most of the non-communist nationalists had cooperated with the Japanese and therefore had tarnished nationalist credentials. An even greater problem was that the local communist movement was structurally weak, centred in the American-occupied south. There were few northern Korean communists known to Moscow. Unlike in Eastern Europe there were no appreciable numbers of communist exiles in the Soviet Union. Most members of the Korean Communist Party in Korea, or the 'domestic communists' as they became known, were imprisoned or in hiding and had little contact with each other or with the international communist movement. When surviving domestic communists did emerge from hiding or jail, they were centred in Seoul, which of course was in the American occupation zone. This presented an awkward situation for Moscow.

In the north the most prominent Korean was the Christian leader Cho Mansik, the head of the Pyongyang People's Committee. Sixty-three-year-old Cho had compromised his nationalist credentials when during the Second World War he called upon students to volunteer and fight for Japan.[6] Nonetheless, he remained well known and respected, and his prestige made him useful to the Soviets. Cho and other conservatives formed the Democratic Party (Minjudang) in November. They were a collection of landlords, prominent professionals and members of North Korea's significant Christian community. Christianity had grown in the north since Kim Il Sung's childhood, but Christians still numbered only 5 per cent of the population. Nonetheless, they tended to be better educated, better represented in the small middle class and active in disproportionate numbers in the nationalist movements. Kim's own family fits the average profile of Korean Christians, who were more often than not from the middle classes, often mission-educated and more open to new ideas. They were strongest in urban areas, especially in Pyongyang. The province where Pyongyang is located, Pyeongan, was also a centre of Cheondogyo (Heavenly Way), an indigenous religious group that had its roots in Donghak, a peasant movement in the late nineteenth century that led an uprising in 1894 directed at corrupt local officials. Donghak's concern with land reform was especially attractive to the communists, who shared this part of their agenda. With Soviet approval the Cheondogyo organized a political party in early 1946: the Cheong'udang. Christians and Cheondogyo members were the most organized non-communist groups in North Korea and the main coalition partners with the communists in the early days of the occupation.

For the Soviets it was easier to find non-communists with whom they could temporarily partner than communists who would, according to their playbook, eventually take over. They needed a leader.

An obvious choice might have been the leader of the Communist Party of Korea in August 1945: Pak Heonyeong. A founding member of the first Communist Party in 1925, Pak was arrested by the Japanese and then released after faking mental illness. He was later rearrested, served six years and released in 1939. Disguised as an itinerant bricklayer, he travelled around the country to re-establish a national party.[7] But Pak, like most of the other domestic communists, was largely unfamiliar to the Soviets and was in Seoul, in the American occupation zone. Another factor working against him was that he had been associated with the Comintern, and Stalin and those around him were distrustful of Comintern members.[8]

Another possible candidate for leader was Hyeon Chunhyeok. On 17 August, in the first days of liberation, the Korean Communist Party in Seoul sent him to Pyongyang to help organize the party there. Hyeon, a native of the city, was the de facto party head in the north, but he had limited authority over other local communists in the industrial and port cities of Cheongju, Sinuiju, Haeju, Heungnam, Hamheung and Wonsan.[9] Hyeon Chunhyeok does not seem to have impressed the Soviets. And he, like the other domestic communists, was little known among his countrymen.

A leader might have been found among the Soviet Koreans. Needing interpreters, some survivors of the 1930s purges were recruited by the Soviets to assist with the occupation. However, as Soviet citizens they tended to have either distant or no connections with Korea. Still another pool of possible candidates could be found among the many Korean communists in China, but they were under CCP authority and in any case not available to the Soviets in the autumn of 1945.

This was the situation that awaited Manchurian veterans of the 88th Brigade when Kim and his comrades arrived in Korea on 19 September, landing by boat in the port of Wonsan. It was the day before the important autumn festival of Chuseok, one of the two biggest holidays of the year.[10] By this time Kim Il Sung was the leader of this small band of about sixty former Manchurian guerillas, or 'partisans' as they are often called. It is not clear how or why he became the leader of this group. There were several other captains and one major, and some of the other ex-guerillas were older and had as much if not more guerilla experience. At 33 he was younger than two-thirds of the group.[11] That his comrades selected him as their leader and spokesperson would seem to be a testament to his leadership qualities and the respect he had earned from them. Some of his comrades had been loyal to him since his role in the Minsaengdan Incident. However, it is also possible that it was not Kim's comrades at all but the Soviets themselves who selected him to represent the group.[12]

For Kim Il Sung the next four weeks would be among the most important in his life. In that brief span he rose from one of a small band of forgotten exiles in a provincial port to one of the most prominent Korean figures in the Soviet zone.

On 20 September, the day after Kim's arrival at Wonsan, the Soviet occupation authorities finally got the instruction from Stalin they were waiting for: they were to create a 'bourgeois democratic republic' consisting of all 'anti-Japanese factions and organizations.'[13]

The occupation authorities were now ready to create an administrative structure in their zone. Kim's band of former partisans, many able to speak Russian and already familiar with working under the Red Army, were extremely useful in assisting with this effort.

The Soviet military dispersed these reliable partisans to various parts of the country. Some were strategically placed in security organs. For example, O Jinu, who later became the highest-ranking military person in the regime, was made police chief of Pyongyang. Since the Soviets made Pyongyang their occupation headquarters, they sent Kim Il Sung there as well, assigning him to the commandant as deputy chief garrison officer.[14] On 28 September Hyeon Chunhyeok, the highest-ranking domestic Korean, was assassinated on his way back from a meeting with the Soviet occupation authorities. Hyeon's death helped open the way for Kim, by removing one potential leader in the communist movement in the north. It is not known who the assassin was or if Kim himself had something to do with it, although that seems unlikely.

Public Debut

Kim Il Sung later described 14 October 1945 as the biggest day of his life. He was selected to be the key speaker at a ceremony to publicly welcome the Soviet forces. The Soviet authorities carefully organized a mass rally of about 300,000 people.[15] Others, including Cho Mansik, also spoke. But Kim Il Sung gave the main address after being introduced by General Lebedev (Nikolai Georgievich) as a 'national hero' and 'outstanding guerilla leader'. Kim stood before the crowd on this bright, clear autumn day, dressed in a Western-style suit and wearing Soviet military medals, including the Order of the Red Banner. In later photos of the speech published in North Korea these Soviet medals were airbrushed out. Kim had to borrow the suit from Soviet Korean interpreter Mihail Kang.[16] The entire event has become known in North Korea as the 'rally to honour

Kim Il Sung'. However, it was not about him but, rather, about the Red Army. Interestingly, Kim's first appearance on the public stage in Korea was to express gratitude for the Soviet liberation of Korea. This part of history had to be rewritten, since North Korean histories later claimed that it was Kim's Korean People's Revolutionary Army that liberated Korea, with the Red Army serving only a minor helping role, if mentioned at all.[17]

Many who attended were surprised at how young Kim looked. He was only 33, and in photos he looked even younger. A rumour started that he was not the real Kim Il Sung, or at least not the Kim Il Sung who was the legendary guerilla fighter. Once born, the idea that Kim was an impostor persisted, at least in South Korea, where in the late 1940s and 1950s it was promoted by the anti-communist government and found its way into the Western press. In the 1960s, South Korean academics examining the records came to a general agreement that the man who stood before the crowds on 14 October 1945 was the legendary guerilla fighter who had led raids on border towns in the 1930s. However, the rumour that he was an impostor was revived and promoted in the 1970s by a South Korean professor, Lee Myeongyong, who argued that there were two different guerillas operating in Manchuria in the 1930s, but the Soviet-picked leader was neither of them.[18] While it is true there were two other Kim Il Sungs operating in Manchuria, it was indeed the Soviet-picked Kim who carried out the raid on Bocheonbo and other exploits. That he was a total impostor is not supported by any credible evidence and is dismissed by almost all South Korean, Japanese and Western scholars, but the rumour still lives on.

Why did the Soviets single out Kim Il Sung? There are many explanations, including the story that he had a secret meeting with Stalin before leaving the USSR. This is unlikely. More probable is that he was the best-known of the communists, largely owing to the publicity given to the Bocheonbo raid in 1937. He appeared disciplined, worked well with Soviet officers and happened to be in the right place at the right time. And, of course, there was the shortage of other suitable candidates. The decision to promote Kim Il Sung was probably not carefully planned by the Soviets. Andrei Lankov has studied this question extensively using Russian archival materials and by interviewing some of the surviving Soviet occupation officers. He has found that the whole process was 'to a very large extent a result of improvisation and *ad hoc* decision'.[19]

Shortly after he arrived in Korea, Kim Il Sung was interviewed by occupation authorities. First the Soviets sought to confirm his credentials. He was asked if he was really born south of Pyongyang, if he was a member of the CCP, what his marital status was and other basic questions.[20] This was followed by other interviews. He must have impressed these interviewers – and we should point out that Kim was very good at impressing people, whether it was his Chinese superiors in his Manchurian days or his Soviet superiors in Siberia. His youth must have been a disadvantage, however, as would his long absence from the country. Yet, while not exactly a household name, he was nonetheless known to many people as a guerilla fighter. He wore a Soviet uniform and spoke some Russian, which would help, and he was not connected with any of the communist factions that the Soviets distrusted. His quick rise is indicated by a meeting he participated in on 30 September 1945. Lieutenant Colonel Grigoriy Mekler, head of the seventh department of the 25th Army, who seemed very much involved with promoting Kim as a leader, arranged for the ex-guerilla to join him in a meeting with Cho Mansik at the elite Hwabang club in Pyongyang. Many years later, in 1992, Mekler recalled the meeting as one in which he sought Cho's cooperation with the Soviets. The salient point is that Kim was also invited along for this important meeting: this suggests he was already on the shortlist for leader. Perhaps he was being introduced to Cho as someone he might be working with in the future.[21]

There is an alternative version of events provided by I. I. Kobanenko, a former party official who served as an officer in the headquarters of Marshal Aleksandr Vasilevsky, commander of the Far East forces. In an interview with a South Korean journalist in 1993, he claimed that in September 1945 Kim Il Sung was sent to Moscow, where he had a secret meeting with Stalin. It was there that he got the nod to be the leader in the Soviet zone. Lankov remains sceptical about the meeting, but this unconfirmed report is often repeated in the literature, even taken as definite fact. While we do not have enough information to dismiss it, such a meeting seems unlikely. Kim was too low in rank to have a personal meeting with Stalin, and if the Soviet dictator had anointed him, it is hard to explain why for several months afterwards Kim did not seem to be the clear leader of the communist movement.[22] Without corroborating evidence, it seems more likely that Kim was quickly emerging as a candidate for leader but was as yet only a candidate that the Soviets were trying out.

An Emerging 'Little Stalin'

Kim Il Sung's public appearance coincided with the organization of a North Korean communist party. On 20 September 1945 Stalin ordered that the Soviets should 'support all of northern Korea's anti-Japanese democratic parties and organizations in order to establish a proletarian democratic power'.[23] On 12 October the Soviet occupation authorities issued a proclamation allowing Koreans to organize political parties, provided they were anti-Japanese and democratic.[24] The following day local communists under the instructions of the Soviets created the North Korea Branch Bureau of the Korean Communist Party. It was done quietly and only publicly announced a week later.[25] While this was supposedly just a regional branch of the main party headquartered in Seoul, in reality it was a separate organization operating under the supervision of the Soviet authorities. Following two name changes, this is the party that rules North Korea to this day. Kim Il Sung was not its chairman. Instead the post went to Kim Yongbeom, a rather minor official. It is not known why or how he was selected other than the fact he was the husband of Pak Jeongae, an active Korean communist who had spent much time in the USSR. The fact that a rather obscure person like Kim Yongbeom was made the branch head over Kim suggests that the Soviets were not yet very certain about their choice of who should lead the emerging state.

Kim Il Sung took over the chairmanship only on 18 December, after Kim Yongbeom died of a stomach tumour.[26] He was elected by the membership, although it is most likely that the decision was made by Soviet officials beforehand. He was now the clearly anointed leader – a decision apparently approved by Stalin.[27]

The date 18 December may well be when Kim became leader of North Korea. According to Fyodor Tertitskiy, based on his study of Russian sources, a list of possible candidates had been drawn up by the Political Department of the 25th Red Army in the autumn of 1945, and by December there were still two candidates in the running, one of whom was Kim. According to Tertitskiy, Lavrentiy Beria, the much-feared head of Stalin's NKVD (later renamed the KGB), may have supported Kim Il Sung. If this was the case then Beria, a brutal sadist, might have been the key figure in the final decision to promote Kim as the future leader of North Korea. If true, it might have been because Kim had been recommended by Beria's intelligence people and he wanted to claim credit for making the decision; or perhaps he was just asserting his power over the military.[28] But whether Beria might have identified with Kim is unknown, since it is unlikely that he ever met the man he promoted.

The decision could always have been reversed, since the Soviets had at this time not given up on the idea of merging the two occupation zones and reunifying Korea. They were not yet fully committed to creating a Soviet-style state in the north, even if they were working in that direction. The situation still seemed fluid, and some sort of neutral, unified Korea under a leadership agreed to by Washington and Moscow, as became the case in Austria, was still a possibility, at least in late 1945. In any case, in mid-December the occupation-controlled press began referring to Kim as 'Commander' and 'Great Guide', suggesting that he was being prepared for leadership.[29]

Kim began his new duties with a rebuke to his fellow Northern Branch party members. In his speech 'Mistakes and Weaknesses of the Northern Branch of the Communist Party', he pointed out that only 30 per cent of its members (membership was low, at around 4,500) were workers. He urged leaders to go out to the farms, factories and mines and organize the workers.[30] He may have been acting on instructions from the Soviets to expand the party. Even if he was, the fact the party was made up of mostly a small number of intellectuals and professional revolutionaries was his concern too. This became a consistent theme of his, that the party should be a mass party with a large membership and that party officials should spend time with the labouring people.

Over the coming months Kim began to consolidate his position as leader, but then, on 1 March 1946, his rise to power was almost cut short. In February 1946 a right-wing group in the south sent agents to carry out assassinations of leftist leaders in the north. Kim was one of their targets. That day a grenade was tossed at him but was caught by a Soviet officer. It exploded in the officer's hand, and he lost an arm.

Meanwhile, Kim's loyal fellow partisans took up key positions in the security apparatus emerging in the Soviet zone. Their numbers were small, perhaps no more than two hundred in the autumn of 1945. Yet they dominated the Peace Preservation Corps, the border constabulary and railroad guards.[31] They also took up positions outside the Communist Party. At first the Soviets worked with a broad coalition of Korean nationalists, at least in theory. The Soviets then orchestrated the political domination by the communists in steps. When Cho Mansik and his conservative colleagues organized the

Democratic Party in November, the Soviets pressured them to include some communist members. Choe Yonggeon, a former Manchurian partisan, was made deputy chair of the party. Choe had once worked with Cho Mansik but later joined the guerillas in Manchuria and became a comrade of Kim Il Sung. Later he served as North Korea's head of state. Kim Chaek, another Manchurian partisan, headed the Democratic Party's secretariat.

The American and Soviet occupation zones were meant as temporary arrangements under the trusteeship that had been discussed and agreed upon during the war. When the Allied powers met at the Moscow Conference in December 1945 to discuss the post-war settlement, they agreed to carry out the four- to five-year four-power trusteeship of the United States, the USSR, China and Britain. Koreans, in general, were still unaware of the trusteeship agreement, and reaction to the public announcement by the powers was met with universal outrage. Massive demonstrations took place in the south. In the north the Soviets demanded all parties were to support the trusteeship. When Cho Mansik opposed the Soviet–U.S. plans for a trusteeship, he was removed as party chair and placed under house arrest. Choe Yonggeon was made the new Democratic Party chair. Thus, the chief non-communist party became a mere puppet organization of the communists, with two of Kim's associates in charge.

Just as Kim Il Sung was emerging as the leader among the North Korean communists, another group of Korean communists began to trickle into the country. In autumn 1945 members of the Yanan faction, consisting of the Korean communists who fought with Mao Zedong in China, began returning to Korea. In January 1946 they formed their own Sinmindang (New Democratic Party) with Kim Dubong as its chair. This briefly appeared as a rival communist party, although there were no real ideological differences. The situation was hardly pleasing to the Soviets. There were now two communist parties: one dominated by veterans of mainland China, and a second that was the only branch of the Korean Communist Party headquartered in the American occupation zone. Behind the scenes they orchestrated some changes. In June 1946 the Branch Bureau detached itself from the Seoul-based main Korean Communist Party; renamed the North Korean Workers' Party (NKWP), it merged with the Sinmindang. The NKWP held its first party congress on 28–30 August 1946. Kim Dubong was named chair and Kim Il Sung one of two vice chairs, the other being a rather minor figure, Chu Nyeongha. There were good reasons to select Kim Dubong as chair: aged 56, he was 22 years older than Kim, better known and well respected. Not just Kim Dubong but many of the Yanan members were older and had held greater positions of responsibility in the independence movement than Kim Il Sung. But Kim Dubong was little more than a figurehead; Kim Il Sung was still Moscow's man and the real leader of the party.[32] Moscow then instructed leftists in south Korea to form a similar coalition in November 1946, known as the South Korean Workers' Party (SKWP).

In March 1948 the Second Party Congress of the NKWP met, and Kim finally got the party position that had eluded him: he was elected chair. The party itself was becoming more to his satisfaction. Kim had complained about the party's narrow membership base, its lack of representatives from the working class and the almost total lack of representatives from the peasant majority. This was corrected with the recruitment of many new members. In fact the NKWP differed from most other communist parties in that a majority of its members were peasants rather than workers. However, few had any training in Marxism-Leninism or much knowledge of communist doctrine. Concerned about this, under Soviet advice, six-month ideological training sessions were conducted for a selected elite at the Central Party School, and an even smaller number were sent to the Soviet Union for further ideological training.[33]

Three years later, after most of the communists in the south had fled to the north or were underground, the two parties merged – or rather, the southern party was absorbed to form the Korean Workers' Party (KWP, Joseon Rodong-dang), which has remained the name of North Korea's ruling party. Kim Il Sung was its chair.

Birth of the Cult of Kim Il Sung

Once the Soviets had settled on Kim Il Sung, they began crafting a Stalin-like cult around him. During 1946 his portrait appeared alongside Stalin's in almost every public place. Songs about him were sung, and in October 1946 the new national university in Pyongyang was named after him. He was praised as 'the leader of all the Korean people', the 'hero of the nation' and the 'Great Leader'.[34] The adulation of the leader started almost with the inception of the new state. An early biography described him as a great general, 'winning every battle'.[35] There was nothing unusual about this. Throughout the Soviet bloc the 'little Stalins' carried out their own cults of personality alongside that of Stalin himself, a development encouraged and fostered by Moscow.

However, there were some distinctive characteristics of the cult that emerged in the late 1940s. Some of the language and symbolism appeared to reflect the influence of the intense emperor worship of the colonial period. For example, in early 1946 the writer Han Sorya referred to Kim Il Sung as 'our sun' (*uri ui taeyang*), consciously or unconsciously using the same sun metaphor that had been associated with the Japanese emperor.[36] Another distinctive North Korean feature were stories of the Manchurian guerillas and Kim's role in directing them. These would grow to wildly exaggerated proportions later, but even as early as 1946 the 'Song of General Kim Il Sung', composed by Kim Won'gyun and played at public occasions, spoke of 'the snowy winds of Manchuria/ the long, long nights of the forest/ Who is the timeless partisan, the peerless patriot/ the beneficent liberator of the working masses/ Great Sun of democratic new Korea?'[37] One feature of this cult was very different from

Stalin's: the glorification of Kim Il Sung's family. Most of this developed later, but even in the late 1940s the phrase 'revolutionary family heritage' (*hyeongmyeongjeok gagye*) appeared in a textbook.[38] Based on the Korean tradition of seeing each son as carrying out their family line, Kim's leadership was being depicted as part of his family tradition of fighting for a progressive, independent Korea.

Kim himself did not create or direct the cult. The actual work of crafting it was done by Korean intellectuals who had no personal connection or ties to Kim Il Sung. The most important was Han Sorya. Han was born in Hamgyeong, in the north, the son of a local official. He moved to Manchuria and then to Seoul and became a pro-Japanese writer. After the liberation he moved to Pyongyang, where he promoted himself as a communist literary figure, based on his brief affiliation with a leftist writers' group. A talented Korean writer, more than any other single person he created much of the style and imagery of the Kim cult. Another major figure was the Pyongyang journalist Han Jaedeok. Han published stories of Kim's sacrifices and heroic efforts to achieve 'national salvation', and in 1948 he wrote an official biography in which he stated that General Kim Il Sung was 'our nation's greatest hero and the sun of our people's hope.'[39] Thus, many of the elements of Kim's cult appeared in these early years, invented by the Soviets and their Korean collaborators. Kim only elaborated on them over the years, and as he did, they came to reflect Kim's own inflated self-image.

Kim Il Sung and the Emerging State

Kim Il Sung became the de facto leader of not only the KWP but the emerging state it ruled. After an initial confusion the Soviets began to construct this state in stages. The first was in February 1946, when they organized a North Korean Provisional People's Committee. They appointed Kim as its chairman and Kim Dubong as vice chairman. In November 1946 Soviet occupation authorities carried out carefully managed elections to provincial and city people's committees. Delegates from these newly elected people's committees met in February 1947 and established the North Korean People's Committee, a legislative body.[40] Significantly, the term 'provisional' was dropped, giving this a more permanent connotation as Moscow had moved closer to creating a satellite state in its occupation zone. The members elected Kim Il Sung to head this new body. All this was of course orchestrated by the Soviets, confirming that Kim was to be the leader of this new state. Kim Dubong was replaced as vice chair of the People's Committee with Kim's partisan comrade Kim Chaek, further consolidating his position. Did Kim Il Sung manage to engineer this change? The answer is not clear, but if he did have something to do with Kim Chaek's appointment he would have needed Soviet approval.

The Soviets were building a state and a party to rule it, and they also began constructing an army and security system to defend it. First, in 1946 the Soviets established a police force as well as railway defence units. They established a Central Security Officers' Training School, which graduated its first class in the autumn of 1947.[41] In February 1948 the Korean People's Army (KPA) was officially organized, although in fact the Soviets had begun forming the army in 1947. Most of its high-ranking officers were partisans. The Soviets played a big role in training the KPA, attaching at least three Soviet advisers to each regiment.[42] Kim Il Sung held no position in the security forces, but many of his partisan comrades did. For example, Kim Chaek headed the Pyongyang Institute, founded in November 1945 to train military officers and political cadres. They did not completely dominate the KPA, however; many military positions went to Yanan Koreans who also had military experience. Yet the partisans held enough positions that Kim was able to exert considerable influence over the KPA. The head of the internal security forces, Pang Hakse, was a former Soviet police officer who was sent over along with other Soviet Koreans to assist the occupation.[43]

Pang became one of Kim's most loyal supporters. By the summer of 1948, as North Korea was moving towards independence, Kim was head of the ruling party, head of the state apparatus, and had close allies in key positions in the military and security forces.

It was not just a new state that Kim was presiding over but a new society. Under Soviet tutelage, North Koreans were carrying out what Kim Il Sung called a 'people's democratic revolution', using the label given to similar reforms being carried out in other Soviet-occupied countries.[44] Industries in the Soviet zone were nationalized. Most of the owners were either Japanese or Koreans who were labelled as 'collaborators'. These industries were confiscated by the state as the Japanese returned home and the business class fled to the south. The most significant measure taken was land reform. Three out of four Koreans were peasants; most were tenants either owning no land or having plots so small that they had to work as sharecroppers for wealthy Korean or Japanese landowners. When the North Korean Provisional People's Committee met in early 1946, one of the first measures it issued was to confiscate the land owned by Japanese, 'national traitors' and landlords who owned more than five *jeongbo* (approximately 1 hectare, or 2.5 acres) and redistribute it to the peasants.[45]

The land reform was carried out with great speed, largely finished in time for spring planting. At a stroke the countryside was transformed from a land of tenants to one of small independent farmers. The actual living conditions of peasants improved only marginally. They had to pay a heavy land tax, and their farms were very small. But probably no other measure did more to win support for the regime. It also served as a rebuke to the American occupation authority and its supporters in the south, where the landlords were still entrenched.[46] It provided a powerful argument for those who argued that the North Korean zone represented the real liberators. Unfortunately, it did little to solve a problem Kim had to face often during his tenure as North Korean leader: food shortages. Most of the good farmland was in the south, and North Korea could never quite produce enough to adequately feed the population.

North Korea was experiencing a true social revolution. Under Soviet direction the Korean communists were constructing a radical new society. The old landholding *yangban* class vanished; the newly emerging business entrepreneurs fled. Instead of the traditional hierarchical society with its many levels of deference in speech and honorifics, all workers were encouraged to address each other as comrade (*dongmu*), no matter their position or age.[47] New social identities were being imposed on everyone by requiring their enrolment in state-sponsored organizations. A North Korean Democratic Women's League was created in early 1946 (later renamed the Korean Democratic Women's Union) and had over a million members by the end of the year.[48] Young people in their early teens to late twenties were organized into the North Korean Democratic Youth League. There was a North Korean Federation of Trade Unions; all workers were incorporated into it.

Probably second only to the land reform in reshaping society was the massive push for education and literacy. Half the population was illiterate and only a small percentage had more than a basic education, but that began to quickly change. The emerging North Korean state rapidly expanded school enrolment and conducted mass literacy campaigns, facilitated by the decision to switch from a mixed script using many Chinese characters to the exclusive use of the easy-to-learn Korean alphabet Hangeul. It created a new educational system, with Kim Il Sung University at its apex. The expansion of schooling provided greater opportunity for ordinary people to get an education for their children, and literacy campaigns enabled many unschooled adults to read. Other reforms included an eight-hour day for workers and legal equality for women. Laws made divorce easier and ended the legal basis of the old patriarchal family system.

Korea's economic recovery from the initial chaos and destruction of 1945 proceeded rapidly, led by industrialization and modernization of society. Abundant supplies of hydroelectric power contributed to the rapid increase in electrification. The number of homes with electricity increased from one in six in 1945 to one in three in 1948.[49] Tiled roofs replaced thatched ones. This much-desired improvement in rural housing was not achieved in South Korea until the early 1970s. Of course, not everyone was happy, and there were some violent protests, mostly by Christian groups. They were quickly suppressed and participants arrested. Many Christians and other dissenters fled south.[50] Thousands of opponents were sent to Siberia, a practice that continued until North Koreans established their own system of political prison camps.

Historians disagree on whether the Soviets were doing all the planning and pulling all the strings or whether the North Koreans themselves were active agents in these transformations of society. Scholars such as the South Korean historian Sŏ Tongman have given greater agency to the North Koreans themselves.[51] The work of Charles Armstrong, Suzy Kim and others looking at captured documents indicates that at the very least, the North Korean communists enthusiastically carried out the radical reforms, even if they were drawn up by the Soviets.[52] As for Kim himself, the same seems to be true. The reforms reflected his vision of society and his own experiences with the People's Revolutionary Governments established in Manchuria in the 1930s. He was not a puppet carrying out the will of his Soviet masters but, rather, a good officer carrying out the orders of his superiors. But most likely, Kim, like many of his fellow Korean communists, did so enthusiastically.

Leader of the DPRK

As Kim no doubt understood, it was clear over the course of 1946 that the Soviets and their Korean communist partners would set up a separate state in their zone; a unified state would come later. When the Soviets and Americans met at the Moscow Conference in December 1945, there still seemed to be hope that the division into two zones would be temporary and a unified government could be created. Washington and Moscow created an American–Soviet Joint Commission to work out arrangements for a unified governing board. However, by the spring of 1946, when the Joint Commission met, it was probably already too late for this. The border between the two zones was being treated as a permanent one, and the outlines of a separate state in the north were already being established. The body's second meeting the following year also got nowhere, after which the USA, seeing no progress and wishing to extricate itself from the peninsula, turned the question of independence over to the United Nations. The UN formed a Temporary Commission on Korea, which decided that elections would be held in spring 1948. When it was clear the Soviets would not cooperate, the UN held elections anyway in the areas that were accessible to them, that is, in the south. This meant there was to be a separate election in the south, which would likely mean a separate government.

In the spring of 1948 North Korea had a government, with Kim at its head, an armed forces and was in the process of a sweeping revolution, reorganizing society on the Soviet model. A few prominent South Koreans still hoped something could be worked out, but their efforts at negotiating some sort of united government came to nothing. The UN went ahead with its supervised elections in May in the south, where people elected a National Assembly. In July the assembly elected Syngman Rhee (Ri Seungman) as president, and with the UN's blessing the Republic of Korea (ROK) was declared in Seoul on 15 August.

Meanwhile, the Soviets prepared for their state. Officials in Moscow drew up a constitution for the DPRK modelled on the 1936 USSR constitution. It was written in Russian, translated into Korean and then presented to Kim and his comrades. The Soviets and their clients proceeded to carry out their own elections in August 1948, which they claimed were secretly conducted in the south as well. An assembly, with two-thirds of the delegates supposedly representing the south, met and was approved by the new government. On 9 September the delegates proclaimed the Joseon Minjujuui Inmin Gonghwaguk (Democratic People's Republic of Korea, or DPRK), with Kim Il Sung as premier. To distinguish itself from its rival, the DPRK adopted a new flag in July, the *Ingonggi* (People's Republic flag), to replace the old national flag that the ROK was using (the *Taegeukgi*). The North denounced the *Taegeukgi* with its yin-yang and trigram symbols as 'feudalistic' and 'imported from China'.[53]

The creation of two separate states was an outcome that few, if any, really wanted. Neither Kim nor any of the other leaders of the newly created DPRK saw the situation of two rival Koreas both claiming to represent the entire nation as more than a temporary measure until national unification could be achieved. Reunification was a prime goal of the DPRK from the beginning of its creation. Southern districts were represented in their Supreme People's Assembly. The constitution of the DPRK specified Seoul as the capital (*seoul* means 'capital' in Korean); Pyongyang was the temporary government headquarters. This was also true of South Korean president Syngman Rhee, who considered the division temporary until the country was reunified under his leadership.

The Leadership of the New North Korean State

Kim Il Sung, although the preeminent leader of North Korea and already the subject of a personality cult, was still first among equals. His fellow partisans held key cabinet posts but were far from dominating it. Only three Manchurian partisans held cabinet positions: Kim Il Sung as premier, Kim Chaek as minister of industry and Choe Yonggeon as minister of defence. The partisans, while holding only a minority of the top positions in the party and the government, were over-represented in the security organs and the military. Still, many key positions were held by the Yanan and Soviet Koreans. Domestic communists held more cabinet posts than any other faction. Most prominent was Pak Heonyeong, the leader of the SKWP. Pak, who held the posts of vice premier and foreign minister, was considered the number-two figure in the regime. It was a bit awkward to have so many South Korean communists in the government, but their knowledge of the South made them important for any reunification plans. In 1948 they were the most serious rivals to Kim and his partisans.

Kim led a comfortably private life during this time. Initially, he came without his family. His wife, Kim Jong Suk, and their children arrived at the port of Unggi, in the extreme northeast of Korea, in November 1945 with a group of partisan women. Kim Jong Suk then joined him in Pyongyang.[54] They lived in a compound for Korean leaders in a pleasant house with a garden and a small pond. Their neighbours were other prominent people in the emerging North Korean state. A frequent visitor was Terentii Shtykov, the chief political officer in the Soviet zone; Kim and Shtykov got along well and played cards together. According to one report, the loser had to crawl under the table.[55]

Kim's friendship with Shtykov could have only strengthened his position. Yet he could hardly have found the situation very satisfying. He was an ardent nationalist who had been catapulted into a leadership position by foreigners, heading a state that embraced only a third of the Korean people, a state that was as much a Soviet as a Korean creation. Even the constitution was drawn up by Moscow; Kim and his comrades had had no input in it. And he was not an independent agent but had to obey orders from the USSR. The Soviet occupation forces had quickly withdrawn, but Shtykov had not left. He now assumed the role of Soviet Ambassador to North Korea but was more of a proconsul, relaying instruction from Moscow. Kim's scope of action was so limited that he had to get permission from the Soviets when he wanted to open an embassy in a foreign country, even a communist one. At this point he was just another 'little Stalin' presiding over a Soviet satellite state, his authority and position dependent on the whims of his foreign patrons.

4
FAILED REUNIFICATION

ON 9 SEPTEMBER 1948 the 36-year-old Kim Il Sung was now the leader of the Democratic People's Republic of Korea. But he was only the leader of half of Korea, and only one-third of the Korean people. And he didn't even control the capital. His goal was to be the liberator of the Korean people, but most were still not liberated. He made it clear that the new state he and his comrades governed was merely the 'base camp' from which they would carry out and complete the liberation of Korea.

These were not just his views. The North Korean leadership in general saw reunification, and thus the complete liberation of the Korean people, as their main task. From their point of view, the liberation of the South with its government under the thumb of the United States was a continuation of the nationalist anti-imperialist struggle. Furthermore, the destruction of the political and social order of the South with its 'feudal' landlord class and their comprador bourgeois allies was also a continuation of the socialist revolution. There was no question about the need for reunification. In his first public statement as premier of the DPRK, on 10 September 1948, Kim Il Sung declared that unification of the fatherland was to have top priority in his government's agenda. In October 1948 he announced, 'The central government, established with the consent of South and North Koreans, will unify all the Korean people and use all its power for the rapid construction of a unified democratic, autonomous, and independent nation.'[1] This remained his goal for the next 46 years he was in power.

The situation in the South was encouraging. In many ways the Rhee regime seemed rather shaky. Peasants were disappointed with its failure to enact land reform. Political strikes by workers and students were common. The politics of the country was contentious and divisive. In April 1948 protests against holding separate elections led to a full-scale insurrection on the island province of Jeju. On 13 October 1948, just one month after the USA transferred command of the ROK forces to the Korean officers, troops sent to the southern city of Yeosu on their way to put down the Cheju rebellion mutinied. They took over the town and set up People's Courts. When more loyal forces regained control and put down the rebellion, many of the rebels fled into nearby mountains and joined local partisans in guerilla resistance. The United States, which had planned to withdraw all troops in the autumn, was alarmed enough to delay the withdrawal until December and then again until March 1949.

All this convinced Kim that the sooner he invaded the South the better. The ROK was weak, its government was unpopular and its armed forces poorly trained and unreliable. But the situation could change if South Korean president Rhee's government was able to suppress opposition and with American assistance build up its armed forces. And Kim knew the ROK Army had some experienced Japanese-trained officers, many from the North, who were vehemently anti-communist. And there was the real possibility that the more populous South, if it grew strong enough, would invade the North. Rhee also passionately desired reunification and made it clear in public statements that he wanted to liberate the North and would try to do so as soon as possible.

It is not surprising, then, that Kim, from the day he assumed the premiership of the new DPRK, prepared for war while he sought Soviet permission and support for an invasion. In early March 1949 Kim took his first trip out of the country since becoming premier, leading an eleven-member delegation to Moscow. On 7 March he had a meeting with Stalin. He had two items on his agenda: to ask for assistance with the new 1949–50 Two-Year Economic Plan and to request Soviet support for a military invasion of the South. The latter was the main purpose of the visit. Kim Il Sung is reported to have told the Soviet dictator,

> Comrade Stalin, we believe the situation makes it necessary and possible to liberate the whole country through military means. The reactionary forces of the South will never agree on a peaceful unification and will perpetuate the division of the country until they feel themselves strong enough to attack the North.

Furthermore, he told him, 'Our people are very anxious to be together again to cast off the yoke of the reactionary regime and their American masters.'[2]

Stalin did not dismiss the idea of an invasion but explained that the situation was not yet favourable. Kim, with his usual decisive, impatient nature and youthful energy, wanted to complete the liberation of the country as soon as possible. Stalin was far more cautious. He feared getting involved in a war with the United States. He pointed out that American troops were still in the South, but even when they left it might be dangerous. In fact he believed that the Americans were withdrawing so that the South could invade the North and that their repeated delays in withdrawing were to give the Rhee government time to get ready. That Stalin so misunderstood the real situation seems surprising, since his people in Korea knew the South militarily was not capable of starting a war and that the Americans did not want to get involved in a conflict on the peninsula. Shtykov, his man in Pyongyang, was well aware that the USA was delaying its withdrawal until it felt that the ROK would not collapse – that is, to give the ROK Army time to deal with its internal security problems. However, suspicious of U.S. intentions and keen to avoid conflict, Shtykov exaggerated the strength of the South in his reports, apparently feeding his superior information that supported Stalin's misperceptions.[3] So Kim returned with promises of economic aid but no support for an invasion. Nonetheless, Kim continued with plans for liberation using a three-pronged approach: building up the DPRK's economy, building up its military and supporting guerilla activity and unrest in the South. He and Pak Heonyeong met with Shtykov, the ambassador, twice in August 1949 and told him there was no choice but to invade the South.[4]

Building Up the Economy and the KPA

North Korea's economy in 1948 was still recovering from the chaos and disruptions that followed nationalization, the expulsion of the Japanese at the end of the war and the flight of much of the local entrepreneurial class. But in 1949 industrial production was returning to pre-liberation levels. Food shortages were still a problem, aggravated by the disruptions of the 1946 land reform, but through a system of strict rationing the situation was improving. The North had almost all the electric power generation on the peninsula thanks to the construction of hydroelectric plants by the colonial regime, and rural electrification was expanding rapidly. In general, the economy of the North, for all its problems, was outperforming the South.[5] This part of Kim's programme for strengthening the DPRK, as he prepared for liberation of the South, was going well.

Kim's more immediate concern was building the Korean People's Army (KPA) into a formidable instrument for liberating the South. Officers in the KPA began training in the Soviet Union. Pyongyang also benefited from the influx of Koreans who fought with the People's Liberation Army (PLA) during the Chinese Civil War. With the war in China going well for the PLA, Beijing, at Pyongyang's request, released many veteran Korean fighters so they could go to the North. In the late summer of 1949 the PLA's 166th Division under General Pang Hosan, which consisted entirely of Koreans, arrived in the

DPRK. This was followed by the 164th Division, together amounting to 28,000 highly trained and experienced troops.[6] They were joined by other veteran Korean communist fighters from China so that about 35,000 experienced fighters in total returned to join the KPA from the summer of 1949 to the end of the year. Another 14,000 returned in early 1950.[7] These former PLA soldiers were given two to four months' training and then were integrated into the KPA.[8] They provided combat experience and established links and goodwill between the PLA and the KPA. The Soviets supplied equipment and training.

Pak Heonyeong and the Guerilla Movement in the South

Kim took direct charge of overseeing economic development and building up the KPA, but the task of supporting rebellion in the South he left with Pak Heonyeong. Pak and his southern communist comrades had the knowledge of and contacts below the 38th parallel, which Kim lacked. Kim had never even been to the southern half of the country and had never developed personal relations with anyone from there. Thus he was a complete outsider to the part of the country that contained the capital, most of the cultural centres and two-thirds of the population. As a result Kim had to rely on Pak and his fellow southerners. Pak and the domestic communists ran the Kangdong Institute, which trained cadres to organize revolution in the South. They sent 3,000 guerillas to the South, including six hundred cadres trained at the Kangdong Institute, to assist with or provoke pro-communist uprisings. They included two important experienced communists, Kim Samyeong and Yi Juha. Many of these cadres were sent to fight in the Mount Odae region of South Korea and another group to the Mount Taebaek area;[9] these were both rugged areas not too far from the North and ideal for guerilla operations.

Pak was optimistic about the prospects of winning over the people of the South and enthusiastically and persuasively promoted the idea. In fact he was more enthusiastic than Kim about the invasion, since he felt the Rhee regime could be toppled by his partisans with the support of the people in the South. Kim was more cautious about this.[10] A partisan himself who worked to gain support of the local people in his Manchurian days, Kim believed in the necessity of winning over the people. But he was a realist who knew the limitations of small bands of guerillas fighters in the face of well-equipped state forces. He put his faith in what the Soviets achieved, defeating the Japanese with a massive force well equipped with artillery, armoured vehicles and air support. His preference, therefore, was to build up a large, modern, heavily armed military. But Kim seems to have believed Pak when he told him that the people of the South would revolt against their own government.

Pak's guerillas, in fact, did not do very well at all in the South. The ROK conducted successful counter-insurgency campaigns against the guerillas in 1948–9 and 1949–50, including setting up strategic hamlets and carrying out frightful reprisals against rebel supporters. And in March 1950 prospects for a successful guerilla campaign were dimmed when both Kim Samyeong and Yi Juha were captured.[11] However, Pak believed and persuaded Kim that resistance to the ROK would be rekindled by a northern invasion. This belief was not wholly unfounded. Peasant discontent over the delays in land reform, student demonstrations at universities and high schools, and frequent labour strikes suggested that the masses of the South would be ready for an alternative. Furthermore, despite the South's successes in counter-insurgency, the winds of change seemed favourable to Pyongyang. The PLA had defeated the U.S.-backed Guomindang in China in 1949, and a triumphant Mao Zedong proclaimed the People's Republic of China on 1 October. By the spring of 1950 the Guomindang held on only to the island of Taiwan. Its erstwhile ally the United States appeared resigned to the imminent fall of that last non-communist stronghold. Politically unstable, with a restive population, a weak military, a foreign patron that seemed less than fully committed to its defence, and with thousands of sympathizers ready to rise up in support of the KPA (or so Pyongyang may have believed), South Korea seemed ready for a quick conquest. By June 1950 the KPA had 150,000 men under arms, compared to fewer than 100,000 in the ROK. It had more experienced troops than South Korea's military, and it had better equipment, including heavy artillery, tanks and planes, which the ROK lacked. For Kim an invasion seemed likely to result in a swift victory and the completion of the struggle for national liberation and reunification.

Personal Tragedies

Kim Il Sung's private life was very private, almost secretive. Hard facts about his family members, unless they were major political figures, are difficult to come by. We have limited knowledge of his marital life, his relations with his children or his romantic liaisons with women, let alone what they might reveal about him. We do know that during these years of his rise to power and preparation for war, Kim Il Sung suffered some personal tragedies. First there was the death of his second son, Kim Manil. The boy was born in Siberia in 1944 and had a Russian name, Shura (Kim Manil). According to the later official accounts, Manil was playing with his older brother, Jong Il, at a pond by their home in Pyongyang when he accidentally drowned.[12] Accounts vary as to the date of this tragedy. Russian sources have him drowning in a well in Siberia before the family moved back to Korea, but other accounts state this occurred more than two years later. According to Mun Il, a North Korean official who later left for the Soviet Union, Kim reacted to news of the death of his younger son by getting drunk and crying.[13]

On 22 September 1949 Kim's wife Kim Jong Suk died in childbirth. She was three months short of her 32nd birthday. There is evidence that Kim Il Sung had affairs with other women during their marriage,[14] yet Kim talked fondly of Jong Suk for the rest of his life and there is no reason to assume he did not love her. She gave birth to his first and second sons and in 1946 to his first daughter, Kyong Hui, who later became one of the most powerful figures in North Korea. Jong Suk played no active role in politics, and her life and death were mostly a private affair; as noted, however, twenty years later she became a major figure in the cult of the Kim family.

Getting the Go-Ahead

Stalin had been reluctant to support Kim's plan for an invasion of the South. Then Stalin changed his mind. On 30 January 1950 he telegrammed Ambassador Shtykov to tell Kim Il Sung 'that I am ready to help in this matter'. He explained he understood Kim Il Sung's impatience, but 'he must understand that such a large matter such as he wants to undertake needs large preparation' and 'the matter must be organized so that there would not be too great a risk.'[15] He then added, oddly,

> I have a request for Comrade Kim Il Sung. The Soviet Union is experiencing a great insufficiency in lead. We would like to receive from Korea a yearly minimum of 25,000 tons of lead. Korea would render us a great assistance if it could yearly send to the Soviet Union the indicated amount of lead. I hope that Kim Il Sung will not refuse us in this.[16]

The next day Shtykov reported that Kim Il Sung received the news that Stalin would support his invasion plans 'with great satisfaction'.

At Stalin's invitation Kim Il Sung and Pak Heonyeong went to Moscow at the end of March, returning on 25 April. It was a long stay in which the two had time to meet with Stalin and other Soviet leaders several times to plan for the invasion. Historians have speculated on what might have caused Stalin to change his mind about supporting Kim's request to send the KPA into the South. Besides the perceived weakness of the ROK, the somewhat ambiguous American position in South Korea was also encouraging. The United States supported the state and wanted to prevent communism from spreading closer to Japan, which all in Washington agreed was vital to U.S. interests; however, the members of the Truman administration and many in Congress did not want to invest too much in a land that remained of peripheral concern. The USA began withdrawing its forces in September 1948, completing it the following year. It allocated funding for the establishment of a 65,000-man ROK Army and left behind a 500-member Korean Military Advisory Group to help train it. It also provided generous economic aid to Seoul. But this generosity soon waned; the U.S. Congress considerably reduced economic aid for 1950 and limited funding for the South Korean Army. Americans were particularly wary of President Rhee's strident nationalism and were concerned over reports of ROK raids along the northern border, as they wanted to avoid the risk of conflict on the peninsula. They provided only small arms for the ROK forces and no tanks, heavy artillery or combat aircraft. Even in small arms, the ROK Army had a mere fifteen-day supply in June 1950.[17] The United States was unclear about the extent of its commitment; the most famous example was Secretary of State Dean Acheson's press conference of 12 January 1950, at which he excluded South Korea from the U.S. defensive perimeter. This press conference could have been interpreted as a signal that the Americans would not intervene. Mao's victory on the mainland and the USA's abandonment of its Guomindang allies were most likely major factors as well.

According to official Soviet summaries of their meetings, Stalin explained his decision to his Korean visitors. He told Kim and Pak that 'changes in the international situation' made circumstances more favourable. The PLA victory in China was a psychological victory for Asian revolutionaries and it showed how weak the Asian reactionaries were. It also made Chinese troops available if needed. The risks for the USA if it entered a war in Korea were higher, since China was now allied to the USSR and the Soviets now had the nuclear bomb. Stalin also referred to 'information coming from the U.S.' that it would not attack, but it is not clear to what he was referring.[18] Still, as always, Stalin expressed his concern about an American intervention. Kim assured him that the war would end swiftly since the people would rise up in support, led by 200,000 communists in the South; the ROK would fall before the Americans understood what was happening. At one point he predicted that the war would be over in three days.[19]

Stalin's support was conditional: he had to inform Mao Zedong of the invasion plans and get the Chinese leader's support before the final go-ahead could be given. Just a little over two weeks after returning to Pyongyang, on 13 May 1950, Kim and Pak travelled to Beijing. This was Kim's first visit to China since the People's Republic of China was declared on 1 October the previous year. And it was his first visit to China outside Manchuria. At the meeting Mao expressed concern over the possibility that the USA might intervene to prop up the Rhee regime in the South, pointing out how close Korea was to Japan. Mao feared that Chinese forces might need to intervene. Kim expressed confidence that the operation would only take two or three weeks and that it would be over before the Americans could arrive; the KPA could handle everything and would not need Chinese military support. Mao seems to have been put off by Kim's certainty on this matter and later told his colleagues that Kim's response was 'arrogant'.[20]

Nonetheless, Mao did not oppose the invasion even if he did not enthusiastically support it. That was enough for Kim to report to Stalin and his comrades in Pyongyang that he had Mao's assent. The last obstacle to the invasion was cleared. Mao in fact reluctantly agreed to back the North Koreans only after Moscow assured him of the invasion's likely success. However, he made it clear that

Chinese forces would not assist if the Americans intervened, unless they crossed the 38th parallel.[21] Meanwhile, a team of Soviet advisers drew up plans and the USSR began supplying more tanks, artillery and other weapons. In late spring Soviet advisers completed their 'Pre-emptive Strike Operational Plan'. By the end of May the Soviet ambassador reported that the KPA infantry was nearly ready for combat and that Kim Il Sung wanted to carry out the 'attack' in late June, before the rainy season began in July.[22]

Before dawn on 25 June 1950 the DPRK launched artillery barrages along the Ongjin Peninsula, the scene of frequent clashes. Within hours it had begun a full-scale offensive along the border. The next day, in a broadcast to his people, Kim announced that the ROK forces had attacked but that the KPA had successfully counterattacked.[23] North Korea's plan was to quickly capture Seoul, strike a crippling blow to the ROK Army and then advance further south as the South Korean state collapsed. ROK forces defended Seoul for two days and then, as Pyongyang had anticipated, they began to crumble. On the third day of fighting, Seoul fell to the KPA, causing horrendous scenes as thousands of panicked civilians fled. Symbolic of the chaos and horror was the Han River Bridge incident. The South Korean military prematurely blew up the only bridge over the river that separated the capital from the country to the south, killing hundreds of civilians as they were trying to escape the city.

With the fall of Seoul on 28 June, defence minister Choe Yonggeon declared three days of celebration.[24] Everything had gone to plan, and complete victory over the South seemed imminent. Pyongyang caught Washington and Seoul completely by surprise. However, after some initial confusion over the scale of the invasion, President Truman acted swiftly. On 27 June, as Seoul was falling to the KPA, he ordered General Douglas MacArthur in Japan to use available U.S. air and naval forces to support the South Korean army. Partly because he was uncertain of support from a Republican-dominated Congress, but also to give an international legitimacy as well as gain allied support, Truman went directly to the United Nations and called for a resolution giving Washington authority to intervene. At the time the Soviet Union was boycotting the UN to protest its refusal to allow the new communist regime in Beijing to take China's seat, which was still held by the Guomindang government (now headquartered on Taiwan). With Moscow absent, the Security Council swiftly passed a resolution that demanded the withdrawal of DPRK forces and called for UN members to assist the ROK. On 7 July the UN Security Council established a unified military command under the United States. The army that North Korea now faced was at least nominally an international force, with sixteen nations contributing men. By the spring of 1951 this included 12,000 British, 8,500 Canadian, 5,000 Turkish and 5,000 Filipino troops. It was, however, largely an American operation, with the USA supplying most of the troops, paying the costs and in command.

Even with the American intervention, Kim Il Sung's forces were still in a strong position. Since it would take weeks to mobilize forces from the United States, Washington relied on the 100,000 troops it had in occupied Japan, which began arriving on 30 June 1950. But these soldiers were mainly involved in administrative and clerical duties and had little combat readiness. The U.S. armed forces had been downsizing since the end of the Second World War from 12 million men and women in uniform in 1945 to 1.6 million in June 1950. There were fewer than 600,000 in the army, and many of these were in Europe. When the first American troops saw action at Osan, south of Seoul, on 5 July, they were forced into retreat along with the ROK soldiers. The KPA continued its offensive, capturing Daejeon, about 160 kilometres (100 mi.) south of Seoul, in early July, then advancing towards Busan in the southeast corner of the country, where the South Korean government had fled.

It was now imperative to complete the conquest before American troops could be fully deployed. However, two things were going wrong for Kim. Although the ROK forces had been overwhelmed by the KPA and Seoul fell in three days, the retreating South Korean troops did not collapse as quickly as he had expected but often put up stubborn resistance. And there was no popular uprising in support of the liberators from the North. Although there was some communist guerilla activity in the southeastern mountains, this was merely from the remnants of partisans that had mostly been wiped out in the 1949–50 campaign. By June 1950 most leftists in the South had been killed, imprisoned or had fled to the North. For the most part, the South Korean population fled or acquiesced to North Koreans, but with some minor exceptions did not rise up in arms against their own government. Kim's expectation that the war would be over in a matter of days was wrong. Still his forces continued to advance southward.

North Korea attempted to bring its revolution to the areas of the South that came under its control. In a radio speech on 26 June, Kim announced that South Korea was being liberated from Japanese and American imperialism and called for the reinstatement of the people's committees that had sprung up in the days after liberation, calling them the 'real organs of the people'.[25] During the two to three months that KPA forces occupied Seoul and other major cities, they attempted to carry out the same revolutionary changes as in the North. They set up people's committees as the local governing bodies. DPRK officials confiscated the property of the ROK government, its officials and 'monopoly capitalists' and drew up plans to redistribute land in the countryside. They released political prisoners from jails, many of whom sought the opportunity to get revenge on the police and others who had persecuted them.

But in what must have been a great disappointment to the North Korean leaders, few South Koreans showed much enthusiasm for their liberators. Instead of embracing them, hundreds of thousands fled. Busan, which became the wartime capital of the ROK, and other southern cites swelled with refugees. Some moderates joined the committees, and the new North Korean liberators had some enthusiastic support from students and labour activists, but overall, most South Koreans were wary of the new regime at best. The brief occupation served instead to create hostility towards the northern regime, especially because it conscripted thousands of young men into the KPA and carried out executions and confiscations of property. The worst atrocities were committed by the North Koreans during their hasty retreat. Many 'traitors' were executed, and others were taken with them as the North Korean forces retreated. It was a brief and bloody occupation.

The Tide Turns

The logistics of moving tens of thousands of troops with their vehicles, artillery and tanks across the mostly unpaved roads were challenging. The situation grew worse with the onset of the monsoon rains, turning roads into mud. On 8 July Kim asked Stalin for 25 to 35 Soviet advisers to serve with the KPA's frontline headquarters, but Stalin refused. He had made it clear that no Soviet military personnel could be directly involved in a conflict with the Americans.[26] Still Kim Il Sung felt confident of victory. This was not so with other leaders, such as Kim Dubong, who did not feel the KPA would be a match for the American forces and so the war had to be won quickly. Kim's optimism was soon vindicated. On 20 July the KPA arrived at the strategically located city of Daejeon 160 kilometres (100 mi.) south of Seoul. There they encountered American forces under General William Dean who were sent to assist the ROK Army and hold the city. Morale among U.S. soldiers was high, many believing just the sight of them would intimidate the North Koreans. They were wrong, and the KPA quickly surrounded and defeated the combined ROK–U.S. forces. General Dean escaped by fleeing into the mountains. After 36 days of barely surviving, he was captured and spent the rest of the war as the highest-ranking UN prisoner of war. The defeat of the hastily assembled American forces was a great morale boost for the KPA, and for Kim it removed whatever doubts he had about achieving victory.

With Daejeon's fall, the way was open to Busan, where the South Korean government had fled. This port city, at the extreme southeast corner of the peninsula across the Korea Strait from Japan, which had become the wartime capital of the ROK, was the last major toehold of the ROK on the mainland. Its defence was vital if there was any chance for the South Korean state to survive. The sooner the North Koreans could capture Busan, the sooner they could bring the war to a victorious end. To achieve this, General Pang Hosan, commanding the KPA's Sixth Division, moved south into the rich rice-growing provinces of North and South Cholla, where he met only light resistance, and from there made a sharp turn to the east towards the city. It was a well-executed manoeuvre, but Pang had to delay his final offensive while waiting for the arrival of artillery and supplies.

Then Kim had a setback. As his forces moved towards Busan from the west, other KPA forces were planning to come down from the north. To do this they took the northeast city of Chuncheon, easily defeating the ROK defenders. Surprisingly, the ROK's Sixth Division managed to pull off a minor miracle. From the disparate remnants of fleeing soldiers they regrouped into a coherent force, counter-attacked and retook the city and held it for five days, withdrawing only after they were ordered to do so. It was a critical delay for the second pincer of the North Korean forces that was swooping down on Busan from the north. Soviet adviser Matvei Zakharov, head of a special mission to oversee operations, credited the 'unexpectedly courageous defense of the ROK's Sixth Division' for creating a key setback in the carrying out of the invasion.[27]

The stand at Chuncheon gave the Americans and the South Koreans time to establish the Naktong Perimeter around Busan – so called since much of it ran along the Naktong river of South Gyeongsang province. The United States Eighth Army was responsible for

110 kilometres (70 mi.) of the western flank and the ROK for the 90 kilometres (55 mi.) of the northern flank. By early August this was the last stand of the UN and ROK forces, and it held. By August the North Koreans had overrun the vast majority of the Republic of Korea, which had been reduced to a small southeast corner about 15 per cent of its previous size. All that was left of the ROK was a tiny piece, the part closest to Japan. As the UN and ROK generals peered at their maps, they could see at a glance just how precarious the position of the South Korean–UN forces was.

Kim, with his love of symbolic dates, probably hoped to reunify the country by 15 August, the fifth anniversary of Japan's surrender, a date known by North and South Koreans as Liberation Day. But that did not happen. As precarious as it might have seemed, the perimeter held throughout August, allowing time for two new divisions of U.S. troops as well as other UN forces to arrive. By late that month Shtykov was reporting that all the KPA forces were committed but were not able to stop a UN counter-attack. Kim himself, he reported, felt under pressure and complained of the difficulty of victory: 'There is no one to consult with. The vice-premiers are no help. Cabinet ministers are doing a poor job. I trusted Pak Heonyeong but Pak was not up to the task and could not handle problems himself.' He complained, Shtykov wrote, 'Some of the North Korean leadership who expected an easy victory are confused, starting to lose confidence in their own capacity, and fear the war will be prolonged.' Kim as usual blamed others rather than take responsibility. He accused commander Kim Chaek of ignoring his instructions, and Pak of misleading him about a large underground Workers' Party in the South. 'Despite the appeals to rise up and help the KPA, the partisans do nothing,' he complained.[28] Shtykov did report that Kim 'throws himself completely into the task. He is concentrating on military matters.' But, the Soviet ambassador went on to report, he neglects other parts of the administration, and his 'work style [reflects] a lack of experience and maturity.'[29]

The Chinese were concerned with the situation as early as July. In August they feared a massive American counter-attack. In late August they were predicting a U.S. amphibious landing on the west coast. At this time Kim sent a personal representative to Beijing to meet with the Chinese leaders and discuss the war situation. The Chinese leaders expressed their worries to him that the North Koreans were not prepared for an American landing on the west coast. Mao pointed to a map of the coast of Korea and noted three areas where the American forces were likely to land, including Incheon. 'We ought to prepare for [the possibility] that American troops might take a circuitous course through landing at any one of these ports to strike the rear of the Korean People's Army,' he told the North Korean.[30] Yet, rather than shoring up the coastal defences, Kim kept focusing on the Naktong Perimeter, hoping for a breakthrough that could bring victory.

Much as the Chinese expected, the USA launched an amphibious landing on the west coast – and right at one of the spots Mao had pointed to on his map. Still, its scale and swiftness probably took even the Chinese by surprise. The UN forces commander General MacArthur brought 75,000 marines and 260 ships to Incheon, negotiating its treacherous tides and sandbars, and landed at the port on 15 September. Kim was caught totally unprepared as the UN forces outflanked and trapped the KPA. His forces were quickly overwhelmed as UN and ROK forces fought their way back into Seoul. By the end of September most of the KPA was in near total disarray, although some troops managed a tactical retreat up the east coast. North Korean forces had been defeated, with an estimated 50,000 killed, captured or missing.[31] The attempt by Kim Il Sung and the rest of the KWP to unify the country under their leadership had disastrously failed.

Kim panicked, grasping the immensity of this setback. He wrote to Stalin on 29 September. Addressing him as 'the liberator of the Korean people and the leader of the working peoples of the entire world', he explained the situation. 'The adversary, suffering one defeat after another, was cornered into a tiny piece of land at the southernmost tip of South Korea and we had a great chance of winning a victory,' but the USA, to 'restore its prestige and to implement by any means its long-held plans of conquering Korea and transforming its militarily strategic bridgehead', launched the attack on Incheon. The military situation, he reported, had now become 'extremely grave'. Street fighting was going on in Seoul, and units in the south were cut off by the enemy and unable to communicate with their superiors. Korea was in danger of being 'a colony and a military springboard of the U.S. imperialists'. Only direct assistance from the Soviet Union or 'international volunteer units in China and other [friendly countries]' would prevent that from happening.[32]

If the United States had been willing to accept the pre-war status quo, the conflict might have ended soon. But Kim was correct about the plans to invade the North. Both MacArthur and Rhee were determined to 'roll back' the North Koreans. The UN resolution had only authorized that the North Koreans be repelled. Some in America and some allies, especially Britain, opposed widening the war, fearing Chinese or even Soviet intervention. But MacArthur wanted the complete destruction of the DPRK, and the South Korean leaders wanted reunification, which now seemed so close. The day after Kim made his appeal to Stalin, ROK forces crossed the 38th parallel in pursuit of the KPA troops. They had no authorization from the UN command to do this, but Rhee and his generals did not bother to wait for any approval to reunify the country. The next day, 1 October, a desperate Kim sent Pak Heonyeong to Beijing by plane to hand-deliver a letter to Mao. The Chinese leader was busy that day celebrating the first anniversary of the People's Republic of China. After the celebrations he received the letter. It read like Kim's letter to Stalin, explaining that the KPA was about to 'win the decisive final victory' when the U.S. imperialists, 'for the purpose of changing Korea into their colonial and military base', assembled a massive force and landed at Incheon. Kim was counting not on Chinese goodwill but on its self-interest in preventing American forces from having a base on China's border. Kim told one of his officials, Mun Il, 'We have lost the war and will lose Korea if we do not get foreign help.'[33]

Pak's mission to China was not his first. Kim had sent him and Pak Ilu some days earlier to inform the Chinese leaders of the situation after the Incheon landing. Pak Ilu was chosen because he had fought with Mao's troops and was reported to have developed a close relationship with the Chinese leader. The two Paks were instructed not to ask directly for Chinese intervention. Kim hesitated to do so probably because Chinese intervention might strengthen the Yanan faction and weaken his own position. According to some Chinese sources, the two Paks asked Mao to send troops anyway and to remove Kim from power. Mao refused to interfere with DPRK politics.[34] But they all shared a lack of confidence in Kim's handling of the situation. If this story is accurate, Kim must have remained unaware that the messengers he sent on 1 October were trying to remove him from power.

Mao called a meeting of the top leaders that evening and a larger one the next day that included his military commanders. While the decision whether to intervene was discussed, Mao made it apparent that he supported doing so. Many of the leadership were reluctant, but, of course, Mao prevailed.[35] After a brief hesitation, Mao sent a telegram to Kim on 8 October that China would send troops to support the North Koreans if the UN tried to occupy the North. He sent it to the Chinese embassy in Pyongyang and had two embassy officials hand-deliver it.[36] Mao's decision to save Kim's regime is in contrast to Stalin's seeming willingness to write it off.[37] In fact even before Kim sent his 29 September letter to Stalin requesting help, the Soviet leader had asked Mao if he would consider allowing Kim to operate a government-in-exile in Manchuria.[38] On 13 October Stalin notified Kim Il Sung that

> continuation of the resistance is hopeless. Chinese comrades refuse to get involved militarily. Under these circumstances you must prepare for total evacuation to China and/or the USSR. It is of the utmost importance to take all the troops and military equipment. Draw a detailed plan of activities in this connection and follow it meticulously. The potential for further struggle against the adversary must be preserved.[39]

The fact that at this crucial moment Moscow was ready to abandon him could not but have had a profound impact on Kim, contributing to his determination not to be reliant on his patrons in the future.

China, which maintained no diplomatic relations with the United States, sent a warning in early October through India's ambassador in Beijing that it would not tolerate a U.S. presence on its border, but Washington ignored this. Perhaps overconfident after the success of Incheon, Washington now gave MacArthur permission to destroy all KPA forces, and on 7 October the UN passed a vaguely worded resolution that approved the use of UN troops to cross the 38th parallel in order to establish a unified government. On 9 October UN forces moved north of the parallel. On 10 October the provincial capital of Wonsan fell to ROK forces as Kim Il Sung, in a radio broadcast, urged the KPA to 'fight to the last drop of blood'.[40] Throughout October UN and ROK forces, which were under UN authority, swept across North Korea, capturing Pyongyang and other major cities while Kim Il Sung and the other DPRK leaders fled to mountainous strongholds near the Manchurian border. On 20 October a triumphant President Rhee visited Pyongyang. Within a few weeks about 90 per cent of North Korea was occupied by United Nations and ROK forces.

Kim was disappointed, and in fact a bit shocked, at how little support there was for his liberation in the South in the summer of 1950. In the autumn he was alarmed by the lack of resistance by his people to the occupation of UN and ROK forces. This lack of resistance and the disarray of the KPA forces account for the swiftness by which the North was occupied. Acting largely on their own, without consultation with General MacArthur despite being nominally under his command, ROK forces and intelligence officials carried out bloody reprisals. Any member of the KWP was subject to arrest or abuse. Since this was a mass party that included a sizeable proportion of all North Koreans, these punishments were unrealistic. North Korea, in a 26-volume official history of the conflict published in 1981, claimed that 15,000 people were murdered in Pyongyang and tens of thousands elsewhere by the occupation forces. While this number is probably exaggerated, ROK military and civilian officials executed thousands of civilians.[41] Farmers were required to return land to their former landlords. When the ROK forces retreated they too took with them tens of thousands of North Koreans, mostly young men, whom they forcibly conscripted. Nonetheless, for all their heavy-handed methods, few ordinary North Koreans put up much resistance to their southern 'liberators' and their UN allies, and many seemed to have willingly cooperated with them. Their failure to actively resist was alarming to Kim Il Sung and his government. His response to this after the war was to make every effort to indoctrinate his people into the goals of the revolution and instil in them unquestioned loyalty to the regime.

Meanwhile, he lashed out at his comrades. On 21 December 1950 Kim Il Sung made a speech at the temporary seat of government in Kanggye. He blamed almost everyone for the setback. He blamed his party cadres and government officials for being undisciplined and his generals for mismanaging the war. He also blamed the failure of the guerillas in the South, and the incompetence of the ministries of transportation and propaganda. Almost no one was spared, even fellow partisans and old comrades from Manchuria such as Kim Il, Choe Kwang, Yim Chunchu and Kim Yeol. Many of them, as well as Yanan veterans such as Mu Jeong, were relieved of their positions. The one person he did not blame was himself, other than by admission that he had not expected American intervention.[42]

Chinese Intervention

By late November the DPRK had been reduced to a few mountainous regions near the Chinese border. Then, on 27 November, the Chinese, calling themselves the Chinese People's Volunteers (CPV) and led by veteran commander Peng Dehuai, counter-attacked. From this point on, the Chinese took effective control over military operations from the North Korean leadership. Overextended and overconfident UN troops were forced into a full retreat. Chinese forces advanced as swiftly as the UN and ROK forces had done weeks earlier. They retook Pyongyang on 6 December and within two weeks had forced the withdrawal of UN and ROK troops from most of North Korea.

As Chinese forces approached Pyongyang, Kim was in Beijing, meeting with Mao and Zhou Enlai and the communist head of Manchuria, Gao Gang, at Mao's office in Zhongnanhai. Kim praised the Chinese troops' bravery but wanted to know how much longer the Chinese would fight. Mao said, 'The [*North*] Korean side should get prepared to fight a protracted war in which [you will] mainly rely on yourself and partly on outside assistance.' Kim pressured China to aim for a quick end to the war: 'We should not give the enemy breathing time.' Kim added, 'We ought to advance in the crest of victory to seize Pyongyang and Seoul and to press the enemy to withdraw from [the whole of] Korea.' Addressing Chinese concern about supplies, he promised to provide food and supplies to the Chinese forces.[43]

Making the same error as the United States had done, the Chinese continued their advance south, crossing the 38th parallel and retaking Seoul on 4 January and then continuing to the 37th parallel. But by late January their offensive was losing momentum. Peng Dehuai, the Chinese commander, decided to halt it. He had little choice, since

UN forces had regrouped and were imposing heavy casualties on his forces, which were also running low on supplies of ammunition and food. This angered Kim, who still thought there was an opportunity to drive the UN and ROK forces back to Busan and liberate all or most of the South. At a meeting with Peng at the Chinese People's Volunteer headquarters, accompanied by Pak Heonyeong on 10 January, he asked why the CPV did not advance 'on the crest of victory'.[44] Peng told Kim that his troops needed to rest and recuperate, and he would not consider another offensive for two or three months. Kim replied, 'In my opinion, the time for the troops to rest and reorganize should be no longer than a month.'[45] 'You are gambling with the fate of the people,' Kim stated, 'and this will lead to disaster.'[46] They discussed the situation again, and the atmosphere became heated. An infuriated Peng replied, 'In the past, you assumed the United States would never send troops to Korea. You never thought about what to do if they did send troops.' He continued, 'You are hoping to end this war by luck. You are gambling on the fate of the people, and that's only going to lead to disaster.' He went on, 'Your underestimation of the enemy is a serious mistake and I will not tolerate it. If you think I am not doing my job, you can fire me, court-martial me, or even kill me.'[47] Peng had a low opinion of Kim and of the leadership, and his contempt for Kim seemed only to increase during the conflict. In one incident Kim went unannounced to see Peng, and a guard at the CPV headquarters detained him.[48]

Beijing did not quite wait until spring but conducted a new offensive in February, which was repelled with enormous Chinese losses. Despite the use of massive assaults – the so-called 'human wave' tactic designed to compensate for their inferior firepower – the UN forces were able to retake Seoul on 15 March. It was the fourth time the city changed hands in nine months. The conflict was now mainly carried out between China and the United States, with the DPRK and ROK leadership on the sidelines. With the two sides arrayed roughly around the 38th parallel, the Truman administration was willing to negotiate a truce. By spring Mao too was ready to accept a stalemate with the peninsula divided approximately where it had been before the outbreak of the conflict. With Stalin's approval he signalled his willingness to begin armistice talks. On 10 July 1951 formal negotiations began as representatives of the CPV, the KPA and the UN command met. They came to an understanding that the boundary between the two would be roughly similar but not exactly the same as the 38th parallel, extending a little below it to the west and above it to the east, to be separated by the Demilitarized Zone. They also agreed to the creation of a Military Armistice Commission. Then progress slowed. The conflict continued unabated for two years after negotiations began.

Stalemate

Chinese intervention saved the North Korean regime, but it also resulted in Kim's loss of control over the war. Once the Chinese intervened actively in the fighting in November 1950, they assumed operational command. Mao, who blamed Kim for his failure to prepare for the defence of Incheon, confined him and the KPA to a subordinate role in military planning and fighting for the rest of the war. In essence the two main opponents in the war became the United States and China. From the summer of 1951 to the summer of 1953 the two powers were at a stalemate, with conventional fighting largely confined to a narrow strip of land. Kim Il Sung spent much of this war in a bunker in Chagang province near the Manchurian border, away from the front lines and away from Pyongyang, again a spectator in the conflict rather than a participant.[49]

The discussions of a ceasefire in late spring 1951 worried Kim, who wanted to continue the war until the enemy forces were defeated and the country reunified. He met Mao in May and Stalin in June to convey his sentiment.[50] He was probably not alone in this: the sentiment was generally shared among the Korean leadership in the North, as it was in the South. Both Kim and Rhee never lost sight of their goal of reunification.

But by early 1952 Kim arrived at the conclusion that there was no point in continuing the conflict. As V. N. Razumov, the Soviet ambassador who replaced Shtykov, reported to Moscow: 'Kim Il Sung does not see any benefit in prolonging the negotiations because the American Air Force is causing horrendous losses to the Korean Democratic People's Republic.'[51] On 16 July 1952 Kim's weariness and concerns over the continual American bombing were expressed in a letter to Stalin. He wrote, 'The enemy almost without suffering any kind of losses constantly inflicts on us huge losses in manpower and material values.' About the bombing campaign, he wrote: 'In only one 24-hour period of barbaric bombing, of only one city, Pyongyang (on 11 July and the night of 12 July), more than 6,000 peaceful inhabitants were killed and wounded.'[52]

The decision to end the war, however, was not Kim's to make. Mao may have found the cost of the conflict bearable, since there were many troops no longer needed for the civil war. There was no shortage of cannon fodder, and the war was a useful rallying cause for his new regime. Furthermore, having fought the Americans to a stalemate added to his prestige. Yet it would seem that Mao too was willing to end the war as it entered its third year. And shortly after his November 1952 election, President Dwight D. Eisenhower, who had promised to end the conflict, visited Korea and made his intention to do so clear. Meanwhile, Stalin's death in March 1953 removed an obstacle to peace as his successors showed little interest in continuing the war. When, in the spring of 1953, the USA carried out the most extensive bombing campaign of the war, raining horrific destruction upon the civilian population of North Korea as well as on the CPV and KPA forces, it was clear that Kim's hopes of reunifying Korea had been dashed, at least in the short term. At that point most of the parties were ready to bring the war to an end. The exception was South Korea.

The ongoing talks of an armistice that had been under way for almost two years were now reaching a resolution when they were delayed over the issue of repatriation of prisoners, since many of the Chinese and North Koreans held by the UN did not want to go home. But Beijing and Pyongyang insisted they all be returned. The issue dragged on for months. Kim was willing to make concessions to achieve the armistice, but Mao was adamant. At the request of the new leadership in Moscow, Mao relented. And though the situation was further complicated when South Korea's president Rhee, still hoping for a victory that would reunite the country on his terms, tried to sabotage the talks by releasing many of the prisoners, the UN, the DPRK and China signed the Korean Armistice Agreement on 27 July 1953. Moscow, worried about his security, instructed Kim Il Sung not to attend, so he sent one of his officials, Nam Il, in his place. Rhee refused to be a signatory to the ceasefire, still bitterly hoping to pursue the war until Korea was united. But he did not have planes wreaking daily death and destruction upon his cities and towns. Kim, a survivor and a realist, understood that this was not the time for reunification. That would come later.

After the signing, and no longer fearing for his safety, Kim gave a public address. Standing in Pyongyang's central square, with devastation in every direction, he told a large crowd that the nation had won a historic victory. The people had crushed an attempt by the American aggressor to turn all of Korea into a colony and a military base for use against the Soviet Union and China. Therefore they had won a victory not just for the Korean people but for all the freedom-loving people of the democratic world. After praising the contribution of the CPV, he cautioned that a complete victory had not been won: the Americans had not been driven from the fatherland and were planning to use Japan in their aggressive war in Asia. Indeed, military aircraft from U.S. bases in Japan had turned supposedly peaceful Pyongyang and farming villages across the North into charred ashes. The KPA had to be strengthened, and the people had to develop greater 'revolutionary vigilance' and rebuild the economy.[53]

This speech summed up Kim's views well. The war was not over until the 'imperialists' had been driven out, the 'lackies' were no longer in power and, by implication, the country was reunited. For this the military needed to be strengthened and the people's 'revolutionary consciousness' further developed.

Korean War 'Victory'

Kim Il Sung proclaimed the war a great victory, since the DPRK and its allies defeated the attempt by the USA and ROK to invade and enslave the people of the North. A later official history declared it a 'righteous fatherland liberation struggle' that fought and defeated the 'USA and its puppets [who] launched an armed attack'.[54] But it was hardly a victory. He failed to bring about reunification, instead bringing appalling destruction and death upon his country and thus only making reunification more difficult. His invasion and the brutality of his brief occupation had the effect of increasing the South Korean people's support for their state, if not necessarily its leadership, and a generation of southerners developed a deep hostility to the Kim Il Sung regime. The war thus strengthened rather than weakened the ROK. Furthermore, it brought about the permanent stationing of American forces in the South. Prior to war the USA was ambiguous about its commitment to defend Seoul; that now changed. The Americans poured in vast amounts of aid money, bankrolled the ROK armed forces, which were now among the largest in the world, and maintained troops right on the border with the North.

An appallingly high number of people, military and civilians, perished in the war, 2 million by conservative estimates. This figure includes 37,000 Americans and 4,000 UN allies killed and around 200,000 South Korean military casualties. Approximately 400,000 South Korean civilians may have died when all factors, including starvation, diseases and other causes related to dislocation, are accounted for. At least 200,000 people from the CPV were killed; some estimates place this figure much higher, as many as 500,000. But it was North Korea that suffered the most. Out of a population in 1950 of about 9.6 million, as many as 400,000 soldiers and 600,000 civilians died from causes brought about by the war. This amounted to 10 per cent of the population, one of the highest rates of death any country suffered in a twentieth-century conflict.

Kim presided over a North Korea in ruins. American bombing had reduced its cities to rubble; few factories and little infrastructure escaped damage. Cities in the DPRK were totally destroyed, as was most of the infrastructure. The United States dropped 635,000 tons of bombs on this small, Pennsylvania-sized country: this was 20 per cent more than in the entire Pacific theatre of the Second World War, and slightly more than the Americans had dropped on Germany. Additionally the Americans dropped 32,000 tons of napalm on North Koreans.[55] No matter what interpretation Kim gave it, the Korean War was, in fact, a serious setback for his dream of reunification under his leadership. Instead, the conflict drove the two Koreas bitterly apart and consolidated their separate systems.

However, the conflict strengthened Kim in several ways. He used it to further consolidate his power and eliminate some of his rivals, as we will see in the next chapter. He was able to free himself from the tight control of Moscow. The short but brutal occupation of the North by the UN and ROK may have had a similar effect as the KPA occupation of the South in rallying people to his state, although it is difficult to determine this. And the destruction of most of North Korea's cities gave him a blank canvas on which to rebuild them in accordance with his vision.

Fittingly, the Korean War ended in a ceasefire, not a peace, for few Koreans regarded the settlement in 1953 as permanent. It was certainly not over for Kim Il Sung. For Kim a battle had been lost but not the broader struggle. He would continue pursuing the goals that he had begun years earlier: to liberate all of the country from imperialism and from its backward, feudal past, and to create a progressive, prosperous, united nation-state free from foreign control, a nation that encompassed all Koreans.

Kim Il Sung was just 41 when the Korean War ended, at the midpoint in his life. He would live for another 41 years, all of them spent moulding North Korea in his image. In 1953 his immediate task was the reconstruction of his devastated country. His larger aim was to create a new Korea, one that was modern, industrial and militarily powerful, a Korea that could reunite all the Korean people. To do this he needed to consolidate his own power, freeing himself from the constraints of internal opposition or resistance to his personal rule and from his dependency on the Soviet Union and China for economic assistance and security. During the next eight years he was remarkably successful in achieving this. The DPRK recovered from the war and laid the foundations for a modern industrial state. At the same time Kim established his personal autocracy, eliminated from power all but his Manchurian guerilla comrades and gained greater autonomy from his two communist patrons.

5

CONSOLIDATION OF POWER, 1953–61

Although the war that Kim Il Sung was so eager to carry out was a disastrous failure, it had the effect of strengthening rather than weakening his hold on power. This might seem surprising, but by 1951 the Chinese were in control of military operations; as we have seen, Peng Dehuai had no time for Kim's interference in them. But the Chinese did not insert themselves into domestic political affairs. At the same time the Chinese presence weakened the influence of the Soviet Union. Militarily dependent on China, North Korea achieved a greater measure of political independence from Moscow.[1]

Kim used this opportunity to remove more potential rivals and power centres. An early target, whose fate is illustrative of Kim's tactic, was Mu Jeong. Born Kim Jeong, he took the *nom de guerre* Mu Jeong (*mu* means martial or military). As a young man he joined the Chinese communists. In 1934–5 he made the Long March with Mao Zedong and became one of the leaders of the Yanan faction, as those who fought with Mao were labelled. He established a military unit with the PLA and then in 1942, with Pak Ilu, formed the Korean Volunteer Army as the military wing of the Korean Independence League. These fighters fought the Japanese in China alongside the PLA. Mu Jeong was highly regarded among Chinese military commanders. After 1945 he returned to North Korea. His prestige as an anti-imperialist, nationalist fighter combined with the fact that he was an eloquent speaker made him a natural leader for the emerging regime. Unlike Kim Il Sung, however, he did not have any connections to the Soviets. Nonetheless, Kim saw him as a rival since Mu Jeong's military reputation outshone his. Kim kept Mu shut out of the top leadership circles. When the Korean War started, his experience was too valuable not to be used, and he was made one of the military commanders. Kim put him in charge of defending Pyongyang as ROK forces advanced in October 1950. With KPA forces in disarray and the rest of the leadership fleeing towards the mountainous town of Kanggye, near the Chinese border, it was a hopeless task. But he was now a convenient scapegoat for the defeat. Later, Mu left for China, and he died in 1952 at a Beijing hospital from stomach cancer. Unlike most victims of Kim Il Sung's purges, Mu was posthumously rehabilitated after the Korean War. His remains were interred in a tomb. While he never re-entered the top pantheon of heroes, he was at least honoured.

Most of Kim's rivals were not treated so gently. An example was Ho Ka-i, one of the principal leaders of the Soviet Koreans and an expert on party organization. Ho was the third highest-ranking member of the party and its first secretary. The job of party secretary, in charge of personnel and promotions, was the position that Stalin had used to rise to power. Kim had tasked Ho with removing disloyal members of the party of all ranks. The issue was why was there so little resistance to the ROK and UN forces when they occupied the North. Where were the loyal party members who should have organized that resistance? Ho simply reissued all party member cards and in the process removed three-quarters of the KWP members. Almost all were low-ranking members from modest backgrounds. This ran counter to Kim's desire to create a mass party made of farmers and workers. Ho, however, wanted a small party consisting of a vanguard on the Soviet model, and felt that its members should be workers, not mostly peasants. Kim's idea was a party that represented the fact that four out of five North Koreans were peasants. Under Ho, however, uneducated peasants were rejected because they could not recite the party platform. This was too elitist for Kim. Not only were Ho's actions countering Kim's vision, but they were a challenge to his authority. Kim argued that it was wrong to force foreign models on Korean society and that the party should reflect Korean characteristics. This was a consistent theme with him: not to be a slave to foreigners or foreign ideas. In September 1951 Ho resisted efforts to reinstate members. At the Fourth Plenum of the Party Central Committee in November 1952 Kim presented a report, 'Some Deficiencies in Party Organizational Activities', in which he attacked Ho's party purges. Ho was removed from his post.[2] Most of those expelled from the party were reinstated. Ho was too powerful, too well connected to the Soviets, and Kim was not yet the all-powerful leader, so he was unable to purge Ho, only to demote him to a lesser post. Ho Ka-i remained an influential figure until the summer of 1953, when Kim launched an attack on him, blaming him for failing to defend and then to repair the Sunan water reservoir, which was destroyed by U.S. bombers. In June Ho went to the Soviet embassy to complain about Kim's attacks on him, stating they were unfair and driven by personal conflicts. He also complained about the excessive 'cult of Kim Il Sung' that was forming in the North. This was an interesting comment since this was more than two years before the new Soviet leadership had begun denouncing Stalin's cult of personality. He found no support or desire to intervene from the embassy and died two days later. Officially it was a suicide, but it is not impossible that Kim had his rival murdered.[3]

Kim Il Sung also worked to undermine Pak Heonyeong and his domestic communist faction. In March 1952 Kim had the Kangdong Institute, chaired by Pak, and other domestic communist-run organizations closed and the trainees transferred to other units. The following month, on 15 April, Pak wrote an article in the *Rodong sinmun*, the official KWP newspaper, which was celebrating Kim's fortieth birthday. The essay he wrote began praising 'Comrade Kim Sung our respected leader' but then went on to praise Stalin. It ended by saying,

'Today as we celebrate the fortieth birthday of our own national leader, we send warm greetings and respect to Field Marshal Stalin who liberated us and supported our heroic undertaking and is the brilliant leader and teacher of the working people of the world.'[4] Kim was reduced to a secondary player as Stalin was credited with the 1945 liberation and the victories of the current Korean War. This was interpreted to all in the leadership circles as an indirect attack on the North Korean leader. Kim must have been infuriated when he read this. He waited for more than a year before he struck back.

Eliminating the Domestic Communists

During the Korean War, while often powerless to decide military policies, Kim was free to conduct KWP business. Kim blamed Mu Jeong, the experienced and respected military commander from the Yanan group, for the military disasters of the early war and had him dismissed from his posts. The prominent Soviet Korean Ho Ka-i was, as we have seen, also purged. While consolidating his hold on the KWP, Kim also strengthened his power over the KPA. In December 1952 he appointed himself marshal of the army, outranking all his military officers.[5] But it was only after the conflict ended that the major purges began.

Kim's first major target at the end of the war was the domestic faction, as Pak Heonyeon and his fellow southerners were known. Relations between Kim and Pak Heonyeong had already seriously deteriorated in 1952. In December of that year Kim gave a speech at a party plenum criticizing factional rivalry and attacking the former leaders of the SWKP. Amid rumours of an attempted coup, Kim had some of the members of this group arrested in early 1953. In March he removed Pak Heonyeong as foreign minister and soon after his associate Yi Seungyeon as minister of state.[6] Yi Seungyeon had been active in the Korean Communist Party since its inception when he joined at the age of twenty; he worked under Pak and had a prominent career in the party, including serving as editor of its newspaper, *Haebang ilbo*, after liberation.[7] Then, in the summer of 1953, he had Yi arrested.[8]

One week after the Armistice Agreement, Kim began his full-scale purge of the domestic faction. On 3 August 1953 he began a four-day trial of twelve of its most prominent leaders. Only Pak Heonyeong was absent. It followed the format of the Stalinist show trials of the 1930s: the arrested were accused of preposterous crimes of treason and then publicly confessed. They were accused of planning a coup, which was possibly true, and more absurdly of spying for the United States and working with the Americans to destroy the communist party organization in the South. Yi Seungyeon confessed to working with a U.S. diplomat who informed him of the Incheon landing. The facts of the trial did not even make sense, since the American diplomat at the American embassy in Seoul with whom he was allegedly collaborating was not in South Korea at the time. Yi and his fellow conspirators' task, according to the allegations, was to orchestrate an uprising in Pyongyang in support of U.S. and South Korean troops. The defendants confessed to all charges, accepted that they should be punished and were executed.[9] It all went according to the script, which may have been personally written by Kim himself if it wasn't left to the head of his internal security forces, the former Soviet police officer Pang Hakse.

Pak remained under arrest until he was put on a one-day trial in December 1955. The former number two in the regime was sentenced to death after he admitted to all charges, including being the chief spy for the USA and having been working for the Americans since 1939.[10] By then the domestic faction was no longer a threat to Kim. They were a relatively easy target. Unlike many of the other rivals, the domestic faction members did not have connections to China or the Soviet Union and thus no foreign patron to give them some protection. And they could credibly be blamed for the failure of southerners to rise in support when the KPA crossed the 38th parallel. Kim felt genuinely betrayed by their false or faulty reports of pro-DPRK support below the 38th parallel. But he had to tread more carefully in his move against the Yanan and Soviet Korean factions, since they were connected to Beijing and Moscow. This meant for Kim that his struggle to eliminate them was intertwined with his effort to free himself from external control.

Reconstruction, 1953–6

Kim's growing power was linked to the confidence he gained from the economic recovery. In the first several years after the ceasefire he oversaw the reconstruction of the devastated country. Many smaller plants were quickly repaired, yet industrial production in late 1953 was at only 36 per cent of its 1949 level.[11] During the last months of the war the U.S. bombing campaign targeted the country's irrigation dams, disrupting agricultural production and contributing to severe food shortages. Hwang Jang-yeop, later the regime's chief ideologist, returning from studying in Moscow, described his shock at how bad conditions were. In Pyongyang few houses were standing. People were living in dugouts in the hillside; beggars filled the streets along with thieves desperate for food. Even for a new faculty member at the elite Kim Il Sung University, food rations were limited; he recalls living on turnip soup. The wife of one his colleagues gave birth in the morning and was standing in line waiting for food rations in the afternoon.[12] The enormously high war casualties meant there was a shortage of younger men. Foreign observers were struck by this shortage of men and the fact that women were doing much of the work in construction and other fields.[13]

Yet within three years economic production had recovered to pre-war levels. However, it was not merely a matter of rebuilding the economy but, rather, of restructuring it so that it was a totally socialist command economy, and one oriented towards building the industrial base that could support a strong military. Family farms were merged into state farms; the remaining businesses, even small shops, were nationalized; private markets almost completely disappeared. Although Kim later gave the sacrifices of the people and his leadership complete credit for the recovery, he knew he had to seek outside assistance. Within days of the armistice Kim supplied the Soviets with a list of aid requirements. A month later, in September 1953, he led a delegation to the Soviet Union to meet with Stalin's successors and negotiate assistance. In November he journeyed to Beijing. Meanwhile, other North Korean officials travelled in the countries of Eastern Europe from June to November, seeking aid. His socialist allies responded generously, the only time all the communist countries cooperated to help a member on such a large scale. The Soviets and the Chinese agreed to new loans, and the Chinese cancelled all previous debts.[14] China helped, not only with loans but by using its Chinese People's Volunteers still stationed in the country to help with construction, thereby somewhat easing the labour shortage.

Thousands of Soviet and Eastern European technicians and advisers poured into the country. Several hundred Soviet Korean technicians and experts came and provided valuable expertise. Thousands of North Koreans went to the Soviet Union and Eastern Europe for training programmes. In addition to outright aid, Soviet bloc countries sold materials at low or even nominal prices and provided loans on generous repayment terms. By one reckoning, aid supplied 33 per cent of the state revenues in 1954.[15] But Kim is also correct in attributing the rapid reconstruction of the country to the efforts of the Korean people. North Korea's foreign aid, while considerable, was smaller than what South Korea received from the United States, and the ROK also had much less to show for it. Their aid was also given for a shorter period of time: South Korea remained heavily reliant on U.S. aid until the mid-1960s, but by 1960 Soviet aid accounted for only 2.6 per cent of the DPRK's revenues.[16]

Kim's effective use of mass-mobilization campaigns involving the entire population for reconstruction projects was key to the country's speedy recovery. He had people clear debris and rebuild houses, schools, factories and other facilities. Calling it 'war by another means', Kim Il Sung organized reconstruction efforts as if they were military campaigns, complete with 'speed-battles' and '144-day campaigns' to reach targets. Ordinary citizens were called upon to make heroic sacrifices for the national effort, and this they did by working extremely long hours while living barely above the subsistence level. Nearly everyone who was physically able, including students, was enlisted to work on building projects. Seong Hyerang, whose sister would marry Kim Jong Il, recalled that during her four years as a student at Kim Il Sung University she spent only one year and eight months studying; the rest of the time was devoted to labouring on construction sites.[17]

One part of the reconstruction in which Kim took a direct personal involvement was the rebuilding of Pyongyang. He personally supervised the rebuilding as chairman of the Pyongyang City Rehabilitation Committee. With little left of the former city, he built a completely new one, designed for display with great squares: People's Army Square, Mao Zedong Square and the largest, Kim Il Sung Square. The city had impressive public buildings, such as the National Theatre and Kim Il Sung University, and a Stalin Street lined with modern apartments.

Kim's concern was not just recovery but laying the basis for a new industrial society. His vision was a centralized command economy that would be based on heavy industry, not radically different from the type of economy constructed in the Soviet Union under Stalin. There was little room for any private enterprise, and all remaining private businesses were nationalized during the first few years after the Korean War. The most important sector of the economy in private hands was agriculture. A year after the war ended, he began to eliminate the family farms created by the recent land reforms and merged them into large state enterprises. He called the process 'cooperativization' (*hyeopdonghwa*), and the big state farms, which were called collectives in most communist countries, he called 'cooperatives'. The process was begun almost surreptitiously by having farmers in the villages share tools, draft animals and other resources and then combining them into one state-owned unit. Kim and his lieutenants felt this was the most efficient way to overcome the problem of feeding his people and producing the surplus that would be needed to support a large industrial workforce. By the end of 1956 over 80 per cent of farming households were part of state farms.[18] In the summer of 1958 the state announced that collectivization was completed. Several million farmers, who had only become small private landowners in 1946 when the occupying Soviets had gifted land to the peasantry, now became labourers for the state.

Rejecting De-Stalinization and Eliminating the Yanan and Soviet Koreans

A key part of Kim's economic plan was to emphasize heavy industry rather than the production of consumer goods. Again he followed the Stalinist model. But that decision stirred some criticism from his Soviet Korean comrades. He faced other criticisms as well. For example, it was felt that he wielded too much power by being both the premier and the head of the party. In the face of criticisms from his fellow comrades, he offered to step down as premier. He proposed that Choe Yonggeon replace him.[19] This was hardly sincere, because he knew Choe was hated by most of the party members and known to be personally very loyal to Kim. This incident indicates that in 1955 Kim had acquired enormous authority, yet he still was not the unchallenged ruler. He had to contend with people in power who had their independent bases of support.

After eliminating the domestic faction Kim moved more cautiously against other rivals. He had no choice, since he could hardly afford to anger their patrons in Beijing and Moscow while depending on Soviet aid and while the Chinese had troops in the DPRK.

Nonetheless, in early 1955 Kim removed Yanan faction member Pak Ilu from all his positions. Pak had served as a liaison between the CPV and the KWP during the Korean War and was known as 'Mao's man' because of his close ties with the Chinese leader.[20] His removal weakened the Yanan faction somewhat. Kim then started a campaign to weaken the Soviet Koreans. On 28 December that year, at a meeting of KWP Central Committee members, Kim criticized Pak Changok, the most prominent of the Soviet Koreans, for excessively copying the Soviet Union. Calling for more Korean themes in art and literature, he introduced the term *Juche*, often translated as 'self-reliance'. This was the first public mention of this term, which would later evolve into the official ideology of the state. The following month, Pak Changok was removed from his position as chair of the State Planning Committee.[21]

At about this same time, Nikita Khrushchev launched his de-Stalinization campaign at a closed session of the Twentieth Congress of the Communist Party of the Soviet Union in February 1956. There the Soviet leader denounced Stalin's cult of personality. Kim did not attend the congress, which is interesting because all the leaders of Moscow's other client states attended – most would not dare fail to show up. But Kim obviously had more independence than the leaders of Mongolia and Eastern Europe. Mao and Ho Chi Minh also did not attend. At the meeting Khrushchev denounced Stalin, his 'cult of personality', his purges and mass imprisonments and executions. This new direction in Moscow was a threat to Kim Il Sung, much as it was to other 'little Stalins' in Eastern Europe. After all, Kim had patterned his role after Stalin. Yet this new direction was not a complete shock. In May and June 1955 he and his foreign minister Nam Il visited Moscow. They were invited to a lunch with the Soviet leadership in which Khrushchev explained that Stalin, for all the good things he accomplished, had committed errors in his later years that were being corrected. Many whom Stalin had arrested were being released and often reinstated in their old positions.[22] Still, the zeal of Khrushchev's attack was disturbing. Kim did what he could to stop de-Stalinization from spreading to his country. He discouraged contacts between Koreans and the Soviet embassy, required that officials obtain special permission to meet 'foreigners', reduced the rebroadcast hours of Korean-language Radio Moscow programmes and closed regional branches of the Institute of Foreign Language, the primary source of Russian-language teaching. Russian was no longer taught to university students.[23]

Initially Kim seemed to deflect the potential challenges to his own power represented by the new Soviet thinking. When the Third Congress of the KWP met in April 1956, Kim used the new criticism of personality cults as a means of justifying his purge of the domestic communists. He criticized the personality cult that had built up around the now disgraced and recently executed Pak Heonyeong.[24] At this point Kim may have underestimated the extent of opposition to his rule. On 1 June 1956 he began a seven-week trip to nine Soviet bloc countries, including Mongolia, seeking economic aid. He visited Moscow twice on the trip, but the main focus was on the countries of Eastern Europe. His long absence provided an opportunity for his opponents to carry out their own 'de-Stalinization'. Some of the Soviet Koreans had hoped that USSR officials would bring up some of their concerns in discussions with Kim. The North Korean ambassador in Moscow, a Soviet Korean, suggested to a high-ranking official that when Kim Il Sung visited Moscow the topic of his cult and 'distortions of socialist legality' should be discussed. The latter was a euphemism for arbitrary arrests, torture and executions.[25] The concerns the ambassador and other Soviet Koreans were sending the Soviets were apparently taken seriously in the Kremlin, and Kim found himself reprimanded for 'improper behavior' at his meetings with Soviet officials in Moscow, including most probably by Khrushchev.[26] Echoing criticisms from Pak Changok and others, the Soviets also criticized Kim for concentrating too much on trying to build an industrial base while neglecting the living standards of his people.[27]

Meanwhile, in North Korea a shadowy group began to organize while Kim was away, hoping to remove him from the head of the KWP and perhaps other positions, though not to purge him from the party. It was principally led by the Yanan faction, which had become the most disaffected group, but it included Soviet Koreans. One member of the Yanan group, Yi Pilgyu, head of the Ministry of Construction and a friend of the purged Pak Ilu, met with the Soviet chargé d'affaires, A. M. Petrov, on 20 July. Yi accused Kim of establishing a personality cult, exaggerating the importance of his partisans during the anti-Japanese struggle and minimizing the contribution of the Soviet army and other resistance forces (like his own in China), for possessing an 'incorrect attitude' towards party members. Yi complained that Kim's word was law and that he surrounded himself with sycophants; that he did not allow any criticism. Yi told the Soviet diplomat that there was a plan to remove Kim Il Sung from the top leadership, as 'There is no collective leadership in the Korean Worker's Party.' Another visitor, Yi Sangjo, the North Korean ambassador to Moscow, complained, 'Everything is decided by Kim Il Sung alone, and the people fawn over him.'[28]

The following day Pak Changok paid a visit to the Soviet embassy in Pyongyang, informing the embassy officials that the move against Kim would take place at the next meeting of the plenum. Two days later Choe Changik came visiting, also informing the Soviets of the plans. So, the de facto leaders of both the Yanan and Soviet Korean factions were involved in the plot and gave notice of it to the Soviet Union. Others involved in the plot also visited the USSR. It is likely they expected Moscow, if it did not actively support the move, would at least not interfere with it.[29] After all, Moscow had supported the removal of hardline leaders in Bulgaria and Hungary.

Kim became aware of the plot against him and postponed the plenum meeting of the KWP from 2 August 1956 until the end of the month, buying himself time to move against it. During August he managed to get a majority of the Central Committee to back him.

Kim's strategy to gain support among party leaders was twofold. He warned them of the instability that sudden reforms would bring, providing Poland as an example. And he also recognized the need for improvements and promised to make corrections.[30] When the plenum met on 30 August for two days, Kim was ready. Although the details of the meeting are not known, we do know that it was heated, with open attacks on Kim's leadership given by members of the Yanan and Soviet Korean factions. They did not call for his removal as party head, but by attacking his cult of personality and his administration of the country they were clearly challenging his leadership. Kim angrily accused his opponents of trying to abandon communism. Pak Changok, Choe Changik and, apparently, others criticized Kim's policies, including placing too much emphasis on heavy industry, and the recent appointment of Kim's guerilla comrade Choe Yonggeon to a top leadership post.[31] Choe Yonggeon, who headed the KPA from its foundation and served as defence minister, was especially disliked, considered crude, arrogant and incompetent. His reputation is illustrated by a story told by defectors. In 1956 Kim had the minister of home affairs investigated for counter-revolutionary activities, but soon after announced he had been found not guilty. Choe argued he should be executed anyway.[32] An old Manchurian comrade, he was fiercely loyal to Kim, which was probably why Kim kept him in a potentially powerful post.

Kim remained in control of the meeting. By the second day it was clear he had the support of the majority of party representatives, and motions for a change in policy direction had failed. By 31 August Kim had full control of the party. This would prove to be the most serious challenge to his authority he would face in his 46 years as leader of the DPRK. Nothing comparable ever happened again. Pak and Choe were arrested, and six other high-ranking officials fled to Manchuria. Some members of the party issued a declaration critical of Kim Il Sung but were quickly arrested too.[33] In general the opposition to Kim seemed poorly organized and largely ineffective.

However, Kim was thwarted in his effort to eliminate his opponents in the way he had eliminated the domestic faction. Neither Moscow nor Beijing wanted to see them become victims of a Stalinist-type purge. Soviet Politburo member Anastas Mikoyan and the Chinese military commander during the Korean War, Peng Dehuai, arrived in North Korea on a joint official delegation in September and called on Kim for restraint. This must have been a stressful affair for Kim. Mikoyan had been the man sent to remove the 'little Stalin' in Hungary,[34] and Peng Dehuai and Kim had an unhappy history. Under pressure, Kim halted his attempted purge. This intervention by Moscow and Beijing appears from later documents to have been a bitter experience for Kim Il Sung, highlighting the very situation that he was so determined to avoid: his country's subservience to outside foreign powers. The humiliation of having to be scolded and pressured by Peng, a man who never disguised his contempt for Kim, must have been especially painful. The effect of this incident was to make Kim more determined to achieve as much freedom of action for himself and autonomy for his country as possible. In fact it was one of the truly defining events of his regime, reinforcing all his fears. Yet for his opponents the Soviet and Chinese appeals bought them only a few months.

In September a chastised Kim convened a new party plenum, where he reinstated purged opposition leaders. He also made some remarks criticizing himself. Dependent on Soviet aid and the protection of the CPV still stationed in his country, Kim had to put aside plans to remove remaining Yanan and Soviet Koreans from power and possibly execute them. But then the international situation moved in his favour. First, Khrushchev's liberalism became tempered by events in Eastern Europe. The violent demonstrations in Poland, which Kim himself had used as a warning against reforming too fast, spun out of control and morphed into a nationwide uprising that led to a new leader. This encouraged an uprising in Hungary. While the new leader in Poland managed to reassure Khrushchev that his regime could work within the Soviet-led bloc, in Hungary there was an open revolt against Moscow, forcing Soviet troops stationed in the country to intervene, at a cost of thousands of lives. Fearing losing control over Eastern Europe, Khrushchev was forced to reverse course on his liberalization plan. At the same time Mao was becoming more critical of de-Stalinization and began carrying out an Anti-Rightist Campaign.[35] It became clear that Moscow and Beijing were not only preoccupied by their own problems but were looking less favourably on regime opponents. The hardline turn worked to Kim's advantage, and he soon had a mostly free hand to deal with domestic affairs.

The Great Purge

Kim Il Sung took advantage of the new situation not just to get rid of the Yanan and Soviet Koreans but to conduct a sweeping purge of the KWP and a reorganization of society. His goal was to eliminate all sources of opposition. The prelude to this purge began in December 1956 when the KWP began replacing membership cards with new ones. The new, permanent ones were issued after investigating each party member. This was quite like the method Ho Ka-i had employed to cull the party membership, something that Kim had denounced. North Korean officials at first reassured their socialist allies that the purpose was to replace deteriorated party membership cards, to rehabilitate former rank-and-file party members and to educate them.[36] But it was in fact the start of a mass removal of all members thought to be connected to Kim's opponents or disloyal in any way.

On 14 February 1957 Kim condemned the 'factional activity' of Choe Changik and Pak Changok in a speech.[37] On 25 November he declared in the party publication *Kulloja* (The Worker) that Choe and those associated with him were 'traitors of the revolution and extremely corrupt elements' whose 'conspiracy was so extremely sinister that had it not been uncovered and crushed in time, it might have brought grave consequences to our Party and revolution'.[38] All but a handful of the remaining Yanan and Soviet faction members were removed from office. Kim Dubong was replaced as president of the Supreme People's Assembly and titular head of state by Choe Yonggeon. Many if not most of the Soviet Koreans, including Pak Changok, fled to the Soviet Union, and some of the Yanan faction members, including Choe Changik, went to China.[39] Those who did not were imprisoned or executed.

The purge went far beyond the leadership. But even before this, on 30 May 1957 the Standing Committee of the KWP issued a directive 'On Transforming the Struggle against Counterrevolutionary Elements into an All-Party, All-People's Movement', which called for a thorough investigation of all party members.[40] The loyalty of every party member was to be checked. Not just party members' but everyone's background was scrutinized and placed into three general categories (*gyecheung*): those deemed most loyal, called the 'core' (*haeksim*), those classified as 'wavering' (*tongyo*) and those considered 'hostile' (*jokdae*). The core class members were known as tomatoes: red all the way through. The 'wavering' apples were red only on the outside, and the 'hostile' members were called grapes. This consolidated and refined one of the most distinctive features of North Korean society: its rigid social structure. Each category became what amounted to a hereditary caste whose status was passed on from parents to children; later this system was elaborated on as subcategories were created. In the late 1950s this new class system served as a means of conducting a thorough purge of party members. Accompanying this purge the North Korean Cabinet issued Decree No. 149, which prohibited people belonging to the hostile class from living near the border, the seacoast, within 50 kilometres (30 mi.) of Pyongyang or Kaesong, or within 20 kilometres (12½ mi.) of any other big city.

Kim's purge was massive. More than 100,000 citizens fell victim to arrests during 1957–9, and about 2,500 were executed, some publicly. This was a number equal to all those previously punished since 1945 and proportionately on a scale not far short of that of the Soviet Union during the Great Purges of 1937–8.[41] Show trials took place of those accused of being South Korean agents, of being saboteurs and of cooperating with the South Korean and American forces during their occupation of the North in the autumn of 1950.[42] Additionally, some 70,000 people are believed to have been relocated to remote areas in the mountainous regions of the north, simply because they came from a suspicious background.[43] In the summer of 1957 Kim introduced another measure: the 'five-households-in-charge system' (*oho damdangje*) of neighbourhood collective security. This revived an old East Asian custom by which families were lumped together into neighbourhood units and held accountable for the actions of their members. Under this system citizens were encouraged to spy and report on each other.

By 1959 Kim had eliminated all but a few of those who were in any way associated with a faction other than his own from every level of the state and the party organization. Only a small number of those outside his partisan comrades now held any position of authority. One such person was the Soviet Korean Nam Il, who had early become a loyal supporter of Kim Il Sung. Another Soviet Korean was Kim's loyal head of the security police, Pang Hakse, whom he put in charge of implementing the purge. One prominent Yanan faction member was left: Kim Changman. He was an interesting case. Throughout the 1950s he enthusiastically championed Kim as party leader. Outdoing others in proving his loyalty, he had first denounced the domestic faction as traitors and collaborators with the enemy and then attacked the leaders of the Yanan faction, including the distinguished Kim Dubong, as American spies. But self-serving demonstrations of total loyalty did not save him from being dropped from the leadership only a few years later.[44]

Kim Il Sung's purge went beyond just eliminating possible opponents, although this was his initial concern. It was an effort to reorganize society, to mould it to his vision of a militant, revolutionary society, disciplined and prepared to carry out the leadership's instructions. He wanted to remove not only all those who might challenge him and all those that might support those who challenged him, but all those whose loyalty in times of war or foreign invasion could not be counted on. This meant placing his fellow guerilla partisans and in some cases members of his family in all the key positions in the party, the state and the military.

With Kim's fellow Manchurian partisans in almost total command of North Korean public life, the entire society became moulded by their guerilla culture. Party propaganda constantly extolled the deeds of the Manchurian fighters. A Bocheonbo Museum opened to commemorate Kim's great military achievement, and in 1957 the event's twentieth anniversary was publicly celebrated.[45] In 1958 the Research Centre for the History of the Korean Workers' Party began a programme of elaborating on the myths of Kim and his guerilla comrades. In 1959 it published the first instalment of the four-volume *Memoirs of the Anti-Japanese Guerillas*.[46] This would soon be a 'must-read' for all citizens.[47] The Manchurian guerillas became not only the heroes of exaggerated stories, memoirs, fiction, films and song but the only legitimate bearers of the Korean communist and national liberation tradition.[48] More than just a source to legitimize the regime and form a basis for national pride, they became the model to be emulated for almost every endeavour. This was accompanied by a general decline in the intellectual level of society, resulting from the purge of many of the best-educated people. Hwang Jang-yeop, the only upper-ranking official to defect to the South, commented on the effects of the purge. North Korean scholars who survived the purges, he observed, were less academically trained and compensated for it by their greater loyalty.[49] This intellectual decline was reinforced by the country's increasing isolation as contact with even Eastern European allies, already restricted, became more so.[50]

Kim now surrounded himself with only those with whom he was most comfortable: his old partisan comrades. They were in general poorly educated. Fewer than a quarter of the party cell secretaries had a secondary education, and many had no formal education at all.[51] In addition most had little exposure to anywhere outside Korea or the adjacent regions of Manchuria. Few societies in the modern world were dominated by such poorly educated, unsophisticated, provincial people than the one Kim was creating. It also meant that he had few around him who could offer useful advice, knew the world or had much technical expertise in economic development. Instead, he was surrounded by people who were like himself.

North Korea's Great Leap Forward

Kim's great purge began at the same time as he launched his effort to accelerate the country's economic transformation. In the mid-1950s his plans to move full speed ahead with building an industrial economy had run into resistance from KWP members. But with them removed, he launched a great push for an industrial transformation, spelled out in a Five-Year Plan, 1957–61. He used the same methods to achieve this that had worked for the recovery: mobilization of the population in military-style campaigns to achieve economic targets. Some of the capital would be acquired in the form of aid from socialist friends, but mostly it was a Korean undertaking, squeezing the farmers for as much of the agricultural produce as possible to feed the growing industrial labour forces, and diverting resources from consumer to capital goods. The emphasis would be on heavy industry: iron, coal, steel, tractors and trucks that could fuel further growth and serve the long-term purpose of building a self-sufficient economy and an industrial base to support a self-reliant military.

In 1958 Kim's Five-Year Plan began to change in character while only in its second year under the influence of Mao Zedong's 'Great Leap Forward'. Mao's effort to transform his poor, agrarian society into an industrial state by setting wildly ambitious targets and employing mass mobilization resonated with Kim. In many ways it was similar to his own methods, including mass mobilization of labour to both revolutionize the population and compensate for lack of technology. Mao too was a former guerilla fighter who led an anti-imperialist movement, who saw his country was a victim of imperialist powers and who had fought the Americans alongside Kim's KPA. It was not surprising that Kim would adopt many of Mao's methods and styles.

What Kim was most influenced by was Mao's exuberance. As the Chinese leader became more ambitious in his efforts to transform his country, Kim too began accelerating his own targets, announcing later in 1958 that the Five-Year Plan would be completed in just three and a half years.[52] Mao boasted that China would soon surpass Britain in steel production; in 1959 Kim proclaimed that North Korea would surpass Japan in per capita industrial output in ten years.[53] The real change in policy was seen at a meeting of the full party leadership in September 1958, just months after Mao proclaimed the Great Leap Forward. Kim unveiled the Cheollima Movement, named after the mythical Korean horse that could gallop or leap enormous distances. Ignoring the obvious influence of events in China, Kim claimed the movement had begun two years earlier, in December 1956, when he visited the Gangseon steel mill to personally direct the work. The plant, not far from Pyongyang, had a capacity for 60,000 tons but was producing only 40,000. Needing more steel, Kim Il Sung ordered that the plant increase its production by at least 10,000 tons. The plant managers told him this was not possible, so Kim went to the plant, stayed there for weeks and personally took over its management. He discussed the problems of production with the workers, and from these discussions they were able to come up with solutions and develop more efficient methods. Then, with Kim encouraging them to put in superhuman efforts, the workers not only met but greatly surpassed their targets, producing 90,000 tons of steel; the plant's output increased even more the following year, to 120,000 tons, becoming a virtual cornucopia of steel.[54] What workers at the Gangseon steelworks achieved under Kim's personal guidance became the model for the entire Cheollima Movement. 'The creative power of our working class and our people is really inexhaustible,' Kim declared, and he tested this proposition in endless campaigns. In a radio broadcast that month, he urged North Koreans to 'rush forward like a flying horse' and fulfil the Five-Year Plan in three and a half years.[55]

Beyond the mythical aspects of this story, what is true was Kim's hands-on approach to problems. He was not a remote figure who gave orders from his guarded palace. Unlike Stalin, for example, he spent considerable time at plants, offices, farms and schools, personally inspecting what was going on, giving instructions, talking with the workers, farmers and students and always giving words of encouragement. And while the achievements this resulted in are so exaggerated that they can seem absurd, Kim did try to learn what was going on and did encourage workers and managers to work out solutions. He drove the population as hard as he could at a time of mass purges and relocations of families deemed untrustworthy, when society was undergoing massive upheaval.

Kim created Cheollima Work Teams, groups of workers commanded to exceed their quotas. These supposedly rose from the workers themselves, first by plant worker Jin Eungwon. The regime created other movements to increase production, seeking to grind out more output from the people. There was a 'Movement to See the Early Morning Stars' to make workers and farmers get up and go to work very early, and a 'Movement Not to Have Soup', which originated in textile factories in order to minimize the time lost in bathroom breaks.[56] In 1959 students were sent to construction sites under the slogan 'One Stretch after One Thousand Shovels'.[57] This was accompanied by the completion of the socialization of the economy. In 1957 cabinet decrees 96 and 102 prohibited the buying and selling of grain.[58] Basic commodities were collected and redistributed by the state, private markets were prohibited and the few remaining private enterprises were taken over by the state. Markets were replaced by a public distribution system in which each household received so much food, clothes, cooking oil and other necessities.

Kim was influenced by Mao's Great Leap in other ways. Like the Chinese leader, he directed the production of basic consumer goods to the local units of government, hoping to make them more self-sufficient so that the central state could focus on heavy industry.[59] When Mao began to consolidate state collective farms into larger units, Kim followed suit, merging collective farms into giant rural communes. The nation's 13,309 cooperatives, which were based in pre-existing villages and averaged 79 households, were welded into 3,880 large units, or around 300 households each. The stated purpose was to create economies of scale that would increase grain production.[60] Kim, who had been so critical of blindly imitating the Soviet model, now seemed to be faithfully following Maoist China's path for development. It certainly had a lot of appeal for him. China in the late 1950s was arguing that its Great Leap Forward was a special road for China and other Asian societies to follow that relied on voluntarist efforts and mass mobilization as a substitute for the shortage of capital and technical expertise. Kim was Chinese educated, a fluent speaker of Mandarin and as a Korean he was culturally closer to China than Russia, so it is not surprising he was more open to Mao's ideas. However, Kim was not just emulating Mao Zedong. Even before 1958, Kim had displayed a concern for local self-sufficiency, perhaps deriving from his experiences with the base areas in Manchuria. There was also a concern drawn from the Korean War for local self-sufficiency in the event of another invasion. And he was already inclined to rely on mass mobilization as a substitute for capital.

Kim resembled and no doubt was influenced by Mao in seeking to learn directly from the people. Like his Chinese counterpart, he sought to overcome bureaucratic inertia, to avoid party officials from being cut off from the masses and to tap the creative energies of the ordinary workers. For farmers he developed the Cheongsan-ri Method (*Cheongsan-ri munbeop*). Following the method he used for the Gangseon steel mill, Kim began visiting the Cheongsan-ri village, now a collective farm near Pyongyang, in February 1960. Conveniently close so it could be an easy day trip from the capital, he commuted there for fourteen days. He closely supervised the work being carried out there, listened to the peasants and managers, and then gave instructions. His attention to the details of daily life went as far as scheduling football (soccer) games so that they did not interfere with busy times at work. He made regular trips to the farm until the autumn harvest in October to observe, listen and supervise. It was reported that 'he was so kind and unceremonious that the people could tell him their minds without any cautions.' He was thus able to listen and learn from the people.[61]

Kim created a parallel system for industrial sites. He began visiting the Taean electric machine plant in December 1961, listening to the workers and giving guidance to them. This became known as the Taean Work System (*Taeanui saeopchegye*). Kim's intention at Cheongsan-ri and at Taean was to set an example for all party cadres to follow. To implement this he created the 'on-the-spot guidance system' (*hyeonji jido*), in which he had high-ranking officials of the KWP visit and work with the farmers and labourers. And he set the example: for his entire reign as North Korea's leader he made thousands of visits to nearly every industrial and agricultural site in the country.

Kim, however, was not Mao. He was more pragmatic and took from the Chinese leader what was useful. He was also more systematic, more consistent in implementing policies. There was no mass sending of officials to the countryside; rather, visits to worksites by officials became a matter of routine. Mao's Great Leap Forward was truly a disaster and led to one of the greatest famines in recorded history. When Mao was informed it was going badly, he refused to listen. By contrast, Kim was quick to see that, despite some successes, the wildly ambitious targets he had set were unrealistic and needed to be modified. He admitted that the fast pace of economic development was creating many 'defects', including manpower shortages and shortages of industrial raw materials, housing and food.[62] So, late in 1959, he decided to modify the production targets to more attainable levels. The year 1960 was declared a 'buffer year', a period of adjustments. There were food shortages as always, but nothing as bad as the mid-1950s, and unlike Mao he did not try to make farmers work on industrial and construction projects while trying to tend their fields. As a result his Five-Year Plan or 'great leap forward' (the term was not used by North Korea) was mostly successful in expanding industrial capacity and infrastructure.

Kim's great leap in industrialization was accompanied by an enormous expansion of education. This was done systematically, in stages. First, four years of primary school was made compulsory in 1956. Three years later, when this was fully implemented, basic education was extended to seven years. When this was achieved in 1967, it was expanded to nine years. By the 1970s at least ten years of formal schooling was becoming the norm for young people. Kim's regime vigorously pursued adult literacy by establishing two-year workers' schools, which were so successful that they were deemed unnecessary and abolished in 1967. The state also created middle school programmes for workers. The idea was to bring the entire population up to the same basic level of schooling.[63] North Korea placed a great emphasis on developing practical work schools. As of March 1959, all students in middle school and above were required to work eight to ten weeks in factories, mines or on other projects.[64] Kim differed from Mao when it came to education. His efforts at building a solid, universal and standardized education system were more systematic, more consistent and more successful. Of course, he had a much smaller, homogeneous society to work with.

But he also did not share Mao's suspicion or contempt for technical expertise and encouraged and required all his officials to see that their children received a vigorous education and training in some area, whether it was in ideology, administration, engineering or economics.

Kim was more flexible and pragmatic and as an administrator more competent than Mao. His great leap forward was more successful. This, however, in the long run proved rather tragic for North Korea. Chinese leaders in the mid-1960s and again after Mao's death in 1976 moved away from the ideologically rigid command economy, towards more market incentives. Kim, however, satisfied with his early successes, never abandoned the path he set. Indeed, in the 1960s, with a few minor setbacks, the economy continued to perform well while remaining under tight control and direction. He saw little need to modify his version of economic development, continuing to adhere to it for decades. Kim Il Sung and his successors continued their on-the-spot guidance, party officials were personally involved in production, and renewed calls for local self-sufficiency in the production of basic consumer goods were issued periodically. Mass mobilization of labour for militarized campaigns became an unchanging part of the life of ordinary citizens. The exhortations, political indoctrination and endless campaigns and 'speed battles' remained the prime means of boosting production. Of course, this was not simply because Kim was more rigid than Mao; it was because he was more successful in placing like-minded people in every position of authority. And not only did he govern far longer than Mao, but he successfully engineered his own succession, ensuring that his policies would continue.

Foreign Policy

Kim eliminated internal opposition while making gains in his efforts to achieve autonomy from Moscow and Beijing. In October 1958 the last of the CPV withdrew from Korea. Their presence was originally designed as a counterweight to the American troops in the South. But it was obvious to Kim that there was no desire in Washington or Seoul for the resumption of war, and the Chinese were not really needed. Their withdrawal eliminated a possible avenue for Chinese interference and gave Kim the bragging rights of declaring that, unlike in the South, there were no foreign troops in his country. Careful to maintain good relations with Beijing, he visited China in late November and early December 1958, observing its Great Leap Forward and expressing his approval. 'We will certainly pass on to our peasants the great results you have achieved with your commune movement,' he declared.[65] He paid the Chinese another visit in 1959 and continued to praise their efforts even as he was deciding to slow down his version of the Great Leap. The point was to maintain good terms with the Chinese.

By this point tensions between Moscow and Beijing were growing as Mao was increasingly contemptuous of Khrushchev's revisionism, and Khrushchev viewed the Maoist regime with increasing alarm, pulling out most of the Soviet Union's technical advisers in 1959. For Kim this growing tension was both an opportunity and a threat. It was a chance to balance each power against the other, giving him greater space, since neither Beijing nor Moscow wanted Pyongyang to fall under the other's orbit. He played this rather well. Praising China, he was also careful to praise the Soviet Union's progress. And he was careful to pair his visits to the two countries. He attended the Twenty-first Congress of the Communist Party of the Soviet Union in 1959 and visited China the same year. At the same time he kept a distance from both. He did not support Beijing when in 1958 it shelled Taiwan-held islands off the Chinese coast, which Moscow opposed. And, to Beijing's displeasure, he praised Khrushchev's visit to the USA in 1959. Yet when attending the Soviet Communist Party Congress in 1959 he stated, 'Solidarity centred on the Soviet Union has always been necessary,' but 'it does not mean that somebody is dominating somebody else; nor does it mean our submission to Moscow.'[66]

Kim's diplomatic skills were dramatically displayed in the summer of 1961. As tensions rose between Moscow and Beijing, he simultaneously established formal treaties of alliance with both. After his diplomats had done their preliminary work, he went to Moscow and on 1 July signed a Treaty of Friendship, Cooperation and Mutual Assistance. This formalized their relationship. Then he immediately flew to Beijing, where he signed a similar treaty on 2 July, just one day later. So concerned was he that these treaties should be signed almost simultaneously, he travelled by air. Kim had a lifelong fear of flying and had previously travelled to the Soviet Union, and Eastern Europe, by train, often taking days. This is one of the only times he overcame this fear; he did so since the timing of these ceremonies was so important.

Kim sought to maintain his much-needed alliances with Moscow and Beijing because he was realistic enough to know how much he depended on their economic and military support. But he also wanted to seal his country off from their ability to undermine his authority. He was especially concerned about too much Russian influence. He had criticized schools for teaching Russian literature and neglecting Korea's literary heritage. After 1956 the amount of Russian music performed, literature published and language taught declined. Instead, the publication of Korean historical works increased. The voluminous official history of the Joseon dynasty, the *Joseon wangjo sillok*, was translated into modern Korean and published. Russian plays were no longer performed; all plays were to be Korean plays. The Korean Society for International Cultural Exchange, which spread Russian culture, was forced to close its provincial branches.[67] The streets named after Lenin and Stalin as well as Mao Zedong were given new, Korean names. Even contact with Russians and Eastern Europeans was restricted. Officials and party members who had foreign wives were pressured to divorce them. Special permission was required to meet foreigners, even of friendly socialist countries. And the new histories, written in the late 1950s, made fewer references to the role of the Soviet Union in the liberation of Korea or of China in the Korean War. Kim was cutting off the Korean people's exposure to all outside culture and making Korea and the communist movement he led the centre of all history and all culture.

Personal Life

During this busy period in his life, Kim remarried and started a new family. When the Korean War turned against him in the autumn of 1950, he sent his son Jong Il and his daughter Kyong Hui to China for safety. They spent two years in Jilin province in Manchuria, where Kim himself had spent much of his youth. Kim spent the next two years in the border town of Kanggye. In 1952 he moved back to Pyongyang, in a new house near the Soviet embassy.[68] Shortly after, he brought his children back to live with him there.[69]

A widower since the death of Kim Jong Suk in 1949, Kim became romantically involved with a secretary to his security guards, Kim Seongae (Song-ae). North Korean sources have never provided much information about her background, but according to one defector she was a secondary school graduate who joined the military in 1947 to work as a radio operator.[70] Her job in such a sensitive area suggests that her background was politically correct. Kim might have started having an affair with her before his wife died. In any case, she was probably with Kim in Kanggye, and when they returned to Pyongyang he entrusted the care of his children to her. They were married in a quiet ceremony in the autumn of 1952, attended by a few officials.[71] She was 28, twelve years younger than Kim. Kim Seongae was kept in the background until the mid-1960s, when her first public appearances were reported.

Kim started a new family with Seongae. She gave birth to a daughter, Kim Kyongjin, born in 1952; a son, Kim Pyongil, born in 1954; and another son, Kim Yongil, born in 1955. Pyongil bore a strong resemblance to his father and like him was gregarious. He was good-looking and personally charming, qualities that served him well later as a diplomat. Sometimes referred to by those in the inner circle of power as 'the side branch', Kim's three children by Seongae never played a prominent role in North Korean politics. Their very existence was unknown to the public, but this was also true of Jong Il and Kyong Hui, Kim's children from his first marriage, until 1980.

The 1961 Party Congress

On 11 September 1961 Kim Il Sung convened the Fourth Congress of the Korean Workers' Party for an eight-day session. His control over the party and its domination by his fellow ex-guerillas was nearly complete. At the previous party congress in 1956 there was a higher percentage of ex-guerillas in the Central Committee than in the past: five of the eleven members of the Standing Committee (Politburo) were former guerillas, versus only two out of seven in 1948.[72] But they were still a minority, sharing posts with Yanan and Soviet comrades. In 1961, by contrast, ex-guerillas held most of the posts in the upper echelons of the party. Of the eleven members of the Standing Committee, the highest body of the party, all were partisans except Nam Il, a Soviet Korean, and Kim Changman from the Yanan faction. Of the 85 members of the Central Committee, only 28 had served at the last congress. Yet all but one of the partisans who had served retained their posts; almost all non-partisans had been demoted or purged. There were now 37 Manchurian partisans and only two Soviet Koreans and three Yanan members, and only one member of South Korea's domestic faction, historian Paek Namun in the Central Committee. Almost all the rest were clients of Manchurian partisans.[73] A few owed their positions to family ties to Kim or his close comrades, including Kim Yeongju, Kim Il Sung's younger brother.[74]

Kim's main business of the Fourth Party Congress in September 1961 was unveiling the new Seven-Year Plan. While it was somewhat more realistic than the previous Five-Year Plan, it was still very ambitious, with a target of a 12.8 per cent annual growth rate. Industrial production was to increase 3.2 times, and agricultural production, which had been lagging behind the country's other economic sectors, was to increase 2.4 times.[75] These targets were extraordinarily high. By comparison, South Korea's new Five-Year Plan, launched the following year, set only 7 per cent annual growth, which was thought unrealistically high by its American advisers. Still, Kim's economic targets were not entirely a fantasy; in the eight previous years the DPRK under Kim's leadership had succeeded in achieving enormous economic successes.

The congress was also an opportunity for Kim to celebrate his achievements, and they were considerable. The country, through the hard work and sacrifice of its people, had made a remarkable recovery from the devastation of the Korean War. In the past eight years he had become the unchallenged master of the country. He had eliminated all his rivals and placed almost every important position in the party, military and state in the hands of his old partisan comrades, the most loyal of his followers. He had achieved a similar control over the economy. It was now fully socialized, under the command of the state, and the state under his command so he could direct it towards his goals. He had created a system to supervise the workers and their workplaces, expanded industrial production, enormously expanded education and was establishing the basis for an industrial economy that would be able to produce the capital goods needed for further growth. He had gained greater autonomy from Moscow and Beijing – while still reliant on them, he was no longer their client but their ally – and had signed a treaty of friendship with both that July. From Kim Il Sung's point of view, the task of leading Korea to its former independence and making it a strong, autonomous state that could maintain its sovereignty and take its place among the progressive societies of the world was not yet completed. Yet it seemed within reach.

Also within reach was his goal of reunification. While a strong, unified, rapidly industrializing DPRK was forging ahead, South Korea seemed mired in poverty, corruption and instability. Despite massive U.S. aid, the ROK was making little economic progress. In 1960 a student-led popular uprising overthrew the regime of Syngman Rhee. This was followed by a short-lived experiment in creating a parliamentary democracy, a year characterized by labour strikes, student protests and general chaos, leading to a military coup on 16 May 1961. South Korea's failure to pull itself out of poverty and backwardness, its failure to create a stable political order, its inability to free itself from economic and military dependency on the United States was in such sharp contrast to what he had accomplished that Kim must have thought reunification under his more successful Korea was inevitable.

It is going too far to credit all this to Kim Il Sung personally; nevertheless, he was the chief agent of North Korea's transformation. He was able to utilize the chaos and upheaval caused by the collapse of the Japanese Empire, the Soviet occupation and the destruction of the Korean War to reshape Korean society. By the late 1950s little stood in the way in his attempt to remake the DPRK into a new society where people were graded by loyalty and where the economy was self-sufficient and able to support a powerful military.

6

DIPLOMAT, MILITANT, GREAT THINKER

In 1961 Kim Il Sung was still only 49, and his regime was still young. He had consolidated his power, eliminated his opponents and appeared to have no real internal threats to his authority. Yet he faced several problems: how to achieve the steady, sustained level of economic growth necessary to transform the DPRK into a self-reliant industrial society; how to navigate the increasingly tense relations between Moscow and Beijing while maintaining the support of both; and how to contain the South in ways that would enable him to achieve his goal of reunifying the peninsula. He dealt with these challenges with a mix of diplomatic skill and militancy, while emulating Mao Zedong as a great thinker.

Dealing with the South

Kim remained obsessed with reunification. It was central to all his policies. But in the first decade after the ceasefire in 1953 he was more focused on strengthening his position at home and building an industrial economy. Reunification would come later. In a meeting with Chinese premier Zhou Enlai in 1958, he explained that if 'we can successfully finish our [long-term] construction plan' then 'it is possible to unite Korea, peacefully.'[1] The South, economically floundering and its political system in disarray, was not an immediate threat, and with the U.S. military presence on the border, reunification by force was not an option. Kim's policy was to concentrate on building up the industrial base of his country, carefully indoctrinate his people, promote support for his regime among the people of the South, and wait until the Americans left, which they would inevitably do. He would not invade and expect the people to support him – that was the mistake of 1950 – but rather wait for the people of the South to rise up against their own government first and then join forces with them: what can be called the 'South Korean revolution first and then unification' policy. And he would not get into another war with the USA.

Nonetheless, he was always willing to take advantage of any opportunity that presented itself to weaken the southern regime and win over the masses below the border. When in April 1960 a student-led uprising overthrew the authoritarian Syngman Rhee regime, Kim proposed a Confederal Republic of Koryo as an intermediate step towards unification. The name was chosen because of neutrality: the other two common names for Korea were Han'guk, used by the South, and Joseon, used by the North. Nothing came of this. In the spring of 1961 Pyongyang proposed meetings with radical student groups, who responded positively, but this effort was cut short by the South Korean military coup of 16 May 1961.

The new military junta was led by General Park Chung Hee. Park had a complicated background; a former Japanese-trained military officer, he had a brother who was a communist and was thought also to be a communist sympathizer. He was arrested by the Rhee administration but was released and recommissioned as an officer during the outbreak of the Korean War. Park was also known to resent his country's dependency on the United States. When coming to power, the officers went after the corrupt business class and seemed to be flirting with totalitarian ideas of economic development. Kim saw an opportunity to drive a wedge between the new military leaders and the Americans and sent Hwang Seongtaek, an official who had fled to the North in 1946, to meet one of the coup leaders, Kim Jongpil. But the new military government of Park Chung Hee executed Hwang.[2] Park then instituted a Five-Year Plan (1962–6) that clearly borrowed elements of state-led growth from the DPRK's socialist allies but let the plan be carried out by the very business leaders his military government had initially arrested. He took on a hard anti-communist line and remained closely allied to the USA. Kim's hopes that he could strike a deal with the new military regime came to an end. Kim did not expect Park's economic plans to be spectacularly successful; he cannot be faulted for this, almost no one outside South Korea did.

The Cuban Crisis and Militarization

In the early 1960s Kim Il Sung decided to put greater emphasis on military development. It was not concerns about the Park regime that brought about a shift in Kim's policy but an event quite far away: the Cuban Missile Crisis of October 1962. When the United States demanded the Soviet Union remove the missiles it had secretly installed in Cuba or face an American military intervention in the island, Khrushchev backed down and withdrew the missiles. Kim was disturbed that the Soviet Union agreed under U.S. pressure to withdraw missiles from Cuba. It called into question just how reliable Moscow would be in a crisis when U.S. forces were stationed on his border and seemed to confirm his worst suspicions about Khrushchev. The Soviet Union's abandoning its ally Cuba and its caving in to the United States only appeared to demonstrate how the DPRK had to rely on its own military prowess.

Kim responded to this at the fifth plenum of the Fourth Congress of the Korean Workers' Party, which met in December 1962. At this meeting, under the slogan 'With a hammer and sickle in one hand and arms in the other', it adopted the 'equal emphasis' policy of placing equivalent weight on economic development and military build-up. The new effort for enhancing the nation's military preparedness consisted of 'four lines': arming the entire population; intensifying training for its armed forces; making the entire country into an impregnable fortress; and providing modern equipment for its armed forces. The policy was put into effect immediately, although it was only officially implemented by name at the Second Party Conference in 1966.[3] To coordinate this military build-up, a Military Committee was reconstituted at the December 1962 meeting. This was a body that had been established by the Supreme People's Assembly shortly after the start of the Korean War and abolished at its end. Its revival now suggested the extent to which the nation would be on a permanent war footing. The committee's membership was not publicized, but party by-laws issued in 1970 stated it operated under the direction of the Central Committee and functioned as a military policy-making body that directed both the armed forces and the defence industries.[4]

It would not be accurate to claim this was a radical shift. Kim always saw achieving his goals from a military point of view. Economic plans were expressed in military terms, with 'speed battles' and calls to 'take the hills' (economic targets). When the Chinese People's Volunteers withdrew at the end of 1958, he created a civilian militia, the Worker-Peasant Red Guards (*Nonong jeokwidae*). What was new in 1962 was the decision to step up this effort to militarize the nation. The Red Guards were expanded until all able-bodied men between 18 and 45 and single women from 18 to 35 were required to join. Members of a hamlet formed a squad, a village a battalion. They were organized into regiments at the county level and corps at the provincial level. Men and women were required to attend training sessions after work and farmers during less busy times on the agricultural calendar.[5] Intensifying training for the military included more political indoctrination to ensure high morale and a sense of purpose. This too had already begun earlier, when Kim ordered more ideological training programmes for troops in January 1961, but was now intensified.[6] The size of the army was a problem: only 400,000 were under arms, compared to 600,000 in South Korea. Ideological training would, the leadership hoped, partly compensate for this. At the same time the size of the military forces continually increased until it matched and eventually greatly exceeded that of the South, despite the DPRK having only half the population. This was done by lengthening the period of military service: in the 1970s and '80s the ROK had a three-year conscription while the DPRK's averaged over eight years. Young men who did not enter higher education began military service after completing secondary school, around the age of sixteen. Later, some of the men served until the age of 28. Thus North Korea had the most onerous military service in the world.

The country was made 'an impregnable fortress'. As Kim Il Sung stated in 1963,

> We have to fortify our entire country. By doing so, we can defeat those who have atomic weapons even though we do not possess them ourselves . . . We have to dig underground tunnels. We have to fortify not only the front line, but also the second and third defense area as well as strengthen anti-aircraft and coast-line defenses. We have to build many factories under the ground . . . when we fortify the whole country, not even the strongest enemy, not even the Americans will be able to invade us.[7]

Accordingly, he had shelters constructed throughout the country, including the Pyongyang subway, which was designed as much as a deep underground shelter as a means of transportation. As they were during the Korean War, underground factory and military installations were constructed around the country. The elaborate tunnels that hid so much of the country's military activity became permanent characteristics of North Korea, to the dismay of later U.S. intelligence analysts heavily reliant on satellite photos. Of no less importance was the fourth policy of developing modern weapons. The production of military hardware, especially from the 1970s, became a central focus of industrialization targets.

Although there was an 'equal emphasis' on military and economic development, in practice the Seven-Year Plan's targets were scaled back. There was a sharp increase in the resources devoted to the military, beginning a policy that was never really reversed. Of course, North Korea had always maintained a large military; it was technically in a state of war and remained, in theory at least, ready to resume the conflict. After 1962, however, there was a vast increase in military and military-related industrial development. According to researcher Joseph Chung, defence spending was 8 per cent of the state budget in 1954 and fell to 3.7 per cent in 1959, then after 1962 rose to 18 per cent, peaking at 30 per cent of the state budget between 1967 and 1972. By the late 1970s the budget devoted to defence spending had fallen somewhat, but it would remain among the highest, if not the highest, as a proportion of state expenditure, of any country.[8]

Kim was driven to take this step towards greater emphasis on military production and military training out of insecurity. But it was also part of his effort to be as self-reliant as possible, to not have to depend on the Soviet Union or China to carry out reunification or any other military objective. He was determined for the DPRK to be its own master, as unrealistic as this might have been. And he looked contemptuously on South Korea as a pathetic client state of an imperial power. Yet the decision taken at the end of 1962 and gradually implemented over the next several years was probably a wrong turn. Scarce capital needed for economic development was now being diverted to military build-up, military drills only added to an overworked population, and the enormous period of military service only made the labour shortage worse.

Balancing Act in the Sino-Soviet Dispute

Kim only compounded his economic problems by leaning to one side in the Sino-Soviet dispute. He had initially proved to be a skilled tightrope walker, careful to be the loyal ally of both Moscow and

Beijing as tensions between the two communist giants grew. From 1956 to 1961 Kim Il Sung made five visits to the Soviet Union, attending three congresses of the Communist Party of the USSR, and made three visits to China.[9] His skill culminated in the two separate treaties he signed almost simultaneously in July 1961 with the two powers. Then he seemed to lose his balance. While attending the Twenty-first Congress of the Communist Party of the Soviet Union in October 1961, he heard Khrushchev's attack on Albania, which was indirectly aimed at the small country's ally the PRC. This was especially hard for him to hear, since in many ways Enver Hoxha's regime resembled his own. Both were small countries led by former partisans with a similar personality cult of the leader, similar economic policies and a similar desire to achieve autonomy within the socialist camp. In response he risked Moscow's annoyance or even anger by signing an agreement on cultural cooperation with Albania in March 1962.[10] In fact Kim and Hoxha became friends, and Albania later became nicknamed in the West the 'North Korea of Eastern Europe'.

In other ways Kim leaned towards Beijing, taking its side in the October 1962 border war between China and India, in contrast to Moscow's neutral stance. He sided with China when it refused to sign the Nuclear Test Ban Treaty of August 1963.[11] He resisted efforts by Khrushchev to get the DPRK to join the Soviet bloc economic organization known as Comecon. Still, Kim maintained a public stance of friendship towards Moscow, which continued to supply needed economic and military aid. But he became deeply upset about how the Soviets backed down in the face of U.S. aggression during the Cuban Missile Crisis; in his opinion they abandoned their Cuban ally.

In September 1963 Kim openly criticized the Soviet Union. He did so in a curious and indirect way: three historians at Kim Il Sung University criticized a Soviet world history published in 1955. They accused the Soviet history of having 'many distortions, falsifications and fabrications which came from the prejudice and ignorance of the authors with regard to the history of Korea'.[12] The Soviets, they charged, were basing their history on Japanese imperialist accounts. Korean history had been 'short-changed' by the authors, who placed the first Korean state in the second century BCE when a state existed centuries earlier, maligned the nationalist and progressive credentials of the late nineteenth-century political leader Kim Okkyun and other bourgeois reformers, and minimized the impact of the Bolshevik Revolution on the March First Movement.[13] Of course, this could not have been published without Kim's approval. The following month, the *Rodong sinmun* responded to Khrushchev's attempt to call a conference of world communist parties to expel China with the editorial 'Let Us Defend the Socialist Camp'. It criticized the idea of excluding China and went on to scold the Soviet Union for trying to interfere with the internal affairs of the DPRK as well as other countries. The Soviet Union was attacked for not supporting Pyongyang's emphasis on heavy industry and a self-supporting economy. It went on to criticize Moscow for 'trying to force the anti-personality cult' campaign on other socialist countries and called Soviet policy 'imperialism'.[14] Thus the editorial made explicit the fears and concerns Kim Il Sung had with the Soviet Union.

Kim was too realistic to break openly with the Soviets; he was too economically and military dependent on them. So he was careful not to make any criticism in his name but to do so only through surrogates. His personal interactions with the Soviet representative in Moscow remained cordial. Nonetheless, Moscow in response to these provocations reduced economic aid, threatening his Seven-Year Plan. When the Soviet leadership ousted Khrushchev in October 1964, Kim took the opportunity to mend relations. Soviet premier Alexei Kosygin paid a visit in 1965, relations improved, and aid and economic exchanges were renewed. Until the end of the Soviet Union, relations between the two powers were strained at times, but after 1965 Kim was careful not to alienate his primary economic patron too much. Moscow, for its part, found it useful to maintain influence in the strategically located DPRK.

In 1966 Kim ended a long silence on the Sino-Soviet dispute by stating that his country maintained an independent position in the international communist movement. The DPRK took no further side in the dispute among big communist powers. Kim would for the most part skilfully maintain correct relations with both, using this as a means of receiving aid while achieving political autonomy. Nonetheless, as relations with Moscow improved, those with Beijing worsened. This was a result of internal developments in China. Kim had his grievances with the Chinese: there were memories of the Minsaengdan Incident, his being sidelined by the Chinese forces during the Korean War and Peng Dehuai's interference in his purges in 1956. Yet he was more comfortable with the Chinese, fellow Asians with whom he and his fellow Koreans shared many cultural links. He remained grateful for Chinese intervention in 1950 when Moscow was ready to abandon him. Kim was inspired by Mao's mass line, his emphasis on voluntarist efforts in overcoming a backward state. China's championship of national liberation wars and its confrontational approach to American imperialism was more to his liking than Moscow's 'peaceful coexistence'. However, in 1966 Mao plunged his country into turmoil with his Great Proletariat Cultural Revolution. The extremist antics of his youthful Red Guards and their backers in the party made the leadership in Pyongyang uncomfortable.

Although Kim in 1967 carried out his own version of the Cultural Revolution, he was less than sympathetic to Mao's. The chaos and disorder, the rampages of empowered students and youth were all revolting to him. The North Korean leader employed mass mobilizations for development campaigns, herded peasants into state farms and conducted major purges, but all these were done in a more systematic and orderly way. According to the Cuban ambassador to Pyongyang, officials made jokes about Mao being senile. Kim told Leonid Brezhnev in a secret meeting in December 1966 that Mao's Cultural Revolution was 'massive idiocy'.[15] And the Cultural Revolution soon turned on him. In 1967 a poster signed by veterans of the Korean War accused Kim Il Sung of being 'revisionist and a disciple of Khrushchev'. Other reports issued by Red Guard publications accused Kim of living like a millionaire and of showing concern for traditional filial piety by making his mother and father revolutionary saints.[16] At one point a train arrived in North Korea from China with the dead bodies of murdered China-based Koreans and a warning to the leadership that they should expect the same fate.[17]

This was compounded by a border dispute. Imperial China and dynastic Korea had demarcated the border in 1712. During the Cultural Revolution the Chinese began to challenge the borders with both the Soviet Union and North Korea. Their dispute with the DPRK centred on possession of Baekdusan, the highest point in Korea, a place regarded in Korean tradition as sacred and the home of the legendary founder of the nation, Dangun. But this dispute appeared resolved in 1970 as the Cultural Revolution began winding down. Premier Zhou Enlai's visit that year marked a return to normal relations.

More Purges

In October 1966 Kim Il Sung called for a party conference. This was a gathering of the KWP leadership between the Congresses, and only the second one. The first was in 1958, during the height of the purges. Kim called the 1966 conference to discuss the faltering Seven-Year Plan. The temporary reduction of Soviet aid had been a blow to achieving its targets, although that was probably only a contributing factor. The plan was overly ambitious, and resources were being diverted to the military. It was decided to extend the plan for three years. It was at this conference that the KWP declared its neutrality in the Sino-Soviet dispute. What is also of interest is that Kim removed the last of the non-partisans in high-ranking positions: Yi Changman, Nam Il and Pak Jeongae, the latter the only woman in the top leadership.[18] There was one non-partisan who became an alternate member of the Politburo: Kim's younger brother, Kim Yeongju. Those in the inner leadership understood that Kim was grooming his younger brother as a possible successor. From then on, he was the de facto number two in the regime.

The following year Kim carried out another purge. His Manchurian partisans held almost all positions of importance. But within the partisans were members of the Gapsan group. These were veterans of the Gapsan Operations Committee. Based on the Korean side of the border, they provided key logistical support and information for guerilla operations, such as Kim's victory at Bocheonbo. While not guerillas themselves in official accounts, they were depicted as working heroically with Kim and other fighters in the anti-Japanese struggle. Tensions arose between them and Kim Il Sung when they began to promote a rival or at least secondary cult of Pak Geumcheol, a founding member of the group and the fourth-ranking member of the party. Kim Toman in the Propaganda and Agitation Department commissioned a film, *An Act of Sincerity*, that centred on the heroic deeds of the anti-Japanese struggle carried out by Pak and his wife. He also rebuilt Pak's birthplace. Only Kim Il Sung and his family were allowed to be so honoured. Furthermore, Pak's pronouncements were issued as 'instructions' (*gyosi*), a term reserved for Kim. There are also hints of policy disagreements. According to at least one defector, the Gapsan members were also critical of the single-minded concentration on heavy industry.[19]

Early in 1967 Kim Il Sung called for a halt to these acts of 'individual heroism'.[20] By this he meant developing any rival cults of personality. He also criticized those who preferred to develop light industries and to improve living standards.[21] At a party meeting in late May 1967 Kim had Pak and all other Gapsan members removed from all official posts and sent to prison camps.[22] This was his last major purge. Kim ruled the DPRK for a further 27 years, and over that time comrades fell out of favour with him. Some were arrested, a few were executed, many more simply demoted, but he found no need to conduct large-scale removals of party and state officials.

Kim's Cultural Revolution

Kim Il Sung followed the removal of the Gapsan group with what can be described as his version of Mao's Cultural Revolution. On 25 May 1967, immediately following the purge, he ordered the inspection of all books. Officials then checked all printed material, and anything that was not approved was confiscated and burned, including many literary classics and almost anything beyond a narrow range of official DPRK-published materials.[23] Books were gathered; some had pages blacked, most were destroyed. This was followed by works of art, sheet music, anything that had a foreign influence – even Beethoven was banned. The cultural purge included some traditional works of Korean literature and artistic forms such as *pansori*, the beloved traditional music and storytelling performance.[24]

The cult of Kim Il Sung was intensified. 'Instructions' of the Great Leader were read at every official meeting of any kind throughout the land; every article and publication, no matter what the topic, included his quotes in bold letters; and newspapers devoted a larger amount of their space to coverage about him. Officials had to quote his instructions at every public meeting.[25] One of the peculiar features of North Korea appeared at this time when party officials began wearing badges bearing his picture. Over the next few years the practice was expanded to include ordinary citizens, until all North Koreans were expected to wear these badges in public.

All this bore a strong resemblance to China's Great Proletariat Cultural Revolution, which Mao had inaugurated the year before.

This might seem odd, since Kim was contemptuous of Mao's great campaign, not publicly but in private. But Kim had adopted Maoist policies before, notably the Great Leap Forward. Yet he did so only by modifying it, adopting what was useful while avoiding some of Mao's impractical measures, such as communes and backyard steel mills. In a similar manner he selected what he wanted from Mao's Cultural Revolution. What he was so scornful of was the disorder of the Chinese upheaval. There would be no Red Guards harassing teachers and going on rampages. Nor did Kim want to shake up the bureaucracy or the party leadership as Mao was trying to do, since he had staffed these with his most trusted associates. Kim's 'cultural revolution' was more orderly, more selective and controlled. Nor did Kim go as far as Mao in assaulting traditional culture, and later he reversed himself on this, embracing and promoting selected parts of his country's heritage.

There was another extremely important difference. Unlike in China, where the Cultural Revolution moderated somewhat in the early 1970s and was abandoned altogether with the death of Mao in 1976, the main features of Kim's cultural revolution only became more intense over time, remaining a permanent force in shaping the ideology, culture and politics of his society for decades.

Kim's cultural revolution, directed by his younger brother Yeongju, had one unique feature: the reclassification of the entire population. Previously, in the late 1950s, Kim had divided the people into three classes (*gyecheung*): loyal, wavering and hostile. These were now further subdivided into 51 *seongbun* (groups), each with their own ranking. There were twelve *seongbun* belonging to the loyal or 'core' class. These comprised workers from working-class families, former farmhands, former poor peasants, personnel of state organizations, KWP members, family members of deceased revolutionaries, family members of national liberation fighters, revolutionary intelligentsia (those who received education after liberation), family members of civilians killed in the Korean War, families of soldiers who were killed during the Korean War, families of servicemen, and families of war martyrs or heroes. There were nine *seongbun* belonging to the wavering class and thirty to the hostile class. The last included those who had served under the Japanese as officials, former landlords, businessmen, merchants, Christians, active Buddhists, shamans, those who had engaged in pro-Japanese or pro-American activities and those who had family members who had fled to the South. In 1980 twelve new *seongbun* were created to reclassify ethnic Koreans from Japan, South Korea, China and elsewhere.[26] *Seongbun* were based on family background, so that each became an inherited status.

Discrimination against people of unfavourable backgrounds was common in other communist countries, and China under Mao in the 1950s had placed people in categories. But no other modern society had such a well-defined, inherited system of social status.[27] Kim had created an unparalleled rigid, hierarchical society. People inherited their status based on the activities of their parents or grandparents. These were not officially publicized, but everyone knew where they belonged. These categories mattered profoundly. Food rations, access to desired goods, housing, jobs, career advancement and admittance to higher education were determined by the classification. The privileged were able to live in Pyongyang. In fact it was difficult for most North Koreans to visit the city other than on official excursions. Children often found out if they were from a lower *seongbun* in their early teens when they were denied the right to join and wear the red scarf of the Kim Il Sung Youth. They then found that opportunities to enter a university, get a good job or live in Pyongyang were mostly closed to them. For most people there was little chance of improving upon their inherited social status. Although people could be downgraded because of improper political behaviour, cases of upward social mobility were rare. In many ways Kim created a society that replicated the heredity-based ranking system of traditional Korea.

The Cult of Kim

Kim's cult had appeared as early as 1946, and as we have seen was directed by the Soviets, modelled after that of Stalin. But the Soviet Union and its Eastern European satellites had gone through de-Stalinization; there was no comparable cult of Khrushchev, though in the Balkans Albania developed something similar around its eccentric dictator Enver Hoxha. Kim had not only resisted similar efforts to end the cult of personality but had directed or at least allowed his subordinates to elaborate on his cult. From 1967 it grew in intensity, without pause, until North Korea became what could be called a 'cult-state'. After that year, Kim Il Sung was generally referred to as *suryeong* (leader), a term formerly used for Stalin and Lenin. He had previously been referred to as *susang* (premier) or *janggun* (general). In the late 1960s it became standard practice to refer to him as the great (*widaehan*) or fatherly (*eobeoi*) leader. Only Kim was given these exalted prefixes to his name.[28] As noted, officials and later everyone wore badges with his picture. Portraits and statues of him appeared everywhere. His likeness hung from a prominent place in every office and every home and was treated as a sacred object to be cleaned daily.

Observers have often tried to analyse the traditional Confucian element in the cult of Kim. Considering how deeply Confucianism penetrated Korean culture, this would be expected. Certainly, the language of a ruler who loved and cared for his people, who ruled them with benevolence and protected them from the Yankee imperialists echoed traditional Confucian language and imagery. Yet the cult of Kim Il Sung was unprecedented in Korean history. The Korean kings were less lofty figures than the Chinese emperors; they lacked the sacred aura of Japanese emperors or of Southeast Asian *devarajas* (god-kings). The cult had a more modern derivation: from that of Stalin, influenced by Mao. It was also echoed and influenced by the emperor cult of pre-war Japan. North Korean schoolchildren paid their daily obeisance to the Great Leader at the school's shrine to him much as colonial Korean schoolchildren attended shrines to the semi-divine Japanese emperor. The practice of bowing ceremoniously in the direction of the imperial palace in Tokyo, the ubiquitous Shinto shrines and the tone of reverence expressed when referring to the emperor all had strikingly similar manifestations in North Korea. Even the glorification of the Kim family resembled that of the Japanese imperial family and its ancestors. Like the Japanese imperial cult, the cult of Kim Il Sung sought to inculcate an almost mystical sense of unity among the people and demanded their total loyalty to the leader. Whatever its traditional, colonial and communist influences, the cult of Kim Il Sung and his family had no real counterpart in any contemporary society.

Kim's cult was unlike Stalin's or Mao's or Hitler's, or like any modern dictator's, in one radical way. It became a cult of his family. That had always been true to some extent. Unlike in the Soviet Union or China, where the Great Leader's parents were almost never publicly mentioned, North Korean propaganda had referred to Kim's 'revolutionary lineage' since the late 1940s. From 1967, however, honouring his family became a central part of the ideology. His mother Kang Banseok, for example, became an object of veneration. A song in praise of her appeared that summer, and on 4 September an article calling her 'the mother of us all' appeared in the party newspaper *Rodong sinmun*.[29] She came to be commonly called 'the mother of Korea' (*Joseon ui eomeoni*). Kim's father Kim Hyeongjik also became a revered figure with his own cult. So did his paternal grandparents. In March 1968, in a publicized public ceremony, party officials laid wreaths on the grave of his grandfather and grandmother.[30]

This heightened cult of Kim's family coincided with the rise of his brother Kim Yeongju to the de facto number two in the regime. Unlike Kim Il Sung's other younger brother, Cheolsu, who died a revolutionary martyr, Yeongju was never a resistance fighter. He attended Moscow State University and enrolled in the Bolshevik

Party's school for higher-level cadres around 1946–7. He may have been sent there by his older brother for training to assume a position of leadership in the Communist Party, although he had not been previously active in the communist movement. His first prominent role was presiding over the 1953 show trials of the domestic faction as the secretary of the court.[31] In the early 1960s he was given a key administration role in the Korean Workers' Party Organization Department (Jojikbu), which through its control over personnel wielded enormous power. He became a more public figure in 1966 when Kim made him a member of the Politburo.[32] By 1970 he was listed as the sixth-ranking member of the KWP, though in reality he was the second most important member of the regime after Kim Il Sung himself. In 1967 Kim chose his brother to carry out his cultural revolution. Soon after, it became clear to most of the inner circle that he was to be Kim's likely successor.

Kim's cult was originally created by Korean propagandists under Soviet instruction to establish his legitimacy as a ruler, but its evolution after he secured power was under his control. The chief architects of the cult in the 1960s and '70s were his brother Yeongju and his son Jong Il, with the latter taking over its supervision in the 1970s. It was a family cult in every respect, crafted by family members, glorifying their lineage. Yet it became so extreme as to seem bizarre. If we analyse the elements of it, however, it becomes much more comprehensible: it had clear Stalinist origins; the influence of the cult of the Japanese emperor and imperial family shaped it; and Kim deployed the Maoist tactic of securing power by presenting himself as so awesomely powerful as to be unchallengeable.

Becoming a Great Thinker

Kim Il Sung was a 'brilliant' commander, an 'outstanding strategist', the 'sun of the forty million Koreans', but only from the late 1960s onwards did he become a 'great thinker', according to North Korean media. On 25 May 1967, in the same speech on censorship that led to book burnings, Kim discussed the transition from socialism. While on the surface this speech was not very remarkable, it was an attempt to lay out a theoretical position that differed from Maoist or Soviet versions of Marxism-Leninism.[33] Soon after that speech, his state and party organs began promoting the idea that Kim was a great thinker. This can be seen in the Ten Principles for the Monolithic Ideological System, drawn up at the time under the supervision of Kim Yeongju.

The first of these principles was 'We must give our all in the struggle to unify the entire society with the revolutionary ideology of Great Leader Kim Il Sung.' The second was 'We must honour Great Leader comrade Kim Il Sung with all our loyalty,' and the third, 'We must make absolute the authority of Great Leader comrade Kim Il Sung.' The others in various ways emphasized the need to obey the Great Leader, learn from him and unite the party under him. Kim Il Sung was not only the supreme and unquestioned leader; he demanded absolute loyalty and obedience. Kim told his party officials, 'You comrades should be able to read, not only the contents of words I speak, but also the thoughts in my head.'[34]

What was new in this was the fourth article in the Ten Principles, which declares Kim a seminal thinker: 'We must make Great Leader comrade Kim Il Sung's revolutionary ideology our faith and make his instructions our creed.'[35] Unfortunately, Kim was not well educated and was a plodding writer and unoriginal thinker with only a basic grasp of Marxism-Leninism. His writings were dull, repetitive and banal. But all this was beside the point. He was now the ideological guide whose principles established the basis of society. His 'thought' (*sasang*) over the next few years was elevated to the ideological basis of the party and society.

This thought was sometimes called Kimilsungism, and more often *Juche*. *Juche* has been translated or interpreted in many ways, most often as 'self-reliance'. *Juche* reflected the nationalist aspirations of Kim – which were shared by most Koreans and were the main impetus of the North Korea revolution – to create a nation-state that was strong and autonomous. North Korea never sought to be completely self-sufficient; the country was obviously too small and lacking in crucial resources for that. Self-reliance meant having an economy that was not dependent on another power as colonial Korea's was dependent on Japan; not being dependent militarily on another power for its defence as South Korea was on the USA; and not being politically dependent on another power as North Korea was on the Soviet Union in its first years. This was not an unreasonable or unrealistic goal. Furthermore, Kim's wish for economic self-sufficiency was not unique. In fact the idea of import substitution was common to many developing countries after the Second World War, from Brazil to India. It was bound up with the anti-imperialism that provided much of the impetus for nationalism outside Europe and North America.

Juche was not a new term. Kim first used it in December 1955 in a speech attacking Pak Changok and others, whom he accused of slavishly following Soviet and other foreign models of development as well as foreign culture, rather than seeking a path to modernization based on Korea's own conditions and promoting Korean rather than foreign culture. Korea had to rely on its own experience and culture. In subsequent speeches Kim used the term *Juche* to call for military and economic and political self-reliance. Only after 1967, however, did *Juche Thought* occupy a central place in the theoretical foundation for the Monolithic Ideological System and an instrument for the glorification of Kim Il Sung. At that time official publications began to suggest that *Juche* was a complete system of thought.

There were several reasons why Kim decided to create his own 'thought'. Partly it was in emulation of Mao. Kim Il Sung, having eliminated all possible rivals at home, may have wanted to establish himself as a great thinker too within the broader international communist movement. The troubled relations with both the Soviet

Union and China in the 1960s that made the DPRK less certain of the reliability of its allies only contributed to the tendency towards self-reliance. It was thus an attempt to achieve an independent position within the progressive, socialist movement, a sort of ideological autonomy that complemented and reinforced the country's political independence.

Developing a Plan for Reunification

As Kim focused more on military development, he pursued a more active approach to reunification. In April 1963 he established the Department of External Intelligence Inquiries to promote revolutionary activities among southerners. Often referred to by foreigners as 'Office 35', it trained agents to work in the South. This worked with two other institutions: the South Korean Liaison Bureau and the Department of Culture. The Liaison Bureau was a channel linking the KWP with communists below the Demilitarized Zone (DMZ). The Department of Culture was founded in 1956 as a propaganda organ aimed at South Koreans and at Koreans living in Japan.[36]

Kim articulated his overall strategy for reunification in a speech at a party meeting on 27 February 1964, 'Let Us Strengthen in Every Way Revolutionary Forces for the Realization of the Great Task of Fatherland Unification'.[37] There were three revolutionary forces, he explained: those at home, those in the South and the international ones; all had to be strengthened to complete the liberation of Korea. Thus there were three parts to the process of reunification. First, people in the North must realize their full revolutionary potential. In other words North Korea had to be made economically, militarily and ideologically strong. Second, the revolutionary forces in the South were hindered by the people's ignorance of their own degree of suppression by their 'puppet' government and of their subjection by the American imperialists. This had to be corrected so that, unlike in 1950, the people would revolt against their government in support of the DPRK. Third, strengthening the 'international revolutionary forces' necessitated promoting ties with developing nations as well as the socialist ones and exploiting the weaknesses and divisions among the imperialists. The main aim here was to force the USA to withdraw its forces from the South.

Kim's work promoting the revolutionary forces in South Korea was hindered by the lack of contacts. When the domestic communists were purged in the early 1950s they were replaced by partisans who had little experience or knowledge of the southern half of the peninsula.[38] Kim, in fact, remained very much out of touch with what was happening in the South, which he and most of those around him had never visited. In 1964 North Korean agents were able to contact a few sympathetic southerners and create the Revolutionary Party for Reunification (Tongil hyeongmyeong-dang). This underground communist organization was headed by Kim Jongtae, a high-school teacher and store owner. It remained small, ineffective and was discovered by the South Korean intelligence officials in 1968. Kim Jongtae was executed and 158 others arrested.[39] Although the Revolutionary Party for Reunification ceased to exist, North Korea insisted otherwise and sponsored radio broadcasts and other propaganda in its name. Pyongyang also used two non-communist puppet political parties, the Democratic Party and Cheongudang, that existed only for this purpose: to attempt to establish contacts with and issue appeals to their South Korean compatriots.[40]

The Militant Turn

Kim's apotheosis as a great thinker, his cultural revolution and his placing of his family at the centre of Korean history was accompanied by a newly militant, aggressive, provocative policy towards the South. Despite a greater emphasis on the militarization of society and the economy after 1962, and his plan for promoting revolution in the South, he avoided provoking a renewal of conflict that he knew he could not win and which would likely only heap more destruction on his country. Yet the border with the South was always tense. Along the DMZ there were constant little crises, ranging from failures to adhere to some agreed-upon protocol, such as having soldiers along the border wear the proper insignia, to exchanges of gunfire. North Korea often seized southern fishing boats in waters it claimed. In 1967 there was an elevenfold increase in such incidents, keeping the American and South Korean forces in a constant state of tension. By the end of the year gunfire erupted almost daily across the border.[41] This included artillery shelling for the first time since the armistice. Kim appeared to have decided to place pressure on South Korea to undermine the government and promote a revolution.

The purge of 1967 included the partisan Yi Hyosun, who was in charge of the Liaison Bureau, the main institution for dealing with the South. Yi, who had taken on the position in 1961, may have had a more realistic idea of just how difficult organizing revolution in the South could be.[42] At the same time, following the purge of the Gapsan faction, Kim placed military men in key positions, with Kim Changbong as defence minister and Ho Bonghak in command of overseeing revolutionary activity in the South. Some historians have suggested that they may have sought to brandish their credentials.[43] However, they were hardly acting on their own, which was barely possible in North Korea by that time. Kim himself appeared to be pushing for a more aggressive stance. In a speech before the Supreme People's Assembly he stated that it was important not to leave the next generation with a divided Korea and that the country should be unified 'as soon as possible'.[44]

It is not clear why Kim sought a more aggressive stance. He may have been influenced by the U.S. military build-up in Vietnam and by South Korea's military participation in the conflict. The ROK had agreed to send troops to support the Americans in South Vietnam. Initially this was troubling for the North Koreans. If the Americans and their South Korean allies were victorious in defeating

North Vietnam, would North Korea be next? Then, as U.S. forces seemed to get bogged down there, he saw an opportunity to weaken the USA and perhaps encourage it to withdraw from the Korean Peninsula. In autumn 1965 he visited China to seek support, both economic and military. Mao made it clear that he did not want Kim to restart the war. Returning to Pyongyang, Kim told the Chinese ambassador that 'war was near' and that in the future, 'Korea will become a battlefield. There is no other solution to this problem [of unification].'[45]

Kim began to draw up possible plans for armed conflict on the peninsula. Initially these were based on a Vietnam-style guerilla campaign, but they were modified in 1964 as a more defensive 'Flying Dragon' plan, which would use both PRC and KPA forces. Another plan in 1965, however, the 'Charging Bull', was based on a more aggressive response to liberate the peninsula.[46] In July 1968 a new slogan appeared: 'Cutting Off the Limbs of U.S. Imperialism Everywhere', it said, 'Vietnam is breaking one leg of the American bandit, we are breaking the other one.'[47]

Another factor for these aggressive acts was Kim's alarm at the closer relations between South Korea and Japan. In 1965 the Park government signed a normalization treaty with Japan. This opened the way for Japanese trade and foreign investment, but it also raised fears among North and many South Koreans that the former colonial power might reassert its economic hegemony over the country. Yet it also provided an opportunity for Kim. The normalization treaty between South Korea and Japan in 1965 was accompanied by huge and sometimes violent protest demonstrations by students and political opposition groups in the South, who saw it as a betrayal of national sovereignty. These demonstrations raised hopes in Pyongyang that there was enough hostility to the government to form the basis for a general revolt. It is not clear how captive Kim was to his own propaganda, but he and his officials seem to have believed that the majority of South Koreans viewed their government as the illegitimate heir of Japanese imperialism, a clique of former Japanese collaborators who were now active collaborators of American imperialism. According to this line of thinking, the closer ties with Tokyo only highlighted the lack of nationalist credentials of the government in Seoul, making the situation more favourable for the revolutionary forces in the South.

Taking advantage of the unrest in the South, Kim's government began training a special force, Unit 124, for operations below the DMZ. One group was prepared for the assassination of South Korean president Park Chung Hee. On 18 January 1968 this group infiltrated the South, and three days later 31 commandos launched a night-time attack on the presidential palace, Park Chung Hee's 'Blue House'. When they were spotted camping out by a local woodcutter, rather than killing him as they were trained to do, they let him go after making him promise not to tell anyone. He went straight to the authorities, but they were slow to act. The commandos were able to get within 500 metres of the palace before being stopped by security forces. Twenty-nine were killed, one was captured and one escaped and fled to North Korea. Just two days later, North Korea seized an American intelligence ship, USS *Pueblo*, off the east coast near the port of Wonsan. If the attacks on South Korea were intended to destabilize the country, it is not clear what purpose the capture of the *Pueblo* served; it was perhaps a fortuitous event. North Korea claimed the ship was in its territorial waters, which the USA denied. The 82-member crew was held captive for eleven months before being released in December. The Americans initially responded with a show of force, sending the aircraft carrier the *Enterprise* into the waters off the east coast. However, rather than opting for military retaliation as Kim Il Sung might have feared, the USA negotiated for the release of the crew, issuing an apology, and the crew signed a confession. Americans were amused by the confession written by the crew: it contained many puns mocking the DPRK which the North Koreans apparently did not understand. The captain swore 'on the sacred honor of the Great Speckled Bird' and 'beseech[ed] the Korean people to forgive our dastardly deeds'.

North Korea continued its provocative acts, sending eight teams of fifteen commandos each, who landed by boat along various points on South Korea's east coast in late October and early November.[48] The commandos, from the same Unit 124, rounded up villagers and harangued them about the socialist paradise in the North. The villagers reported them, and most of the North Koreans were quickly killed and captured, but only after leaving 63 southerners dead.[49]

Kim again misjudged the level of support his regime had among his countrymen in the southern part of the peninsula. The activities of 1968 seemed senselessly reckless even to Pyongyang's closest allies. The Romanians, one of North Korea's communist allies, for example, described the Blue House attack as an 'incredibly daring and narrow-minded' act that would only exacerbate tension.[50] Kim responded to the failures as he had during the Korean War: by blaming others and conducting a purge, this time focused on his generals, not political rivals. Between December 1968 and January 1969 he removed Kim Changbong and Ho Bonghak, as well as Kim Gwanghyeop, the vice premier, Seok San, the public security minister, and Ri Yeongho, commander of the KPA marine corps.[51] Altogether, at least ten partisan generals were removed from top posts and were replaced by more technocratic-minded officials, most of whom were also ex-guerilla fighters who had been serving in civilian posts.

Whether or not the work of a small group of military men or the product of internal politics, the events of 1968 reflected the fact that Kim Il Sung and those around him appeared to have interpreted opposition to government policies in the South as sympathy or potential sympathy for the DPRK. In fact the situation in the ROK was much less ripe for communist revolution than it had been. In the early 1950s land reform had been carried out in the South. The countryside was now the home of often conservative small independent farmers. The North's invasion of the South had hardened anti-communist attitudes among many southerners, and in the 1960s the country was beginning to make real economic progress. While anti-Americanism was common among South Koreans, there was also a great reservoir of goodwill towards the USA as well as a growing number of people enamoured with American culture. Furthermore, the stridently anti-communist regime of Park Chung Hee had developed extensive and effective intelligence services that made serious infiltration of the South and the creation of any large-scale communist organization extremely difficult. North Korea was also limited since Kim had purged most of the South Korean communists with knowledge and contacts and placed the Liaison Bureau in the hands of partisans with little experience in the South.

Kim's regime committed one more provocative act. In April 1969 North Korea shot down a U.S. EC-121 spy plane. This may have been an opportunistic move rather than a planned one, when the plane came in reach of anti-aircraft guns. The following month, Nikolai Podgorny visited Pyongyang. Upon his arrival on 16 May he gave a speech, a kind of dressing-down for Kim, warning him against any more such actions that could ignite a conflict.[52] The message for Kim was clear: Moscow's treaty was a defensive one; it was not designed to protect him from American retaliation if he went too far.

North Korea's provocative actions hardened resistance to the North in the South and led to the destruction of the modest network of revolutionaries that Pyongyang had established in the ROK. But they served some useful purposes for Kim. The fact that Washington did not respond militarily to the seizure of the *Pueblo* or to the shooting down of a U.S. aircraft told him just how much the Americans wanted to avoid armed conflict in the peninsula. Later, Kim and his successors would engage in further aggressive acts and then seek to negotiate with the Americans, frequently winning both concessions and demonstrating the DPRK's military prowess to their people. The military provocations promoted the sense of a nation threatened by outsiders. Residents of Pyongyang were required to wear backpacks in case they had to evacuate and to dig emergency shelters. Troops were sent on marches through the main streets of the city – a move likely to impress on the populace an atmosphere of urgency and preparedness.[53] Kim found creating this sense of a nation under threat of military attack by the American imperialists and their southern lackies helpful in keeping his people ready for war and under his control.

7
THE SUN KING

FROM 2 NOVEMBER to 13 November 1970 Kim presided over the Fifth Congress of the Korean Workers' Party. This was nine years after the last one. By its own rules these were supposed to be held every five years, but it was now Kim Il Sung's party and he was in total control, so it met when he decided it should. Speaker after speaker praised him in terms that exceeded those of the last congress. He was proclaimed not only the 'leader of the forty million Koreans' but also 'the sun of their hearts'.[1]

Kim's partisan comrades of course dominated. But many of those present at the last congress were gone. Only 31 of the 85 members of the previous Central Committee of the KWP were still among the 117 members in 1970. The missing members included many military officials who were removed after 1968. Many of the missing members were not purged but simply demoted or reshuffled to other posts. There were newer, younger members at the middle and lower ranks of the leadership. Most of these owed their positions to their partisan connections. Some were members of Kim's family by blood or marriage, such as Ho Tam, the foreign minister married to one of Kim's cousins on his mother's side.[2] Then there was Kim's younger brother Kim Yeongju, who though officially ranked sixth in the party hierarchy was in fact the second most powerful person at congress after Kim himself. Nepotism extended to his inner circle of old partisan buddies, who also had family members in key party positions. They were almost all males. Fewer women were represented than in the past, none in the top ranks. Only four of the Central

Committee members were women, and this included Kim's wife, Kim Seongae. Five women were alternative members of the Central Committee, including the wives of Kim Il and Choe Yonggeon.[3]

The highlight of the congress was Kim Il Sung's hours-long speech in which he summarized the achievements of the previous years and outlined the objectives for the coming ones. He mentioned the success of the Seven-Year Plan. Yet it had to be extended by three years to meet its targets, and it is not clear that it did so even then. For the first time, he boasted, the country was self-sufficient in grain, although agricultural production in fact fell short of its targets. The DPRK had 'created a technological revolution', transforming the country from a developing state to an industrial socialist one. In truth the country had made less progress in developing advanced technology than Kim claimed. All the same, while he exaggerated his achievements, they remained impressive. At the end of the Korean War two-thirds of Kim's people were peasants; now, nearly two-thirds lived in cities, working in factories, offices and shops. More people than ever lived in modern homes with electricity and indoor plumbing. He boasted of the new nine-year compulsory education system, and he had a right to be proud of his regime's achievement in this area. And he cited as one the great accomplishments of the 1960s the creation of the Monolithic Ideological System and the expansion of the country's military strength.[4] But he also admitted that the country was far from self-sufficient in military weaponry and that its military technology was not yet advanced. However, he boasted about the superiority of the political and ideological consciousness of the country's soldiers.[5]

Much of his address was devoted to the external situation, about which his tone was darker and more militant: 'Comrades, the situation in our country still remains tense and strained. The U.S. imperialists continue to step up their aggressive maneuvers, and their schemes to touch off a new war are becoming more and more undisguised . . . In our country, the threat of war is growing bigger with each passing day.' He repeated the importance of the four lines of military strength: arming the entire population, intensifying military training, turning the country into an impregnable fortress and developing modern military equipment. Dealing with the problem of unification, he called on South Korean 'revolutionaries' to advance the liberation movements by opposing 'the colonial rule' of the USA and the 'fascist tyranny' of the Park Chung Hee government. He urged the South Korean people to overthrow the Park government, drive out the Americans and establish a 'peace-loving neutralist' regime. Then both sides could build a 'unified democratic government' through free elections or establish a confederation as a transitional step.[6]

While Kim urged the South Korean people to rise up, he instructed his people to 'buckle down to a further acceleration of war preparations'. He stated, 'We must never be captivated by a pacifist mode and in particular, must strictly guard against the revisionist ideological trend of war phobia to prevent it from infiltrating our ranks.'[7] Be prepared for war, was his message, not just with the United States but with 'Japanese ruling circles'.[8] Japan had a pacifist constitution and relied on the USA to provide for its defence, but Kim knew that he could stir up the people on both sides of the DMZ with fears of Japanese military revival and link that fear with both the Americans and the South Korean regime.

Overall, his address and the congress itself suggested continuity, not change. And there were no major changes in his personal life or his rule around this time. Yet there were several significant developments in the decade that followed. He developed a pattern of off-and-on confrontation with South Korea and the USA, followed by efforts to improve relations and lower the tensions with his rival the South and its superpower protector – a pattern that was continued by his successors. He elaborated on his role as a major thinker, and he reached out to make himself a leader of the developing world. But the most important development was to finally settle on a successor and in doing so make North Korea a dynastic state.

Dialogue with the South and Confrontation

Kim Il Sung's aggressive tone at the fifth KWP congress reflected the confrontational attitude he maintained towards the South. Even his removal of the military group and the chastisement he received from Moscow did not end his acts of provocation against the ROK. These included small incidents along the DMZ and the continued seizing of South Korean fishing boats. On 11 December 1969 North Korean agents hijacked a civilian aeroplane with 51 passengers; a little over a year later, on 23 January 1971, they attempted to hijack another plane. Even more provocatively, on 22 June 1970 agents set off a bomb at South Korea's national cemetery in an attempted assassination of Park.[9] That these acts were condoned if not ordered by Kim is suggested by a speech he gave at a party meeting in April 1971. In especially militant language, he called for the need for struggle against American imperialists, Japanese militarists and their agents in the South.[10] His goal was to destabilize the regime in the South and keep up the state of war that helped to mobilize the DPRK population and keep his people in a state of readiness. But he was careful not to start any action that would lead to war, which of course he knew he could not win as long as the Americans were in the South.

Kim was personally responsible for the tensions on the peninsula. The Park Chung Hee regime was almost totally focused on economic development. Park, a former general concerned with making his state militarily as well as economically stronger, distrusted the North and was staunchly anti-communist but was not interested in provoking his northern neighbour or taking any action that could cause a resumption of fighting. The USA did not want conflict. Moscow clearly indicated that it did not approve of Kim's provocative actions. Neither did Mao, who also made it clear that he did not want a renewal of conflict. Kim had removed the most militant members of his regime in 1969, scapegoating them for the provocations of 1968 that achieved little, yet he continued to stir up tensions. Given his total command, these tensions were purely manufactured by his policies. Kim appeared willing to cooperate on a peace plan, as he did in 1960 and even in early 1971 when he had his foreign minister present an 'Eight-Point Plan for Addressing the Problem of Unification through Peaceful Negotiations'.[11] But these were simply tactics to see if he could weaken Seoul's alliance with Washington. He did not want war, but he wanted to keep his country ready for one, to probe the South and its alliance with the USA for weaknesses and to do anything that would undermine the ROK. It was all part of his desire to complete reunification. No matter what he achieved north of the DMZ, he would only feel successful when he had personally liberated all of Korea and placed it under his rule.

However, on 15 July 1971 the international situation changed dramatically with the announcement that Beijing and Washington had been meeting secretly and begun planning for a visit by President Nixon to China. In February Nixon arrived in Beijing and met with Mao Zedong and other leaders. Initially the news was a disturbing shock to Kim; his reaction indicates he was taken by surprise. 'Nixon's visit to China will not be a march of a victor but a trip of the defeated,' he declared, 'it fully reflects the destiny of U.S. imperialism which is like a sun sinking in the western sky.'[12] This was not what Beijing intended at all; the visit was a tactical move to ease tension with the USA in order to use Washington as a counterweight to Moscow. To Kim this suggested that Beijing might follow Moscow's earlier mellowing of its stance towards the USA, and this threatened to undermine China's future support for his regime. However, he was also quick to realize that it suggested an opportunity. The Americans were eager to get out of Vietnam and wanted Chinese help. With better relations with China, there was the possibility that they might also seek to leave South Korea.

Authorities in Seoul reacted with equal shock and surprise, and also wondered if it would mean the loss of American support. Yet the Park regime also came to see it as an opportunity. Taking the initiative, Park started with the problem of divided families and had the South Korean Red Cross contact its northern counterpart. This was an emotionally charged issue in the South, where several million people had siblings, parents and other close relatives across the DMZ. They had no contact with them or even knew if they were still alive, since the two Koreas maintained no telephone or postal links. Kim, rather than being sympathetic, viewed anyone with relatives on the other side with suspicion and assigned them to the low-ranking 'hostile' category, and frequently relocated them to remote parts of the country. But he saw an opportunity to open talks, even if he had no desire to reunite separated families. He responded favourably to the proposal for talks. When the two sides met on 20 August they did so for only four minutes; yet that meeting, the first since the Korean War, was of symbolic significance, publicly signalling that the two sides were ready to negotiate.

Both Kim and Park were now cautiously optimistic that the new geopolitical situation would work to their advantage. For Park it could ease tension and enable him to focus on the ROK's rapid industrialization. This was not a road to peace, but space for South Korea to take advantage of its greater population and what seemed to be its successful development plans to overtake the North economically and militarily and so undermine the DPRK's claim to be the 'successful' Korea. For Kim it was a way to get the Americans to leave. Secretly Kim arranged with the Park regime an exchange of official meetings. Kim sent his vice premier, Pak Seongcheol, to Seoul, and Park sent the chief of his Central Intelligence Agency, Yi Hurak, to Pyongyang. After these secret talks North and South Korea issued a joint communiqué on 4 July 1972. This stated three fundamental principles for unification: first, unification must be carried out independently, without outside interference; second, it must be achieved peacefully; third, it must be implemented in an act of great national unity, based on the homogeneity of the people, with the differences in ideas, ideologies and systems worked out later.[13]

Kim and Park formed a North–South Coordinating Committee, which held three meetings: one in Seoul from November to December 1972, a second in Pyongyang in March 1973 and a third in Seoul three months later in June. But little progress was made at the meetings. South Korean officials wanted to proceed with gradual confidence-building measures. Family reunifications would be a good first step, and from there they might gradually work on bigger, more difficult issues. Kim's purpose was to take advantage of the warming U.S. and Chinese relations, and the American desire to extricate itself from conflict on mainland Asia, to encourage the Americans to withdraw. For this reason he demanded the withdrawal of all U.S. troops as a precondition for any talks on substantive issues. But ROK officials rejected this. The DPRK representatives also insisted that South Korea's national security laws, which gave the government broad powers to arrest communists or communist sympathizers, had to be repealed before any family reunions or other humanitarian issue could be pursued. The ROK, meanwhile, demanded the DPRK end its propaganda campaign for the Revolutionary Party for Reunification. It was not long before Kim realized that the talks were not going anywhere useful for him. The USA had no intention of withdrawing or reducing its support for the ROK, and Park had no intentions of making any concessions that would lead to this result or derail his own plans to build up his country's military potential. In fact Park was moving the focus of his economic development plans to heavy industries such as steel and industrial equipment, which could be the foundation for self-reliance in military production.

After seven meetings between August 1972 and July 1973, the Red Cross talks came to an end.[14] The North–South Coordinating committee ceased to meet after mid-1973. Mid-level meetings continued at Panmunjom from December 1973 to March 1975; with little promise of any breakthrough, these too fizzled out. Kim also turned down a proposal by President Park in 1973 for dual admission to the United Nations. This would have meant a de facto mutual recognition of each other's regime. Instead, Kim returned to the rhetoric of military confrontation with the South. North Korean officials told Hungarian diplomats in 1976 that 'Korea cannot be unified in a peaceful way.'[15]

Yet Kim still hoped to see the USA leave. So, ignoring Seoul, he decided to appeal directly to the USA. In March 1973 he called negotiations with the United States over a peaceful solution to the problems on the peninsula.[16] When the Nixon administration ignored this, the Supreme People's Assembly in March 1974 issued an open letter to the U.S. Congress calling for direct peace treaty negotiations.[17] These efforts were treated as they indeed were: an attempt to cut a deal with Washington to abandon its ally in the South. Instead, Washington adhered to a policy of no bilateral negotiations with Pyongyang. Any talk of a peace settlement had to involve Seoul.

Kim's regime never stopped carrying out hostile acts against the South. On 4 February 1972, even as the secret talks with Seoul were being conducted, Kim's navy kidnapped five southern fishing boats, wrecking one. After the peaceful initiatives of 1972–3 failed to get anywhere, North Korean provocations continued to test South Korean and American responses, keeping tensions between the two Koreas high, and attempting to destabilize the ROK. Kim also kept the people of the North in a state of military readiness and kept his military prepared for eventual war if one should occur, both of which were part of his desire to create a militarized, loyal citizenry. Most of these were measured actions, such as capturing another fishing boat on 30 August 1976, not actions that would actually lead to war.[18] Some were secret preparations for a possible future war, such as the construction of tunnels under the DMZ. The DPRK constructed tunnels under the border capable of providing passage for substantial numbers of troops. The first was discovered in November 1974. It was 3.5 kilometres (2 mi.) long, ran 1.2 kilometres (¾ mi.) under ROK territory and contained a narrow-gauge railway capable of transporting one regiment an hour. Three more were found in 1975, 1978 and 1990. The second 1975 tunnel was even wider, capable of being driven through in small vehicles and transporting a division in an hour.[19]

Sometimes Kim carried out bolder moves. On 15 August 1974, celebrated as liberation (from Japan) day in South Korea, a gunman made an attempt on President Park as he was making a televised speech. The assassin missed Park but fatally wounded his wife. This was a shocking act, done indirectly: not by a North Korean agent but by a Korean resident in Japan working for a North Korean front organization. This made it harder for the assassination to be traced to Pyongyang. Only once did an incident involve the USA, when in August 1976 North Korean soldiers attacked and killed two American officers who were trimming a tree in the DMZ. The USA responded with a show of force, but, as with earlier incidents, there was no military retaliation. Meanwhile, Kim watched for signs that the situation might change in his favour. The election in 1976 of Jimmy Carter, who pledged to withdraw all U.S. forces from Korea, was one of these. Unfortunately for Kim, President Carter was persuaded by his advisers and members of Congress not to do so.

Kim's Sixtieth Birthday and the Centrality of *Juche Thought*

While the negotiations were going on with South Korea, Kim was busy celebrating his birthday and writing a new constitution that formalized his almost limitless power and enshrined his thought as the foundation of the state. In April 1972 Kim reached sixty, an important landmark in Korean tradition. Sixtieth birthdays, known in Korean as *hwangap*, are often elaborately celebrated. The fanfare that accompanied the Great Leader's birthday, however, was unprecedented in Korean history. Amid enormous, well-choreographed demonstrations, a massive statue painted in gold was unveiled on Mansudae, a high hill overlooking the Daedong river in Pyongyang. This was a spot that, ironically, had once been the site of a shrine for the Japanese emperor. A vast marble museum was opened at Myohyangsan, a famous mountain north of the capital, dedicated to recording the heroic deeds of the Great Leader. Its 92 exhibition rooms dealt with the milestones in recent Korean history: Kim's heroic and successful anti-Japanese resistance, his liberation of Korea, his direction of national defence during the Korean War and his construction of the socialist state after the war. Most interesting were the rooms filled with gifts sent from all over the world to honour the Great Leader, a tribute to his global stature and his many admirers abroad. Badges with the Great Leader's picture were mass-produced for the birthday celebrations. All North Koreans now wore these badges, of which there were three types: for students, adults and party members. They were worn everywhere except at home.[20]

Around the time of his sixtieth birthday Kim Il Sung had his officials draw up a new constitution. The 1948 constitution was written by the Soviets and translated into Korean, and as such was a standard Soviet-style one. Now Kim needed to shed this last vestige of the days of Moscow tutelage for one that reflected his ideas. The new 1972 constitution, sometimes called the *Juche* constitution, could just as easily be called the Kim Il Sung constitution, since it both enshrined his thought and reflected his leadership style. Article 1 declared the DPRK to be an independent socialist state, an emphatic declaration of Kim's concern for autonomy from outside control. Article 4 stated, 'the Democratic People's Republic of Korea is guided in its activity by the *Juche* idea of the Korean Workers' Party, a creative application of Marxism-Leninism to the conditions of our country.'[21] This, incidentally, was one of the last public references to Marxism-Leninism, which by 1980 disappeared from the party's by-laws;[22] by the end of the 1970s it was rare for North Korean publications to mention Marx, Lenin or any thinker at all except Kim Il Sung. His 'thought' was the ideological foundation of society. North Korea continued to call itself socialist and used some of the language of communism, but no longer called itself Marxist or Leninist or even mentioned the terms.

Other articles enshrined the Cheollima Movement, the Cheongsan-ri method and the Taean system, all innovations of Kim's that supposedly improved production by harnessing the enthusiasm of the workers.[23] The constitution concentrated state power in the president, a title Kim Il Sung now assumed. The term used for president, *juseok*, was the same as that used for Mao Zedong (and usually translated as 'chairman') but different from the term *daetongnyeong* used by South Koreans. All leading posts were filled at the recommendation of the president, and the Central Court, the highest judiciary, was also accountable directly to him. The president was the commander and chief of the armed forces and chair of the National Defence Council. In other words the president was an all-powerful figure with no real checks or limitations on this authority.

Becoming the Global Stateman

After 1972 Kim increasingly sought out a role as a global statesman. This was partly a product of his inflated ego, a desire to be recognized around the world as a great leader. But there were practical reasons for this as well. As part of his strategy to pressure the USA to leave the peninsula and to isolate the government of South Korea, he sought to win international support for his cause. By having himself and the society he created admired by the world, especially by developing countries, he aimed to demonstrate to southerners that he was the true leader of all the Korean people. And it served to impress upon his own people that he was a truly extraordinary leader, universally admired, and that they were living in a truly wonderful society.

In the early 1970s Kim permitted a small number of journalists from non-communist countries to visit, taking them on carefully managed tours and sometimes granting them an interview. They were often impressed with what they saw. On a visit in 1971, Alain Bouc from the French newspaper *Le Monde* commented favourably on the level of industrialization, noting that all the vehicles he saw, from bicycles to trucks, were locally manufactured. He described the countryside as characterized by 'beautiful, well-irrigated rice paddies, worked on by tractor'. The cities and towns were neat, with central squares that had pretty flower beds. He saw 'no idlers, street peddlers or useless occupations'.[24] Another foreign journalist on a twenty-day tour that year commented, 'Three things impress the visitor: The well-cared-for children, the adoration of Premier Kim Il Sung, and massive construction.'[25] Harrison Salisbury from the *New York Times*, on his 1972 visit as the first prominent American journalist to enter North Korea since the Korean War, reported that the country had made a 'tremendous technical and industrial achievement'. Visiting the Hamheung-Heungnam area on the east coast, he saw 'endless vistas of industrial smokestacks'.[26] Another American visitor that year, John H. Lee, observed 'a well-organized, highly industrialized socialist economy, largely self-sufficient with a disciplined and productive labor force'. He noted that 'although consumer goods are sparse and factory equipment is sometimes outmoded, the overall industrial plants compare favorably to anything in Asia outside Japan.' Unlike most developing countries, he commented, modernization in North Korea seemed evenly developed, without the usual disparity between the cities and the countryside.[27] Several years later another Western journalist contrasted the orderly industrial society of North Korea with South Korea, noting the lack of slums, prostitution or children selling gum, all of which could be seen in Seoul.[28] Journalists were often impressed with Kim Il Sung himself, who seemed to enjoy meeting them. He was described as outgoing and physically vigorous.

It was not Westerners he was targeting with his charm offensive but members of the developing world. Kim most likely genuinely felt a kinship with much of the postcolonial world. He shared its anti-imperialism, the sense of victimization at the hands of the great powers, the desire to be free from foreign domination, and in many cases shared with leaders the experience of being an independence fighter. The relative success of the DPRK's economic development, its ability to free itself from economic or political dependency on a great power, offered a model to other developing countries. Many political leaders in Asia and Africa and some in Latin America were attracted to Kim's fierce anti-imperialism. Furthermore, not a few leaders were also attracted to his ability to consolidate absolute power. Kim cultivated ties with the socialist regimes of Vietnam and Cuba, which can be described as developing nations. He offered Vietnam relief aid after floods in 1957 and military aid after 1965. He offered to send experts in cave tunnel construction, and 87 North Koreans piloted planes for Hanoi. Kim sent food aid to Cuba after Hurricane Flora destroyed much of the crop in 1963. A close relationship between Kim and Fidel Castro's regime followed. Che Guevara came to visit and later told the American journalist I. F. Stone that North Korea was the most impressive part of his Asian tour.[29]

Kim's efforts to reach out to the non-socialist developing world began in the 1960s. At that time every issue of the KWP journal *Kulloja* had a section devoted to a developing country. In 1965, overcoming his fear of flying, he made his first visit to the non-socialist world with a trip to Indonesia. Kim had already begun cultivating good relations with the neutral government of President Sukarno. He supported Indonesia in its border dispute with Malaysia in the early 1960s and even offered diplomatic and military assistance. Kim travelled to Bandung, the site of the first Non-Aligned Movement conference, ten years earlier. There he celebrated his 53rd birthday. However, there were many distractions, and it was only in the 1970s that he made his major push to win recognition from the developing world as a major leader and sought their support in his efforts to pressure the USA to leave the Korean Peninsula. In the spring of 1975 he made his second foray into the developing world, again overcoming his fear of flying. After stops in Eastern Europe he visited Algeria and Mauritania. Around this time he also began to go out of his way to welcome visitors from developing countries, treating them to lavish entertainments.

North Korea initially had some success in gaining support from developing countries for its demand for the withdrawal of all foreign troops from Korea. At the Non-Aligned conference in Lima in August 1975, it became a full member. A committee of the general assembly in 1975 passed a pro-North Korean resolution on the Korean Question that called for the withdrawal of all foreign troops from the peninsula. At another Non-Aligned conference, in Colombo, the member states endorsed Kim's stance on Korean unification. By the early 1980s the DPRK had established relations with 110 countries around the world. It had more missions abroad than its rival South Korea, and its voice was heard more loudly in developing world forums. A constant stream of leaders from Africa and other developing countries visited Pyongyang, where, no matter how small their countries were or how little actual strategic or economic importance they might have had, they were sure to receive an enthusiastic welcome from the thousands of North Koreans who dutifully turned out on the streets to greet them. Ten foreign leaders visited in 1978. In an outreach effort, North Korean performance troupes and exhibitions were sent around the world. These were given much publicity at home, also contributing to the official line that the DPRK, its culture, its socialist path and especially its leader were globally admired.

Kim sent experts abroad in military training and development. He carried out aid projects in twenty African countries. These were mostly small-scale, low-tech undertakings such as building a cement plant in Somalia. When dictator Jean-Bédel Bokassa of the Central African Republic (or Central African Empire as it was called then) visited Kim's official residence, Kumsusan Assembly Hall, during a state visit to the DPRK, he requested that a similar palace be constructed for himself, and the North Koreans agreed to build it.[30]

As part of the global outreach, *Juche* was reinterpreted as a universal philosophy. In 1979 Kim established an Academy of Juche Sciences in Pyongyang under the direction of party ideologist Hwang Jang-yeop. It sought to ensure that the universal principle of *Juche* was applied to every field: music, sports, science and more. North Korea developed an ambiguity about its role in the world at large. At times its universality was highlighted. *Juche* study societies were organized around the world under the supervision of the International Institute of the Juche Idea, Tokyo, created in 1978. 'The Great Juche idea has become the thought of the time,' the DPRK's international monthly *Korea Today* proclaimed in 1979, 'Many heads of state and people of all states . . . express their admiration, saying President Kim Il Sung shows mankind its way like the sun with his immortal *Juche* idea. The success of the experience of Korea serves all nations building a new society as a priceless model.'[31]

Creating a Dynasty: The Rise of Kim Jong Il

Turning sixty, the unofficial beginning of old age in Korean culture, could only have reminded Kim of his mortality and the need to find a successor. In this way Kim was different from Stalin, Mao and most modern dictators, in that he planned for his succession while still a vigorous middle-aged man. But his plans to have his younger brother Yeongju succeed him were running into problems. Yeongju began having health issues. It is not clear what these were. A high-placed defector, Sin Gyeongwan, said he was prone 'to lose consciousness abruptly'.[32] Another report suggested he suffered from a peripheral nervous system disorder.[33] Whatever it was, Yeongju would outlive almost all his contemporaries, dying in 2021 at the age of 101.

Yeongju was hospitalized in late 1968 and from 1970 was frequently absent, spending time at a clinic on Mount Myohyang and making trips to health clinics in the Soviet Union and Eastern Europe. This, like almost all such information, was kept secret from all but the inner party circle. In May 1972, when South Korean security chief Yi Hurak arrived in Pyongyang and met Kim Il Sung as part of the unpublicized negotiations the two sides were carrying out, he insisted that Kim send his brother to Seoul. It was known within the ROK government that he was the real number two and the likely successor. Kim explained to Yi that this was not possible since his brother was on leave due to illness.[34] Yeongju's illness provided a vacuum. Kim wanted a number two and potential successor he could trust absolutely, a concern that was heightened by the Lin Biao affair. Mao Zedong had designated his military commander as his number two in 1969, and since he was in his late seventies he was viewed as the likely successor. Hailed publicly as the Great Leader's 'closest comrade-in-arms', Lin Biao plotted to assassinate Mao in 1971 and was killed in a plane crash as he tried to flee the country. Kim needed someone who was totally trustworthy, not a Lin Biao. Yeongju was such a person, but if his brother's health did not improve, he would have to look for someone else.

Meanwhile, Kim's wife, Kim Seongae, emerged as a major figure. For more than a decade of marriage she remained in the background, out of public view and never referred to in the media. Only in August 1964 was she publicly mentioned as Kim's wife. In November of that year she became vice chair of the Democratic Women's Union (formerly the Women's League). By 1967 she was rising fast enough behind the scenes to pose a threat to Pak Geumcheol, the leader of the Gapsan faction. According to one defector the animosity of the two towards one another was a contributing factor to the 1967 purge of the Gapsan faction.[35] When in 1969 Seongae took over as chair of the Democratic Women's Union she gave the organization, and herself, a higher profile, constructing a new headquarters on Kim Il Sung Square. At about this time her picture first appeared on the front page of the *Rodong Sinmun*, where she was shown greeting foreign guests.[36] In January 1971, at a meeting with farmers, Kim Il Sung told them that the 'words of Kim Seongae are the same as mine.'[37] A rather extraordinary statement. Seongae promoted the cult of Kim's mother, Kang Bangseok, and downgraded that of Kim's first wife, Kim Jong Suk. At the Democratic Women's Union headquarters, visitors upon entering were greeted with twin portraits of Kim's mother and his deceased wife. Seongae replaced the picture of Jong Suk with her own.[38]

Seongae went further in consolidating her position, promoting her own natal family, especially her brothers Kim Seonggap and Kim Seongho, to prominent positions in the Pyongyang chapter of the party. She attempted to weaken the ex-guerilla group by reducing the special government assistance to them. Her rise must have reminded the inner circle of Mao's wife Jiang Qing's rise in China at the time, including Jiang's undermining of the influence of Mao's old comrades. The parallels are striking. But Seongae was most likely trying to engineer power to her family rather than make a play as Kim's successor. Possibly she sought to make her oldest son, Pyeongil, still of university student age, a candidate. However, she had a rather slender support base: just a handful of family members holding mid-level party posts.

Seongae's position was weakened by Kim's son and daughter by his first wife, Jong Il and Kyong Hui, who did not get along with their stepmother. They were especially angry to find their own mother being demoted in status. Sin Gyeongwan, a North Korean defector, recalls the following story, which took place at Kim's sixtieth birthday party. The party was well attended by ex-guerillas, officials of the Central Committee of the party and generals of the military, who bowed to and served liquor for Kim Il Sung in traditional Korean style. Then it was time for Kim's family to do the same. When it came to Kyong Hui's turn to bow and serve, she burst into tears. The guests asked, 'Why are you crying?' Kyong Hui answered, 'Because my mother [Kim Jong Suk] passed away without seeing this birthday party.' She apparently wailed and called out for her mother. Older female ex-partisans began to cry too. Male ex-partisans such as

Choe Yeonggeon and Kim Il also shed tears. So the birthday party turned into a 'sea of tears'.[39] The incident was interpreted as a rebuke to Seongae. Over the course of 1973–4 she was pushed aside in a concerted effort led by Jong Il and supported by many of the old partisans, and retreated from public view.

Kim Jong Il

Kim in the end selected his eldest son, Kim Jong Il, as his heir. It is not impossible that Kim had always considered making his son his successor and that his younger brother Yeongju was only a temporary placeholder. In any case by 1974 it became clear to the inner circle that Jong Il had been chosen. Much of his early life seemed to have been a preparation for this. Jong Il attended the elite First Pyongyang Middle School and the First Pyongyang High School. In elementary school he was elected chair of the Children's Union (Sonyeondan) and in high school vice chair of the school's Youth League. In 1959 he accompanied his father to Moscow to attend the Twenty-Second Congress of the Communist Party of the Soviet Union. He seems always to have played the role of leader. As a student at Kim Il Sung University, he is reported to have initiated a movement to read 10,000 pages a year, focusing on the works of Kim Il Sung.[40] After graduation, Kim Jong Il was placed in key positions in the party. His first position, in 1964, was in the Organizational and Guidance Department of the Central Committee of the KWP. Since this department dealt with administrative affairs in the various branches of the party, it meant that while still in his early twenties he was involved in important and sensitive work. It was the same office that his uncle Yeongju had headed. In this position he would have worked with much older and high-ranking party officials, including those at the ministerial and vice-ministerial levels.[41]

In 1967 the 26-year-old Kim Jong Il was appointed to head the culture and art guidance section of the Propaganda and Agitation

Department of the Central Committee. This was just after the Gapsan purge during his father's cultural revolution, in which he played an active part.[42] At about the same time Kim Il Sung removed the sitting director of the Propaganda and Agitation Department, who was associated with the Gapsan faction, and replaced him with Kim Guktae, the son of the partisan leader Kim Chaek, a close comrade of Kim's who was killed in the Korean War. In 1969 Kim Il Sung made his son the deputy director, but since Kim Guktae was ill, he in fact ran the department. Thus, at 28, Kim Jong Il oversaw state propaganda during a time when the cult of Kim was intensifying, and he played a major part in that effort.

Jong Il, a man of artistic interests, became the virtual tsar of the arts. He directed the Baekdusan Production group, which produced films; the April 15th Literary Production group, which wrote novels; the Mansudae Art Troupe, which created theatre productions; and the Mansudae Art Studio, which produced paintings. He used these organizations to focus on the cult of his father. Under Kim's direction the arts and entertainment were aimed at glorifying the deeds of his father and those dedicated to him. Since the films people watched, the plays and popular operas they attended, the stories they read and the music they listened to were all under his control, Jong Il was instrumental in shaping and promoting the cult of his father. He also supervised the restoration of historical sites associated with his father's life, such as Mangyeongdae and Bocheonbo, and oversaw the celebrations of his father's sixtieth birthday in 1972.[43]

It is not certain exactly when the elder Kim made the decision to make his son his chosen successor. The first clear sign was a speech Jong Il gave to propaganda workers on the 'Kimilsungization of the Whole Society' in February 1974. Focusing on promoting the Ten Principles for the Monolithic Ideological System, it indicated that he had taken over his uncle's role as the chief ideologist of the regime, and that he had also taken over his uncle's role as successor. From 1975 Jong Il's portrait began to appear alongside his father's at military offices, although it appeared in party and government offices only after his official anointment as successor in 1980.[44]

Around this time Kim Jong Il began to branch out from propaganda to become directly involved in the administration of the party and the state. He used a campaign to intensify study sessions among party workers as a means of assuming a supervisory role over them. Gradually the young Kim built up an elaborate party guidance system in which he placed those loyal to him in every civilian organization. Designated party officials and administrators began to send reports to him directly.[45] In this way he began building and overseeing a vast surveillance system. He also took a direct interest in economic development, directing the Three Revolutions Small Team Movement, in which young people were dispatched in teams of thirty to fifty people to factories and collective farms to assist and encourage workers and farmers.[46] Emulating his father's achievement, he created his own version of the Cheollima Movement: what he called the Three Revolutions Red Flag Movement, in which teams of workers would lead others in spurring production. This began after he visited the Gomdeok coal mine in December 1975. There, like his father, he was able to lead the workers to heroic feats of production.[47] He also may have set up Office 39, a party bureau designed to secure foreign currency and goods for the elite, perhaps in 1974.[48]

While those in the party and state administration understood that Jong Il was assuming the position as the number two person in the regime, this was all happening in the background. Kim saw to it that his son was never mentioned in public. On his 31st birthday in 1973 the *Rodong sinmun* praised his new innovations in the arts but without referring to him by name.[49] Instead, the media began to refer to a mysterious 'Party Centre' (*dang jungang*), a term that initially puzzled outside observers, who only gradually began to be understand this as referring to Kim Il Sung's eldest son. The great publicity given to the Three Revolutions Small Team Movement and the Three Revolutions Red Flag Movement were clearly intended by Kim Il Sung to promote his son, yet his name was never mentioned in public, nor did his picture appear anywhere in the media.

Several reasons have been suggested as to why Kim Il Sung promoted his son in such a strange, indirect way. He may have been concerned about unfavourable reactions from his two benefactors, the Soviet Union and China, and he might have been worried about undermining his efforts to achieve a leadership position in the Non-Aligned Movement. Kim may also have had his personal doubts about his son's ability. Furthermore, there is some hint of internal opposition, although this is not known for certain.

Kim continually gave more responsibility to his son until an incident occurred in the summer of 1976 that shook his confidence in Jong Il's ability to lead. In the Joint Security Area, the section of the Demilitarized Zone where DPRK, ROK and U.S. forces directly face each other, a 30-metre (100 ft) poplar tree blocked the line of sight between a United Nations checkpoint and a northern observation post. The Americans insisted on removing the tree, but the North Koreans claimed it was planted by Kim Il Sung and could not be moved. On 18 August 1976 a group of Korean Service Corps personnel, escorted by a UN security team consisting of Captain Arthur Bonifas, his South Korean Army counterpart Captain Kim, the platoon leader First Lieutenant Mark Barrett and eleven South Korean and American personnel went to the Joint Security Area to trim the tree. As the trimming began, they were approached by fifteen North Korean soldiers led by Lieutenant Kim Chul, nicknamed the 'Bulldog' by the Americans for his aggressive confrontations. Bonifas, a graduate of the prestigious West Point military academy, who was three days from ending his one-year tour of duty in Korea, ignored Kim Chul's demand that they cease trimming. The North Koreans, reinforced by 28 more soldiers, then attacked the UN team with crowbars and axe handles. Bonifas and Barrett were killed and most of the UN troops wounded.

According to Sin Gyeongwan, the incident occurred under the direction of Jong Il. He ordered the North Korean security guards to stop the Americans 'in a certain way' from cutting down the tree.[50] In carrying out his instructions the soldiers at the scene went too far. The Americans responded with a show of force. Naval vessels and an aircraft carrier moved into the area. Kim Il Sung panicked, fearing an American attack, and ordered the population to prepare for war. Thousands of reservists were called up for emergency duty. Jong Il went even further, and under his instructions his brother-in-law Jang Seongtaek ordered a hasty evacuation of Pyongyang. Hundreds of thousands suddenly moved from their homes, in many cases given only several hours' notice, creating a chaotic situation.[51] Kim Il Sung expected American air strikes, but none took place. Park Chung Hee did not want the situation to escalate into war and neither did President Ford. In Operation Paul Bunyan, named after the legendary lumberjack, a task force of 23 American and South Korea vehicles came on 21 August without warning three days later, and a crew with chainsaws cut down the tree. Then Kim Il Sung did something highly uncharacteristic. Later that day he sent the Americans a message expressing 'regret' for the incident.

As always, Kim found scapegoats and demoted several officials in the defence ministry. But the real blame fell on his son Jong Il, although, according to one defector, he did not know about the evacuation order issued by Jang Seongtaek and was furious about it.[52] Although neither was punished after this incident, the public reports about the Party Centre almost disappeared. The KWP publication *Kulloja* referred to the 'Party Centre' 378 times in 1976, almost all before the incident but seldom after that, and only four times in 1978.[53] Jong Il still wielded great power and was actively involved in party work, but he kept a lower profile. Did Kim have his doubts about his son? We do not know for certain, but it appears he felt he had given him too much responsibility too soon. There also may have been some internal opposition to Jong Il. In his opposition to Kim

Seongae's attempt to undermine the old Partisan families, Jong Il scored many points with them, but there still appeared to be some resistance. It is possible that Jong Il, with his insistence on imposing strict guidance rules, may have been too hard on cadres, generating party unrest. One high-ranking ex-guerilla, Kim Donggyu, was quietly purged in 1977, possibly for being critical of Jong Il's ability to lead.

Creating the Kim-Centred Society

No leader in modern times ever succeeded in creating a society so moulded to his personal vision as did Kim Il Sung. This could be seen in Pyongyang, which by the 1970s had become a display city, more akin to the temple and palace cities of the Maya or the Aztecs than any other modern one. It was a city with broad main boulevards and wide squares dominated by monuments to Kim Il Sung and his revolution. His golden statue on a hill towered over the city. Yet it was a strangely lifeless city, with sparse traffic and little visible activity. Pyongyang was hardly an outlier; every city, town, village and even the mountainsides were dominated by posters, statues and shrines to the Great Leader and his revolution. Kim Il Sung's cult had become all-pervasive. Virtually all art, literature, film and music was directed at glorifying Kim Il Sung, the revolution and the Great Leader's philosophy of *Juche*. Every aspect of life was focused on or linked to the leader and his family. From the 1970s the bride and groom at wedding ceremonies, wearing their Kim Il Sung badges of course, pledged, 'We, as an eternal husband and wife, commit totally to the Great Leader and swear that we will build a revolutionary home.'[54]

At public events people presented flowers and bowed before his image. The calendar revolved around his birthday on 15 April and from the 1980s around that of his son Jong Il on 16 February. While most learning, literature, art and history focused on Kim, his family, the anti-imperialist struggle against the Japanese and the Americans, and the glorious achievements of the revolution, very little was devoted to the Korean traditional past or to the outside world. Art and literature in all communist states served the revolution, but in the 1970s in Kim's Korea this was carried to an extreme found nowhere else. In the late 1960s Kim Il Sung put his younger brother Yeongju in charge of glorifying him as a great thinker while his son Jong Il took command of the task of focusing the arts and entertainment on glorifying his achievements. Jong Il zealously produced stories, plays, songs, 'revolutionary operas' and films about the anti-Japanese resistance and his father's heroic leadership in liberating the country. In fact the elder Kim himself supposedly composed the lyrics to one of the early 'revolutionary operas', *Pi bada* (Sea of Blood, first performed in 1971), the story of mass killings under the Japanese. Most musical output consisted of songs extolling Kim's leadership, such as 'Song of General Kim Il Sung', 'Long Life and Good Health to the Leader' and 'We Sing of His Benevolent Love'. One can hardly imagine an artistically more confined or sterile environment. Artists who tried to find any form of creative expression did so within extremely narrow parameters. A painter might express the beauty of nature through his or her depiction of snow as it fell upon Kim Il Sung in a winter scene from his wartime guerilla camp.[55] Only films were allowed a slight bit of creativity.

International news consisted mainly of reports of foreign praises of the Great Leader and meetings of *Juche* study clubs in various countries. Access to any source of information other than that controlled by the state was so severely controlled that few North Koreans had much real awareness of the outside world other than the limited and distorted information they were given. Even literature from other socialist countries like the Soviet Union was severely restricted. Radios and, later, televisions were adjusted so they could only receive the official Central Korean Broadcasting Service. The chief newspaper, the *Rodong sinmun*, was devoid of any real news but was a vehicle for disseminating the official line on various aspects of life. Provincial newspapers were virtually identical in content to the main newspaper in the capital. Even university professors could be surprisingly ignorant of even basic developments in the world.[56] North Korea by the 1960s had become a truly totalitarian society where almost every part of life was controlled by the state.

Kim Il Sung wanted his subjects to possess the will to resist an invasion with a ferocity that was absent in 1950. He therefore saw that they were continually involved in military drills and exercises. A constant state of alert prevailed, as public rhetoric suggested that an invasion was imminent at any moment. Music, dramas, school lessons – every medium was used to promote a militarily ready society. The vocabulary of public announcements, no matter on what subject, was laced with fierce, militant rhetoric. International events were either interpreted as a sign that the United States and its allies were planning an invasion or used as warnings for the need for preparedness. In the wake of the Cuban Missile Crisis, Kim argued that the nation must be prepared to expel the 'Yankee imperialist' invaders and their South Korean allies as well as aid revolutionaries in the South. The increased U.S. involvement in Vietnam and the breakdown of talks with the South in 1972–3 were also occasions to increase combat readiness.

Military training and political indoctrination went together and began from childhood. Starting with preschool day-care centres, much schooling involved political indoctrination and military-like drills and exercises. Small children learned to march with toy guns and were taught dances such as 'My Heavy Little Machine Gun'. Even maths lessons used problems such as 'how many American wolf-bastards remained after so many had been killed?'[57] Considerable time was spent on carefully choreographed dances and marches that were like massive military drills. When boys reached sixteen years old they went into military service, except for a few who went on to college. Military service was extraordinarily long, and as we have seen reached a total of twelve to thirteen years before it was shortened to 'only' eight years.

North Koreans were required to attend regular study sessions. Ordinary citizens spent much of their non-working time attending these. Everyone was assigned a workstation at their factory, farm, office or shop. North Korea initially followed the Soviet bloc practice of a couple of hours a week of indoctrination, but in the early 1960s study sessions became daily. Workers typically spent thirty minutes reading parts of newspaper articles and editorials and then ten or fifteen minutes discussing them, led by low-level cadres. North Koreans had to study and memorize the teachings of the Great Leader and from the early 1980s those of Kim Jong Il. In the 1960s North Korea adopted the Chinese practice of self-criticism sessions, called 'meetings on drawing upon the results of life' (*saenghwal chonghwa*). In the early 1970s these became weekly for city folks and every ten days for farmers; although obviously modelled on Maoist practice, they were later attributed to the innovative genius of Kim's son Kim Jong Il.[58] And on top of this there were the constant mobilization campaigns to meet some special target, in which people did 'voluntary labour' on weekends and evenings.

So much time was taken with official activities that there appeared to be no room for any private life. Nor were there any non-official organizations of any kind. Religious life, other than the quasi-religious cult of Kim Il Sung and his family, was suppressed. By the 1950s there were no functioning churches. Buddhist and Cheondogyo temples were closed, with the exception of a few museum temples at historical spots. Any form of religious activity ceased to exist except at the most hidden level. There was an official Korean Christian Association, but it was disbanded in 1960. In 1974 it reappeared, apparently for propaganda purposes and to function as a means for Pyongyang to obtain contacts with Christian organizations in the South.[59] It served no actual religious role. Foreigners were sometimes taken to sham religious services at one of two churches that seem to still exist for this purpose. Overall, the DPRK went further than most other communist states in suppressing all religious and in fact all non-state or non-party organizations and activities of any kind.

State-sponsored activities began young. Boys and girls from age nine to thirteen belonged to the Children's Union. At fourteen they could join the Kim Il Sung Socialist Youth Union. The membership to this organization was more selective, with those from bad family backgrounds excluded. The highly organized life of youth and the heavy indoctrination that characterized education were typical of communist countries. What distinguished North Korea was the intensity of the indoctrination over so long a period. Young people, especially secondary and college students, often spent much of their time on 'voluntary' service, such as helping with the planting and harvest, or on public construction projects. Dating and romance were initially disapproved of, but this began to change in the mid-1980s when themes of romantic love reappeared in literature, music and drama.

Keeping Watch over the People

Kim sought to root out all disloyal activity. By the late 1960s he had constructed a system of surveillance and control that went beyond that of any contemporary society. In the late 1950s he began placing families into small groups with a leader that was responsible for all members. From 1971 this became known as the 'five-household team', but it was not necessarily composed of five households, it could be much larger – up to fifteen or twenty.[60] Another institution that his regime created was the *inminban* (neighbourhood association), according to which thirty to fifty neighbouring families in urban and rural areas were lumped together as a minor unit of administration. It functioned as a means of organizing the people for neighbourhood cleaning and repair campaigns and for tasks such as collecting night soil for fertilizer. These were supervised by an *inminbanjang* (neighbourhood head), usually a middle-aged woman who was also responsible for disseminating the latest state directives. The *inminbanjang* also served as a means of keeping track of everyone's activities. She checked all visits to each home and kept track of all activities in the neighbourhood. To assist her, residents of apartment buildings took turns as security guards. Special units of police carried out 'midnight patrols' accompanied by the *inminbanjang*. These were often random inspections of homes; all people were subjected to them.[61] Security officials would check people's radios to see that the mechanism that fixed them to state radio stations had not been tampered with, and that there was no unauthorized literature or goods. People had to register to stay overnight at another home, even that of a relative. Travel of any kind away from one's city or town required a permit.[62] Permission to travel was challenging to obtain for city dwellers. It was even more so for farmers. Fearing an exodus of farmers to cities and towns, the state made it extremely difficult for rural people to travel anywhere. Since each collective farm had its own school, a store – or what might better be described as a distribution centre – and a medical clinic, there was little reason for a resident to leave, making them virtual prisoners on their collectives. Most restricted of all was travel to Pyongyang. A trip to the capital was a rare privilege.

All these elaborate surveillance systems were supervised by the special security police, which underwent several name changes. In 1973, under the name the State Political Security Department, it became an independent branch of the government, headed by Kim Pyeongha, a distant relative of Kim Il Sung. In 1982 Kim removed his relative, and it was renamed the State Security Department and brought directly under Kim Jong Il's control.[63] The security police, assisted by a network of informants including the *inminbanjangs*, watched over citizens in much the same fashion as in all police states. A separate Military Security Command operated as a secret police system within the Korean People's Army.

Kim created a political prison system often called by outsiders the 'Gulag' after the system of prison camps of Stalinist Russia. North Koreans called them *gwalliso*, which can be translated as 'place of custody' or 'management centre'. Some were divided into 'revolutionization zones' and the 'total control zones'. The former were for prisoners with some chance of rehabilitation. They lived and worked under harsh conditions and spent their 'free time' memorizing the works of Kim Il Sung. These zones had a high death toll. Those who survived and had showed 'correct thought' could be released, although they would have the stigma of being former political prisoners. The total control zones were death camps with the harshest conditions and no attempt at rehabilitation, no hope of release. As in the Soviet Gulag, prisoners were often put to work in mines under extreme conditions, many mining for coal. The population of political prisoners grew with the purges of the late 1950s, but the number is not clear. Estimates are that by 1980 about 150,000 to 200,000 people were held in the camps, a number that may have remained the same over the next thirty years.[64]

Political prisons were gradually consolidated into a few enormous camps. In the 1980s there were about a dozen political prisons with up to 50,000 inmates in each. Most of the camps were located in remote, narrow mountain valleys where the steep mountainsides acted as a natural barrier. Rather than fitting a conventional image of a prison, they were more like a string of villages. Perhaps the most unusual feature of North Korean prisons was the practice of incarcerating the entire families of political prisoners, from grandparents to children. Thus prisoners often lived in huts with their children and even their parents. Blood relations were most important. Sometimes the spouse of a political prisoner would be spared by being forced to divorce his or her partner and cease any contact.

By the 1970s when this system was perfected, Kim had created an extraordinarily regimented society. There were no private organizations of any kind. No religious institutions. Buddhist temples that once dotted the countryside were gone except for a few historical ones kept as museums. There were only state-run and party-run organizations, such as for women, youths and labourers, and everyone fitting these categories had to join and participate. Kim kept everyone busy working volunteer hours, participating in campaigns and attending official meetings and study sessions, while being constantly watched.

The Kim-Centred Hierarchy

The society Kim directed was not only the most regimented and controlled in the world, it was one of the most hierarchical, with Kim and his family at the apex. He had created a rigid and finely articulated social structure with its 51 *seongbun* (more were created later), where all power and privilege was concentrated into a small elite, the highest *seongbun* within the core class making up perhaps less than 1 per cent of the population. This top tier of society lived in a separate and restricted section of the capital. The gap between the elite of higher-ranking KWP members, top bureaucrats and military officers and the rest of the population became more marked over time. By the 1980s, if not earlier, those at the very top enjoyed a lifestyle unimaginable to ordinary people, driving expensive German cars, drinking French cognac and having access to other imported luxuries.

The hereditary nature of the ruling elite also became more pronounced as time went on. By the time of Kim Il Sung's death in 1994, most of the younger high-ranking officials were the sons, nephews or in-laws of the old guard. North Korean politics by then could be seen as a rivalry among powerful elite clans. The elite sent their children to special primary and secondary schools and for higher education to elite institutions such as Kim Il Sung University in Pyongyang or the technical-focused Kim Chaek University. In theory universities were open to all based on scholastic achievement, but family background and ideological purity counted as much if not more than merit. The egalitarianism and social mobility of the first years of the DPRK was replaced by a rough replication of the rigid, ranked structure of society based largely on bloodlines that was characteristic of traditional Korea.

But to a greater extent than in pre-modern times, all power and privilege radiated out from the centre, and at that centre was a single person, Kim Il Sung. Around him was the innermost ring of his immediate family, then other family members, his close ex-guerilla associates and their families, with the most powerful ones having intermarried with his own. An example of the latter was Ho Dam, a key official who from the 1970s served in a number of important posts and was one of the best-known figures in North Korea. He was married to a cousin of Kim Il Sung.[65] And then there were the vast client networks of these great families. Kim ultimately controlled all access to power and privilege. More than Louis XIV had ever succeeded in doing, he had made himself the sun king.

8
STABILITY AND STAGNATION

In 1980 Kim Il Sung called a congress of the Korean Workers' Party. This Sixth Party Congress was the first in a decade and the last he held. It met from 10 to 14 October in the recently built February 8 House of Culture. A grandiose building with a classical colonnade, it contained various military related offices and a great auditorium for public events. The congress was the biggest gathering of party officials to date; more than 3,000 attended along with Communist Party delegations from China, the Soviet Union and one hundred other countries. Kim had several purposes for the meeting. One was to make changes in the KWP rules and by-laws. These eliminated all references to Marxism-Leninism, as had been done in the 1972 constitution, and made the 'Juche-ization of the whole society' the party's aim.[1] But Kim's main purpose was to confirm his son Kim Jong Il as his successor. This remained unstated, but everyone within the leadership clearly understood.

Kim, now a robust 68-year-old, had presided over a party dominated by old partisan comrades.[2] It was an ageing leadership of people who were rather unsophisticated, possessed a modest education and few technical skills, and whose outlook was shaped in the mountain retreats of Manchuria and in the Korean War. In other words, it consisted of people like himself. None had the intellect, the charisma or any other special strengths or an independent base of support that would make them a threat or alternative to Kim as leader. Their main qualities were unquestioning loyalty, personal ties to him – in many cases forged in their youth – and ruthlessness in carrying out their leader's commands. It was not a group likely to initiate innovations, nor one by experience and aptitude well prepared to deal with the challenges of the rapidly changing international environment of the 1980s.

Along with these older men, and they were all men, were some younger emerging leaders, the second generation. Most of them were related to Kim or his close comrades. Only two of them were in the Politburo. One was the 47-year-old O Gukyeol, also the son of a close partisan comrade and the second-youngest member of the Politburo. The other was Kim's son Kim Jong Il, who at only 38 was by far its youngest member. Many of the younger members of the upper echelons of the KWP were graduates of the Mangyeongdae School for Children of the Revolution, where top officials sent their sons and daughters.[3] North Korea was emerging as a state ruled by a tiny hereditary elite, largely consisting of Kim Il Sung and his family, his partisan comrades and those related to them by blood or marriage. The party, the state bureaucracy and the military were dominated by this little group of families and branch families. Each would develop their own patronage networks. These elite families were careful to place members in all the major centres of power. It was becoming an inbred group, as powerful families formed alliances based on marriage.

While his son Jong Il was the real reason for the congress, Kim made no official announcement that he was the designated successor. He didn't need to, since all party officials had known this since 1974, and by 1980 he was clearly the second most powerful and most feared member of the party. But few ordinary North Koreans had ever heard of him or knew he was the mysterious 'Party Centre'. Kim's strategy, a rather clever one, was simply to get people used to the idea that his son was an important, especially brilliant leader heading the next generation of the 'revolutionary lineage', so that his succession would seem so natural that it did not need to be announced. Kim was trying to get not only the North Korean public to accept the succession but his Soviet and Chinese patrons as well. And it is possible that he was also making sure all the party members were on board with his succession plan, but it is hard to imagine that by 1980 any of them could have possibly opposed it. Besides, Kim was making nepotism and hereditary succession a rule among the elite.

The highlight of the congress was Kim Il Sung's lengthy address to the delegates, which, as in the past, acted as a way of summing up the achievement and goals of the revolution. Kim's speech, which lasted for four hours, provides a valuable window into his thinking. Kim spoke of 'a brilliant victory in the building of socialism'.[4] Kim was not without justification for praising the country's economic achievement with pride. Into the 1970s North Korea maintained an impressive level of economic development. Two and a half decades after the Korean War North Korea had become an industrialized nation. No more than a third of the population was rural; in Asia only Japan was as urbanized. Kim was not alone in thinking things were going well. Later, many North Koreans would look back on this time as one of promise and prosperity, at least compared to later periods. Hwang Chang-yeop, the party ideologist who defected to South Korea in 1987, recalls the years before 1980 as a time of comfort and high morale among party workers.[5] Other defectors have echoed these comments. The system overall was working. People were receiving their food rations as well as other necessities. Factories were turning out their products, education was still expanding and immunization programmes were improving health.

There was cause for optimism as well for Kim's great obsession, the reunification of Korea under his leadership. The year 1980 was a terrible one for South Korea. Amid growing unrest in response to his increasingly autocratic rule, Park Chung Hee was assassinated on 26 October 1979 by his own security chief, the head of the Korean Central Intelligence Agency, after he refused to consider compromising with the opposition. The months that followed, the so-called Seoul Spring, saw open political debate calling for dismantling the security state Park had constructed and for open and fair elections. Instead, a military clique headed by General Chun Doo Hwan seized effective control of the state on 12 December 1979 and in May cracked down on all opposition, arresting its leaders. Chun then ran for election for president unopposed. The arrest of opposition leader Kim Dae-jung led to an armed uprising in the southwestern city of Gwangju, which was put down by sending in paratroopers. Some 1,000 civilians were killed. Chun, who ordered the retaking of the city, remained hated by the majority of South Koreans. The events of 1980 radicalized many of the student and labour organizations, some denouncing the USA, which supported the Chun regime, and calling for the withdrawal of American forces from their country. All this must have been very promising, even exciting, for Kim.

The political turmoil in the South was accompanied by a sharp economic downturn. GDP shrank 6 per cent that year, which was compounded by rising oil prices and a bad rice harvest. Some foreign observers speculated that South Korea had reached the limits of its economic growth based on its model of a low-cost and submissive workforce producing labour-intensive goods for the international market. There was also a concern that it was entering an era of greater political instability that followed the assassination of Park Chung Hee in 1979. But South Korea was not North Korea, trapped in a rigid system and following an outdated model for economic development. What happened in the 1980s was truly remarkable. The country resumed economic growth in 1981 and went on to have the highest rate of economic expansion in the world for most of the decade while transitioning to a stable, democratic political system. Kim of course did not foresee this in 1980, but neither did most other observers at the time.

After the early 1970s access to the DPRK was more difficult, but the country permitted some Western journalists to cover an international table tennis tournament in 1979. One, American journalist Bradley Martin, noted of his visit that 'the overriding impression was of Northern success, up to a point – not failure.' Even though he was 'deeply troubled' by the intense ideological indoctrination that he found carried out throughout society, he was impressed by the level of industrialization. He observed that the 'people appeared adequately housed and clothed' and that 'there was austerity apparently rather evenly shared, but I saw no sign of destitution. All this seemed to set North Korea apart from other developing nations.'[6] Another academic visitor to North Korea at the time noted that it was producing everything from metal lathes to large refrigerator ships, excavators, bulldozers, electric transformers and electric locomotives, 'all signs that notable gains have indeed been made on the economic construction front'.[7] However, much of the North Korea that visitors saw was a Potemkin village to impress outsiders and hide the country's lack of development. This became even more true after 1980 when the economy was stagnating. In one example, after foreign visitors complained of the lack of public phones and taxis, some public phones were installed in areas of the capital where foreigners were likely to visit, although they were found nowhere else and not used by the public.[8]

The year 1980 was a turning point for Kim Il Sung's society. After that year its trajectory went from at least limited success to one of almost unmitigated failure. Its economy stagnated, then declined. Living standards deteriorated as the country sank into poverty, and its people went hungry, becoming among the most malnourished in the world. Its international position deteriorated as North Korea went from a developing world leader to an isolated pariah. And perhaps most importantly for Kim's sense of self-esteem and purpose, South Korea rose to become an international success story, a dynamic economic powerhouse increasingly recognized as such by the rest of the world. Yet Kim was not a complete failure; the political system he created proved remarkably durable, and control of it was kept in his family.

Kim Turns Seventy

By the time of his seventieth birthday in 1982 the entire country was dotted with shrines to Kim Il Sung. The places he visited – and he travelled frequently throughout the small country – became sacred sites marked with commemorative plates. His quotes were carved into prominent rocky outcroppings and mountainsides across North Korea. Songs in praise of him dominated the airwaves. On his birthday, to celebrate this new milestone in his life, an Arch of Triumph, larger than the original arch in France it was modelled on, was constructed. In addition, a Tower of Juche was built to honour his contribution to human thought. At 170 metres (560 ft) tall it was the highest stone structure in the world (today the second tallest behind the 2007 San Jacinto Monument in San Antonia), and it is topped with a red torch. And the Kim Il Sung Stadium, a massive sports arena holding 100,000, was opened.

By the 1980s adoration of the Great Leader and his family came to pervade every aspect of North Korean society to an extent that it struck most foreign observers as incomprehensibly bizarre. His name was preceded by such honorifics as 'Ever-Victorious Iron-Willed Brilliant Commander', 'The Sun of the Nation', 'The Red Sun of the Oppressed People of the World' and 'The Greatest Leader of Our Time'. Kim Il Sung became the infallible leader, and his *Juche Thought* the infallible truth. The religious-like cult of Kim was a central feature of North Korean society. Workers and students began their days bowing before his portrait and placed wreaths at his statues on holidays. His birthday, 15 April, was a major holiday. His home town of Mangyeongdae was a place of pilgrimage. His life and his various heroic activities were the subjects of most of the nation's output of films, plays and operas. Kim Il Sung was portrayed as an international figure admired by the oppressed throughout the world. North Koreans were told of tributes to the Great Leader that constantly came in from abroad.

Glorification of Kim Jong Il

Kim used the preparations for his seventieth birthday as a means to highlight the role of his designated successor. Two months prior to it he declared 16 February 1982, Jong Il's fortieth birthday, a national holiday, and the day before he was awarded the title 'Hero of the DPRK'. The state published an official biography of the young leader that told of his birth in a cabin on Mount Baekdusan. The entire period from 16 February to his father's birthday on 15 April became known as 'Loyalty Season'. That same year Kim Jong Il published *On the Juche Idea*. It became required reading and was given the kind of praise that had previously been reserved for his father. It also signalled a new role for him as the official interpreter of his father's thoughts.

After 1982 Kim Jong Il was nearly as public a figure as his father. He never spoke in public, but he was portrayed standing alongside his father in ubiquitous posters. Officials wore badges that depicted both father and son. Jong Il was referred to as 'Great Leader' but with a different term, *jidoja*, somewhat less exalted than the term *suryeong* used for his father. He was also referred to as the Dear Leader (*chinaehan jidoja*). In June 1983 Kim took his son with him on a ten-day visit to China, introducing Jong Il to the leadership in Beijing as his successor. Jong Il also began to issue *gyosi* (instructions). The term *gyosi* was an important one for Kim Il Sung. The term is used for religious cults in South Korea and has a connotation of something akin to sacred teachings.[9] When he travelled around the country visiting offices, factories, farms, schools and military facilities as part of his on-the-spot guidance, Kim Il Sung would issue *gyosi*, which were carefully copied down. These were often publicized in the media and acted as guidance for the whole nation or for all similar institutions or worksites. They were sometimes placed on placards and chiselled in stone, as a constant reminder of the glorious day on which the Great Leader came to visit and gave guidance. Kim took this seriously, and when Pak Geumcheol of the Gapsan faction issued *gyosi*, it contributed to his purge from the party. Now, Jong Il joined his father as one who could issue instructions.

Although standing close together in public portraits, Kim and his eldest son were very different personalities who in private led very different lives. While Kim Il Sung was physically imposing, Jong Il was short and physically unimpressive. Kim was gregarious and a people person, constantly meeting people, chatting with ordinary folk, genuinely happy when surrounded by workers, farmers, children and families and of course basking in their adoration of him. He would have made a good politician in a more open, democratic society like that which was emerging in the South. Jong Il, by contrast, was never comfortable in public settings and appeared dour and distant. He never gave speeches or made any public utterances at all, leading to rumours in the West that he suffered from a speech impediment. This later was disproved after he came to power and met foreign leaders, who often found him a good conversationist with a surprisingly self-deprecating sense of humour, which his father lacked. Jong Il was comfortable in small groups, where he matched his father's political skills and his ruthlessness. But his artistic temperament, his love of films, theatre and culture, was unlike his father, who showed little interest in the arts.

A Complicated Family Life

Jong Il's private life was very private, more so than even his father's. In fact it was kept largely out of his father's sight. He loved to party. His drinking parties were notorious within the KWP inner circle. They lasted all night and included singing forbidden South Korean and Japanese songs, and beautiful dancing girls. These were more than bacchanals; they served as a way for Jong Il to bond with and observe those who were loyal to him. Indeed, he often sipped water while watching his comrades get very drunk. Invitation to these parties indicated that one was in the rising leader's good graces. The parties were kept secret from the public and from his father, who did not approve of such behaviour, although no doubt he heard rumours of them and possibly knew these to be true.

Jong Il loved women, as did his father. The elder Kim was in many ways a conventional, conservative Korean male. He maintained at least the appearance of a proper family life. He seems to have to been generally close to both Jong Suk and, after her death, Seongae. Kim did have affairs while married to Seongae, although almost nothing is known about them. Nonetheless, he acted as and perhaps in his mind was a faithful husband. Kim knew that his son was a playboy, attracted to actresses and entertainers. He arranged a suitable marriage for him to Kim Young Sook, the daughter of a high-ranking military officer, in 1973. Jong Il was 32, well beyond the normal marital age. At the end of that year they had a daughter, Seolsong, meaning 'snow pine'. It was a name Kim Il Sung gave her, perhaps a reference to his own days in the pine forests of Manchuria. She was not Jong Il's first child. In the late 1960s, when he began to work for the Propaganda and Agitation Department, Jong Il became infatuated with a popular actress and film star, Seong Hye-rim. She was five years his senior and the daughter of a former editor of the official party newspaper. She became his mistress in the late 1960s, eventually divorcing her husband, the son of a prominent North Korean writer. They had a son together, called Kim Jong Nam.

Jong Il's relationship with the actress Seong Hye-rim was kept secret from his father for some time. Kim would not have approved of his son's marriage to an actress, even if from a good family, and he would not have approved of his son taking a married woman as his mistress.

Much of what we know about Jong Il's relationship with Hye-rim comes from her sister, Seong Hye-rang, who defected to Switzerland in 1996 and wrote a memoir that is an important source of information about the Kim family. She writes that Young Sook was 'insignificant to Kim Jong Il, apart from being a legitimate wife in front of Kim Il Sung.'[10] This sort of sharing of family history was not tolerated, yet Hye-rang survived in quiet exile. Her son, Ri Il-nam, was not so lucky. He defected to South Korea in 1982 and was shot dead in Seoul by North Korean agents in 1997.[11] After 1980 Jong Il lost interest in Hye-rim, who began to have mental and physical health problems. It is believed that at one time she too defected and joined her sister, only to return to North Korea. She died at a Moscow clinic in 2002.

Jong Il next took up with a Japanese-born dancer, Ko Young-hee, and they had two sons, Kim Jong Chul and Kim Jong Un, and a daughter, Kim Yo Jong. Kim Jong Un became the leader of North Korea in 2011 and Kim Yo Jong became the most powerful woman in the history of the state. Ko Young-hee died of cancer in 2004. The relationship with Ko Young-hee was even more unacceptable, since Ko was born in Japan and did not belong to a family with good revolutionary credentials. Jong Il kept the relationship secret from his father for some time, although he eventually found out about it.

While Jong Il kept his private life as out of sight of his father as possible, at the same time he worked closely with him, becoming his chief adviser and indispensable assistant. Kim increasingly relied on Jong Il to carry out many of the daily responsibilities of governing and to report to him on the activities of other party leaders. In general, he was pleased with his son's performance. In May 1986, at the Kim Il Sung Party School's 49th anniversary, Kim publicly announced that the political succession had been satisfactorily resolved.[12]

Although the succession was going relatively smoothly, the same was not true of the economy. For the first two decades after the Korean War, Kim seemed to be achieving his plans to transform North Korea into a modern industrial state. North Korea's real economic growth was probably 7 or 8 per cent from 1954 to the early

1970s, far above the global average. But by the late 1970s it was growing at half that rate, and by the mid-1980s it was barely growing at all.[13] Of particular concern to Kim was how this compared with his rivals in the South. Up to the early 1960s his economy had been outperforming the ROK, but by the 1970s it was lagging far behind. Kim's economic ambitions consistently exceeded reality. Even when industrial development was proceeding well, such as during the first years of the Seven-Year Plan for 1961–7, it fell short of its overly ambitious targets. But in the 1970s this gap between the goals and the actual achievements was becoming greater. Kim disguised this by simply declaring wildly inflated economic growth while not publishing any real statistics. Sometimes this becomes a bit absurd. For example, after he launched a Six-Year Economic Plan for 1971–6, he declared his aim to achieve its unrealistically high targets ahead of schedule, in time for the thirtieth anniversary of the founding of the KWP in October 1975. This was an effort to duplicate the achievement of the first Five-Year Plan in the late 1950s, when by mobilizing the population the state was able to meet economic targets one and a half years early. And he used the old methods of mass mobilization campaigns and created the Revolutions Teams Movement to spur workers on rather than offer incentives, roughly a reincarnation of the Cheollima Movement of the 1950s. On the eve of the 10 October anniversary, Kim Il Sung proclaimed that this effort was successful: the Six-Year Plan had been completed sixteen months ahead of schedule, with industrial production having grown in the past five years at an annual rate of 18 per cent, well over the 14 per cent target.[14] Yet in early 1976 North Koreans were still being urged to fulfil the targets of the plan, despite the previous claim that they had already been achieved. Then one more year was added in 1977, a so-called 'year of readjustment' whose major task was to ease 'temporary strains' on the economy.[15] The following year Kim inaugurated a Second Seven-Year Plan, launched for 1978 to 1984, but many of its targets were similar to the ones already said to have been completed by the previously development plan. The Second Seven-Year Plan was declared a success, but only after being extended by two years. Even the announcement of its completion was given quietly, amid routine reports, which was perhaps a tacit admission of failure.[16]

Kim's Economic Failures

North Korea was following the pattern of most command economies, which made real progress in the early years of development but then had difficulty sustaining growth due to over-centralization, lack of market incentive and a stifling system that hindered innovation and individual initiative. Alongside these inherent problems with the socialist command model he had adopted, Kim created many serious economic problems of his own. A major one was his insistence that the economy give equal emphasis to military and economic development, which resulted in an enormous drain on the economy. Military production, referred to as the 'second economy', was the main growth area through the production of artillery, tanks, military vehicles and small arms. In the 1980s military production made some strides towards producing more sophisticated weaponry. Overall, however, although the 'second economy' may have outperformed the civilian industrial sector, its output was not sufficient to free North Korea from reliance on military aid from its socialist allies. It did enable the DPRK to supply much of the arms for its huge military, yet it diverted resources from other needed economic development projects.

Then there was Kim's love of grandiose but ill-conceived projects. Striking examples were those associated with the Four Projects for Nature Remaking, which Kim enthusiastically launched in 1981. All typified his favourite way of approaching economic problems: by carrying out massive, labour-intensive projects. All were disastrous failures. The most ambitious one was the West Sea Barrage, an 8-kilometre (5 mi.) sea wall with three lock gates and three dams at the estuary of the Daedong river. Built to reclaim desperately needed arable land, it was a costly failure. It created much less land than expected, and what it did reclaim was too salty for agriculture. Furthermore, it interfered with the drainage of the river, causing industrial, farm and urban waste to back up. Another project was diverting streams into the Daedong through a massive tunnel underneath a mountain so they could generate electricity. But this proved to be impracticable, and, after expending much effort, the project was abandoned.[17]

Kim also squandered resources on prestige-based projects of little economic value, but which he thought enhanced the image of his leadership. In the late 1980s he went on a construction spree in preparation for the Thirteenth World Festival of Youth, held in Pyongyang in 1989. These were clearly his attempts to emulate the construction efforts the South had carried out for the Summer Olympics in 1988. But while the South used the Olympics to complete needed infrastructure, such as the Seoul subway system, other prestige projects of Kim's included a virtually unused Pyongyang-Kaesong Express Highway and the Ryugyeong Hotel. The latter, a good example of Kim's love of the gigantic and tasteless, was the world's tallest hotel. But it never opened due to structural flaws and was hardly needed in a city that received few visitors. It remains today a strangely elongated pyramid-shaped 105-storey structure on the city skyline, a symbol of economic folly and failure.[18]

The greatest weakness in his plans to develop his country was a shortage of energy. When the DPRK was declared independent in 1948, Japanese-built hydroelectrical plants produced abundant energy, which was exported to the South. But as the country modernized it became woefully short of energy. Few new hydroelectric projects were implemented, and many of those were ill designed. Coal was produced, but mining techniques were primitive and inefficient. Much of the mining was done by prisoners working under appalling conditions, which reduced the incentive for more efficient, labour-saving technology. Instead, North Korea relied on petroleum imported from the Soviet Union at nominal 'friendship' prices. Kim became increasingly dependent on this as he developed energy-intensive heavy industries and made substantial use of petroleum-based fertilizers to improve agricultural production. What he received was never quite enough to supply the country's needs, but the DPRK lacked the foreign capital to buy energy on the international market. As a result, by the 1980s energy shortages were a bottleneck to further development.

Chronic food shortages also plagued the economy. At no time after 1945 was North Korea able to accomplish more than barely meeting the population's minimum nutritional requirements. As was the case in many communist countries, priority had always been given to industry, but nonetheless the regime made heavy investments in agriculture. At first the DPRK relied on economies of scale that resulted in consolidating farms into large cooperatives and some mechanization. This was clearly insufficient. In the 1960s Kim had launched his 'four modernizations' in agriculture, which consisted of mechanization, electrification, irrigation and chemicalization (chemical fertilizers and pesticides). Still, even with this heavy and costly investment, agricultural production was insufficient to meet basic needs.

A major problem for North Korea was the shortage of foreign exchange. It produced little that anyone wanted to buy. Its manufactured goods were too shoddy to sell abroad. North Korea's exports were mainly to its socialist allies, and these consisted primarily of raw materials, as the country is rich in mineral resources: the DPRK contains over 80 per cent of the peninsula's mineral wealth, including iron, coal, gold, copper, silver, molybdenum, manganese, magnesite, nickel and tungsten. But poor mining practices and the country's isolation from international markets hampered their exploitation.[19] Lack of foreign exchange is why the country was forced to default on its modest loans to purchase modern equipment in the early 1970s.

One source of hard currency was the remittances from Koreans living in Japan. Since its formation in the 1950s the Chosen Soren (Chocheongnyeon), a pro-Pyongyang organization among the Koreans in Japan, had provided an important source of revenue. There were approximately 600,000 to 700,000 Koreans resident in Japan, many of them brought over during the Second World War to work in factories and mines. As the result of an agreement worked out between Tokyo and Pyongyang, 80,000 Korean residents in Japan, including some Japanese spouses, migrated to North Korea, mainly between 1959 and 1967. After 1967 the agreement ended and the migration slowed to a trickle.[20] These Korean Japanese were not allowed to return to Japan, although many wished to when they discovered the harsh realities of living in North Korea. Instead they were held hostage and forced to write to family members back in Japan, requesting they send money to support them. There are widely different estimates of the size of these remittances. Whatever the amount, they were an important source of foreign exchange but far short of what the country needed.

In the late 1970s Kim's regime turned to more illicit methods of obtaining foreign exchange. He created a special bureau of the KWP known as Bureau 39, or more commonly Office 39, to help earn foreign exchange. This became notorious for carrying out illegal activities, such as the manufacture of methamphetamines and other narcotics, the manufacture of counterfeit cigarettes and later counterfeit American currency, as well as smuggling. Even before the creation of this office, North Korean diplomats were expelled from several countries around the world for heroin smuggling. All these efforts produced only modest results while damaging the country's international reputation. In the mid-1980s the state inaugurated new efforts to earn foreign exchange. It instructed all organizations, from factories to handicraft shops, to find ways of producing exportable products. Rural folks were ordered to pick medicinal herbal plants, and children to raise rabbits to sell their skins. The KWP, various branches of the military and the government maintained separate trading companies to partly support themselves by promoting exports.[21]

Yet Kim Il Sung appears to have had no desire to change. His address to the delegates at the 1980 party congress praised the traditional methods of economic development and organization: the Cheollima Movement, the Cheongsanri method, the Taean Work System. Each he hailed for its great successes. He also singled out the Three Revolutions Team Movement for strengthening the ideological foundations of production, although it probably did nothing to halt the slowing of economic growth. Rather than talk of reform, Kim attacked self-serving economic officials, which may have been a veiled criticism of those who were more pragmatically inclined in economic affairs.[22] Kim Il Sung's response to economic problems was to mobilize more labour. He sent students to labour projects or to work on farms, and he utilized soldiers to work on construction and to help with harvesting. Fridays became Friday Labour Day, when government workers were to work on farms and construction sites.[23] These efforts only made life harder without reversing the country's economic slowdown. Yet it must have been particularly alarming to Kim that his economy was slowing down at a time when the South Korean economy was booming. In the 1980s the ROK broke into new export markets, such as steel, automobiles and electronics. Propelled by successful exports, its growth rates reached an average of 12 per cent a year in 1986–8, when they were the highest in the world.

Kim declined to follow the path that China under Deng Xiaoping was taking. He was certainly aware of it, since it was discussed when he visited China in 1982, the first time in many years. He made another visit the following year and at the encouragement of his hosts travelled to Shanghai, where Chinese officials introduced him to some of the economic reforms they were undertaking. In 1984 he sent his foreign minister and his vice premier to China, where they visited Deng's new special economic zones, set up to attract foreign investment in China.[24] In September 1984 the Supreme People's Assembly enacted a Joint Venture Law allowing foreign companies to build plants in North Korea with local partners. But the law was never implemented, and rather than embracing China's path in carrying out economic reform, Kim took advantage of an improvement in ties with the Soviet Union to avoid doing so. As Beijing appeared to tilt to the West, Moscow decided to strengthen ties with Pyongyang as a counterweight. Kim took advantage of this change in Soviet policy and in the spring of 1984 boarded his specially equipped luxurious train and paid a six-week visit to the Soviet Union. Soon after, Moscow stepped up economic aid, much of it in the form of trade on favourable terms.

This new injection of Soviet aid was extremely important in propping up the flagging economy. Trade with the Soviet Union increased in the 1980s, nearly doubling from 1980 to 1988, with imports exceeding exports by 30 to 40 per cent.[25] In 1980 the Soviet Union accounted for 24 per cent of the DPRK's foreign trade, a figure that rose to 37 per cent in 1987.[26] Soviet economic support made it easier for Kim to ignore the basic structural problems of the economy and continue with his accustomed methods of development. Even with the aid, North Korea's economy was largely stagnant from 1984 to 1989. The industrial plants were becoming obsolete, food shortages were becoming more severe and efforts to increase foreign trade failed. Meanwhile, consumer shortages were dealt with by encouraging the people to get by with less.

Economic Naivety

It is not clear how well Kim understood the economic problems he faced. Concerned about the new industries South Korea was rapidly developing under Park Chung Hee, he became aware of the need to update the country's technology, which was based on that of colonial-era Japan or the 1950s Soviet Union. But instead of working on technology transfer agreements as South Korea did, he simply purchased entire industrial plants, such as a complete French petrochemical complex. Some of the purchases were economically pointless, such as a Swiss watch factory. These were too sophisticated for North Korea, which did not have the trained technicians to operate them, nor could it afford to buy expensive replacement parts. Since the country did not have the foreign exchange to pay for them, it had to borrow the money from international banks.[27] Thus Kim entered the global financial markets without seeming really to understand the risks. Chronically short of foreign exchange, the DPRK was almost immediately unable to meet its debt obligations. It was forced to reschedule its debts with western Europe in 1980 but quickly fell behind the repayment schedule and had to reschedule its debts with Japan in 1982. Again in 1984 it rescheduled its foreign debt, only to cease making payments almost immediately afterwards.[28] It simply defaulted on its loans.

Kim, however, does not seem to have appreciated the damage this did to his country's creditworthiness. On 20 June 1977, in an interview with the French newspaper *Le Monde*, he dismissed the trade deficit as 'a temporary difficulty', then blamed the whole problem on the 'the economic difficulty of the advanced capitalist countries of the West caused by the [oil shocks, meaning] they are unable to purchase our goods'.[29] Although Kim was quick to blame and punish subordinates for any failures, the minister of external economic affairs, Kong Jintae, who was responsible for the debacle, not only was not punished but was promoted to vice premier. Nor was the minister for foreign trade, Kye Ungtae, held accountable for ill-advising Kong.[30] Kim does not seem to have taken the debt seriously enough or understood its implications enough to blame anyone for it.

Kim's inability to fully grasp the economic situation of his country or to understand basic economics is suggested by his conversation with the South Korean film director Shin Sangok and Sangok's actress ex-wife Choi Eun Hee. Their story is so truly bizarre that it would stretch credulity if it were not confirmed by both U.S. and South Korean intelligence sources.[31] Kim Jong Il the film fanatic was disappointed by the poor quality of his country's films. To rectify this he had the popular South Korean actress Choi kidnapped while she was visiting Hong Kong. When her ex-husband and on-and-off lover (they later remarried) Shin went to look for her, Jong Il had him kidnapped too. They were reunited in North Korea and asked to make films for him, which they did. Talented actress that she was, Choi was able to totally charm Jong Il, and she and her husband won his full confidence. Kim Il Sung, meeting them in December 1984, stated he was 'very satisfied with their work'. After making several films in the North they conned Jong Il into letting them film in Vienna, where they slipped away to the U.S. embassy.[32]

Choi Eun Hee, amazingly, walked around sufficiently unchecked that she was able to secretly tape-record conversations with Kim Jong Il, which were an incomparable source of information to the American and South Korean intelligence agencies about the reclusive future leader of the DPRK. Unfortunately her interactions with Kim Il Sung were rare. The couple met Kim Il Sung at a reception line on New Year's Day, 1985. In the recording Kim and his wife Seongae make small talk about their films. Then Kim changes the topic and talks about a recent proposal from Seoul that both North and South Korea join the United Nations. That, the Great Leader declares, would divide Korea forever; 'Instead, what we are proposing is to retain the system and autonomy of North and South while uniting [in a confederation] and enter the UN as one country. That way would not perpetuate the division.'

He goes on to explain:

> It's impractical to ask the South Korean government to get rid of their rotten system there overnight . . . They have a

> $50 billion debt. Fifty billion: think about it! Fifty billion is not a simple problem. Our debt is $1 billion. We are going to earn foreign currency and thus within a couple of years we are going to fully pay it back. Do you know what [Japanese lawmaker] Tokuma Usunomiya said to me? The Japanese give a lot of money to South Korea, but that amount is equivalent to what the South Korean government has to pay each year as interest on its loans!

Kim was proud of the small debt North Korea had, but it was a debt (somewhat larger than the amount he gave) that the country was defaulting on, while South Korea's was wisely spent, and the country not only was able to repay its loans but became a creditor nation. The conversation ends when interrupted by an official, who offers a hardy New Year's greeting. 'Long live the Great Leader!' he declares. 'Thank you,' Kim Il Sung replies.[33]

Kim Il Sung and the Rise of South Korea

In 1980 Kim still believed he would eventually reunify Korea. But South Korea's economic and political rise in the coming decade would challenge this notion. Already by 1980 South Korea had caught up and surpassed North Korea in economic output and certainly in living standards. Its 9 per cent annual growth rate in the 1970s was probably much higher than the real rate in the DPRK; its education system was expanding at a greater pace; its export earnings were many times higher; and even its military was modernizing faster. In the 1980s the gap in economic strength between the two countries widened enormously while the ROK broke out of its international isolation and established a stable democratic political order.

Yet at the start of the decade Pyongyang could still find signs that history was on its side. The South, whatever its economic achievements, was occupied by foreign troops and was economically in debt to its former colonial master Japan; furthermore, it was ruled by a military whose officer corps was subordinate to the American military. Student radicals, labour and social activists and intellectuals in the South often challenged the ROK political and social order. They often echoed the DPRK's own propaganda in questioning the legitimacy and nationalist credentials of their government. Kim Il Sung firmly adhered to the belief that he was the true legitimate leader of all Korean people, and it was not hard for him to interpret the dissent in the South as signs of popular support for this claim. Meanwhile, his propaganda organs continued to depict South Korea as a hell on earth. Reports of famines appeared regularly, along with those of oppressed farmers and workers living under extremely harsh conditions who could only dream of the standard of living the people of the DPRK enjoyed. People suffered from hunger, farmers were swindled out of their land and workers laboured in appalling conditions and suffered horrific punishments if they complained. All this while under the brutal rule of the American imperialists and their South Korean puppets.[34]

Not all this propaganda was completely false. South Korea's remarkable industrial transformation had come at a heavy social cost. In the late 1970s there was considerable social and political unrest from political, student and labour groups and from a burgeoning middle class uncomfortable with the restraints of Park Chung Hee's increasingly authoritarian rule. Tensions in 1979 led to labour strikes, demonstrations and confrontation by a younger generation of political opposition leaders. All these events suggested the South Korean system might be unravelling. Assuming the role of the main champion of national unification, Kim Il Sung reintroduced his call at the sixth party congress for a Confederal Republic of Koryo, which he had first proposed two decades earlier. Fishing in troubled waters, the DPRK proposed the resumption of talks and even used South Korea's official name Republic of Korea for the first time. Seoul responded by referring to the North as the Democratic

People's Republic of Korea. A series of low-level talks were held from February to August 1980 to prepare the way for a meeting of prime ministers. However, the consolidation of power by the new military rulers who had seized power in the 12 December 1979 coup and their crackdown on dissent in the spring of 1980 removed the opportunities for the North to exploit the political divisions in the ROK and dashed immediate hopes that the system might unravel. The consolidation of power by the Chun Doo Hwan regime and the resumption of the economic boom in 1981 further dimmed those prospects. The DPRK broke off all talks in September 1980 and resumed its loudspeaker tirades along the DMZ, suspended since 1972.[35]

The Seoul Olympics

When in 1981 the International Olympic Committee awarded the 1988 games to Seoul it came as a blow to Kim's ambitions. This provided South Korea with an opportunity to move out from the shadow of the USA and overcome foreign-held images of a backward, American client state. Seoul hoped it would serve as the 1964 Tokyo Olympics did to highlight Japan's recovery after the Second World War, to show off the new country of bullet trains and dynamic modernization. For the South Koreans it also offered possibilities to break out of diplomatic isolation as well as open channels to North Korea's allies in the communist world. And it served to counter those in its own country who still looked to the North as the more legitimate Korea. Kim obviously understood this and spent the next seven years doing what he could to undermine the Seoul Olympics. This took several paths. One was to destabilize the South perhaps enough to make the Olympic committee reconsider its decision, or at least cause countries to avoid participation. Another was to frighten people from attending. In 1985 he demanded North Korea co-host the Olympics. The International Olympic Committee considered the DPRK proposal for a 'Pyongyang–Seoul, Korea Olympiad' and in 1986 provided a more modest proposal: an offer to hold table tennis, archery, football and cycling events in the North. Pyongyang rejected this.

In 1982 North Korea carried out an assassination attempt against the South Korean president Chun Doo Hwan while he was visiting Gabon. But the most dramatic attempt to create a crisis in the South was on 9 October 1983, when the DPRK attempted to kill Chun during his visit to Burma. In Rangoon a platform where ROK and Burmese leaders were to speak was blown up, killing seventeen senior ROK officials, including four cabinet ministers, as well as members of the Burmese government, although failing to harm Chun. This was a carefully planned operation that was probably approved of at the highest levels. It seems quite reckless, and it damaged the DPRK's international image.

Kim also tried to frighten away participants in the Seoul Olympics by reminding them that there was a state of war going on in the peninsula. He or his son ordered a bombing at Seoul's Gimpo airport on 14 October 1986 and the destruction of Korean Air Flight 858 in November 1987. The latter occurred when North Korean agents placed a bomb on a plane returning to Seoul from Baghdad. All 104 passengers, mostly South Koreans working in the Middle East, and 11 crew members were killed. The two agents were traced to Bahrain, where one committed suicide while the other, a female agent, survived and confessed. Her testimony suggested the incident was again planned at the top level. Kim's propaganda organs issued warnings of a widespread AIDS epidemic: the state's official news magazine carried reports of people claiming they would not go because they feared contracting the disease.[36] There was no AIDS epidemic in the South, and this disinformation campaign was not very effective.

Was Kim himself personally responsible for these acts of terrorism? Most historians and pundits have put the blame on Kim Jong Il, and there is circumstantial evidence to support this. It is held that Kim Jong Il needed to prove his credentials as a warrior. It has been pointed out that Jong Il appears to have been the mastermind behind the ill-conceived attack on U.S. and ROK servicemen attempting to prune a tree in the DMZ in 1976, for which his father became furiously angry at him. Could he have been behind the assassination attempts too? After the late 1960s we almost never find military or civilian officials knowingly taking the initiative on anything without the Great Leader's permission. So if someone ordered the Rangoon attack without his approval, it is most likely to have been his son Jong Il. And if so, did his father know of this beforehand? The elder Kim had supported terrorist attacks before, such as the 1974 assassination attempt on Park Chung Hee, so it is conceivable that he knew and supported, even approved of these attacks, disapproving only of their failed execution.

None of these attacks did anything to weaken the South Korean regime or the U.S. support for it, or win over many hearts and minds below the DMZ. And they were repeatedly viewed by Kim's own allies as reckless and dangerous. Yet he continued with them. Creating crises and ratcheting up tensions with the ROK and the USA made some sense, since it supported the fiction that the DPRK was always in danger and that the people must be vigilant and prepare for whatever sacrifices may be necessary. It also tested the response capabilities and resolve of his foes. But terrorist attacks seem harder to justify in pragmatic terms. In so many ways Kim was careful and rational to avoid war, calculating when to cool down a crisis he had created. He never forgot the lessons he learned fighting the Japanese or the Americans in the Korean War, battling a larger, well-armed enemy, which was why he was so concerned to more than match the size of South Korea's army and have a heavily equipped armed forces with an industrial base to support it. But Kim Il Sung's rationalism, his pragmatism, had its limits. Just as he never quite grasped the need to rely less on mass mobilization and more on capital inputs to improve the economy, he never seems to have fully grasped the pointlessness of his regime's acts of terrorism.

Beijing saw the Rangoon incident as counterproductive and reckless. Alarmed, Chinese officials encouraged Kim Il Sung to open a dialogue with the United States and the South. The United States also indicated that it would talk directly with Pyongyang if the talks included the ROK. North Korea agreed to the three-way talks between the DPRK, ROK and USA. Little, however, came of this, since North Korea insisted that the talks lead to a bilateral agreement with the Americans, excluding the ROK, a demand that was acceptable to neither Seoul nor Washington. In September 1984 the DPRK Red Cross offered assistance to the South after severe floods struck that country. Seoul accepted the offer of food, textiles, cement and medicine to the victims, taking it as an opportunity to resume talks. A discussion about a joint Olympic team, of family reunions and other issues continued into 1985. North Korea rejected an offer to open the country for trade, and the South rejected a proposal for a non-aggression pact. Talks came to an end when Pyongyang objected to the Team Spirit military exercises.[37] Held each spring, the joint exercise between U.S. and ROK forces was a sore point with Pyongyang. It was useful for domestic propaganda, since it highlighted the presence of American troops in the South and could support the propaganda line that the imperialists were always plotting an invasion. Team Spirit also provided an excuse whenever North Korea was negotiating with its southern counterparts for ending or delaying talks. Negotiations resumed, leading to an exchange of art performances and family union visits in the summer and autumn of 1985. But this minor thaw in relations soon ended when the DPRK again demanded a non-aggression pact between the two countries and the ending of joint military exercises between the ROK and U.S. forces.

Olympic Defeat

Meanwhile, Kim kept urging friendly countries to boycott the Olympics. But by 1987 Moscow and Beijing had clearly indicated they were participating, and already their athletes were coming to the ROK and inviting South Korean athletes to their country. For a while there was the prospect that the South Koreans could undermine their own Olympics. In the spring of 1987 President Chun Doo Hwan, nearing the completion of his seven-year term of office, reneged on his promise for free elections and instead handpicked his successor, another general and a co-conspirator in the 12 December 1979 military coup, Roh Tae-woo. Massive demonstrations continued daily throughout the country as the public rose in anger over being denied a say in the selection of their next leader. This must have brought the same hope to Kim as events in 1961, 1965 and 1980 did. But the situation was resolved rather suddenly in late June when Chun and Roh agreed to a free election, released jailed opponents and ended most censorship. In December 1987 Roh was elected when the opposition was split between three candidates. But the opposition won an overwhelming majority in the newly empowered National Assembly, and Roh sought to govern according to democratic norms. Rather than plunging into instability, South Korea entered 1988 as a young functioning democracy. Consequently, Kim's hope for the collapse of the political and social order in the South was more remote than ever before.

The Olympics went smoothly: only Albania, Cuba, Ethiopia, Madagascar and the Seychelles answered North Korea's call for a boycott. The games, the first in twelve years in which all major countries participated, were a great success, enabling South Korea to show off its economic achievements. The Olympics took place in September 1988, when the DPRK was celebrating its fortieth anniversary. For Kim, who loved anniversaries, the symbolism was not lost.

Fading Leadership of the Developing World

Another setback for Kim in his competition for legitimacy with Seoul was his loss of support from countries in the developing world. Since the mid-1970s the Non-Aligned Movement had regularly passed pro-DPRK resolutions at summits and meetings of foreign ministers. And each year the members placed a North Korean drafted resolution before the UN (of which the DPRK was not a member) calling for the withdrawal of all foreign forces from the Korean Peninsula – that is, for American troops to leave South Korea. In 1981, at a conference of foreign ministers in New Delhi, the representatives of the Non-Aligned Movement failed to place the Korean unification issue on its agenda, despite DPRK efforts. The next year, in June 1982, at a meeting of foreign ministers in Havana, the movement did not support a DPRK-sponsored resolution calling for the withdrawal of U.S. troops from Korea and the dissolution of the UN command.[38] Foreign leaders from African and other developing nations still came to visit Kim in Pyongyang and were given extravagant welcomes, but their number diminished somewhat and the DPRK's alternative model of development became less appealing.

Seoul was increasingly winning over support from developing countries, putting itself forward as a model of successful economic development. It offered a chance for lucrative trade opportunities, and its diplomats were more skilful than Kim's poorly trained representatives, who were often ignorant of local norms and customs. And the 1988 Olympics assisted Seoul in presenting itself as a rising economic power with much to offer developing countries. By contrast Kim's regime was losing its appeal as a result of its sponsorship of terrorism directed at South Korea, especially the Rangoon bombing, its default on international loans, the extremism of its leadership cult and its promotion of a hereditary succession.

Splendid Isolation

In the 1980s Kim Il Sung became, like his country, more isolated. Part of the problem was that he had fewer peers in whom he could confide. Choe Yonggeon, often crude and blunt, was one of the few who could be open with Kim. He died in 1976. O Baekyong, a close friend who fought alongside Kim at Bocheonbo, a top commander in the Korean War and who served on the Military Commission, died in 1984. Choe Hyeon, another old guerilla comrade, died on 9 April 1982, just three days before Kim's seventieth birthday.[39] Few high-ranking officials were closer to him than Choe Hyeon, who remembered Kim when he was just one of the partisan leaders and of no more importance than he was. In fact being five years older made him a sort of older brother. He was one of the few who could speak frankly with Kim, who trusted and respected him. With their passing, Kim was increasingly surrounded only by those who constantly flattered him and tended to his needs.

Kim was physically more isolated, spending his time behind closed doors in one of his many walled palaces, often located in scenic places. One, in Pyongyang, was situated on a hillside overlooking the Daedong river. Another favourite was on Myohyang mountain, about 100 kilometres (60 mi.) from Pyongyang. It has been reported but never confirmed that by the time he died, Kim and his son together owned a hundred 'villas'. One seaside mansion had an aquarium-like glass wall that looked out under the sea. They were luxuriously furnished. Kim Young-song, an architect who defected, was involved in the building of one of these mansions. The one he worked on, he reported, had 'a tile roof, but straight rather than curved as is traditional. All windows are imported from Austria. The furniture all comes from Japan.'[40] Kim was, of course, used to getting anything he wanted. When he visited Yugoslavia he stayed at the Bled Hotel on the eponymous lake. He liked his hotel room so much that he bought its entire furniture and had it shipped back home, where it ended up in a storage room.[41]

Kim no longer ate with ordinary people as he travelled but had his own special food, grown in special farms, orchards and greenhouses. Each individual piece of fruit or vegetable was carefully selected. Even the rice he ate was specially grown, with each grain individually polished and every imperfect grain removed.[42] In addition, to keep him young and vigorous officials searched for special elixirs.

Kim Il Sung's exalted status and his growing isolation from the people he ruled is demonstrated in his sexual life. Kim adhered to the Chinese belief that a man could prolong his life and expand his years of physical vigour by having frequent sex with young women. According to this theory, just having close contact would be enough to absorb their *ki* (in Chinese, *qi*), their vital life energy. After the Korean War Choe Yonggeon organized a small corps of young female companions for Kim. Over the years this was expanded to become several different groups. The *Kippeunjo* (Happy Corps) were drawn from actresses and singers, and they entertained at night and may have sometimes slept with Kim Il Sung or Kim Jong Il. Kim Jong Il, who was attracted to entertainers and deeply involved in the arts, supervised the organization of this group. The *Manjokjo* (Satisfaction Corps) provided more explicitly sexual services. The *Haengbokjo* (Felicity Corps), recruited from female party workers, served as bodyguards and did menial labour tasks.[43]

Girls for these groups were selected at a young age, around thirteen years, and were trained in comedy, dancing, singing and sexual activities. Kim generally waited until they reached fifteen before sleeping with them. These young girls differed from the comfort women, the thousands of young Korean women conscripted or tricked into sex slavery by the Japanese during the Second World War. These girls were told, and probably usually believed, that being selected to serve the Great Leader was an honour. The girls and their families were generously rewarded, and the officials found suitable husbands for them once their service was terminated after a few years.

But they had to keep the nature of their employment secret; the public, other than a few in the inner circle, knew nothing of this.[44] There were girls for some higher-ranking officials as well.[45]

Kim still travelled about the country doing on-the-spot inspections and giving speeches as well as instructions to local officials, but less often in the 1980s than previously. Fewer inspections made it easier for officials to prepare and make sure that he saw only the most ideal farms, factories, schools and offices, and nothing that would disturb or bother him. He was becoming an increasingly remote figure, more removed from the reality of the society he ruled. He understood that reforms in China, the crumbling of the Soviet Union and the rise of South Korea were posing unprecedented challenges to his regime, but it is less clear that he fully comprehended the full extent of his own country's economic troubles.

9

FADING DREAM, FAILING STATE

KIM SPENT his last years weathering a series of crises. His country became isolated as most of his socialist allies abandoned socialism and some became allied with the West. The nations of the developing world drifted away; even China, while remaining communist, opened relations with Seoul and kept a distance from Pyongyang. More critically, from 1990 the Soviet Union ceased supplying economic and military aid, then disintegrated, with the Russian successor state having little interest in maintaining close ties with the DPRK. Kim's North Korea was looking increasingly like an anachronism. As his rival, South Korea, continued its transition to democracy, support for Pyongyang declined among its youth and leftist intellectuals. Perhaps most seriously, the economy went into a sharp decline, exacerbated by the loss of Soviet aid, especially cheap petroleum. So fast did the economy deteriorate that outsiders wondered if the regime would collapse. By 1994, the year of Kim's death, rather than preparing for the inevitable reunification of the peninsula under his leadership, his concern was the survival of his regime.

Facing a Geopolitical Crisis

The unfavourable turn in geopolitical events was swift and no doubt shocking for Kim. The greatest blow was the collapse of the Soviet Union and its allied regimes. In 1988 Moscow began direct economic contacts with Seoul through the Soviet Chamber of Commerce and Industry. In September 1988 Hungary and South Korea exchanged ambassadors and began negotiations towards full diplomatic recognition. The Soviet Union and the ROK exchanged trade missions in 1989, and in September 1990 President Roh and Soviet leader Mikhail Gorbachev met and agreed to establish full diplomatic relations. In April 1991 Gorbachev went on an official visit to South Korea. The USSR's trade with the ROK increased after 1988, while its trade with the DPRK sharply declined. Meanwhile, 1989 saw the collapse of most of the communist regimes in Eastern Europe, an extraordinary pace of change in the Soviet Union and talk about the 'collapse of communism'.

Moscow, which was so concerned with North Korea's strategic importance just a few years earlier, now was more interested in establishing economic ties with South Korea. In 1989 the Soviet Union ended major weapons shipments and ceased its joint military exercises. In September 1990 foreign minister Eduard Shevardnadze officially informed the DPRK that Moscow was suspending further large-scale investments.[1] In an even greater setback for Pyongyang the Soviets began insisting on payment for oil and imports in hard currency. These developments amounted to an enormous economic blow, since the Soviets accounted for half of the DPRK's foreign trade, much of its oil and most of its new technology inputs. North Korea's faltering economy had been briefly buoyed by the increase in Soviet aid; that aid was drastically reduced until it came to an end altogether. Then, in December of 1991, the Soviet Union itself dissolved. The impact of this can hardly be exaggerated. For all its trumpeting of 'self-reliance', North Korea remained dependent on Soviet economic and military support. When relations between Moscow and Pyongyang soured after 1962, the DPRK economy was hard hit. Kim Il Sung quickly improved relations after 1965, and while never fully comfortable with the Soviets after that, he was careful not to rupture relations and actively sought to keep the aid flowing. Now it stopped. In 1992 the new Russian state under President Boris Yeltsin made it known that the Soviet–North Korean Treaty of Friendship, Cooperation and Mutual Assistance of 1961, especially Article 1, which committed Moscow to the defence of the DPRK in case of armed conflict, was no longer in effect.[2] The treaty was formally nullified in 1996. That Kim's influence among developing countries continued to decline only compounded the growing sense of isolation. He was no longer seriously competing with South Korea for influence abroad. By the early 1990s South Korea was winning support with rural development programmes in Africa, while North Korea's effort focused on smuggling ivory and rhino horns to earn foreign currency.[3]

Isolated and ignored by the world during the Seoul Olympics, Kim hosted the Thirteenth Festival of Youth and Students in 1989 by way of compensation. Some 22,000 young people from 177 countries attended. But the games were a costly burden the state could hardly afford, and whatever domestic purpose they may have served, they drew little international attention. Meanwhile, Seoul made some efforts to improve relations with its northern rival. On 7 July 1988, President Roh Tae Woo issued a six-point declaration that defined the DPRK as part of a 'single national community', not as an adversary.[4] In subsequent addresses he called upon both Koreas to work on a Korean Commonwealth. This was not a new idea and resembled Kim's own proposal of a Democratic Confederal Republic of Koryo. Pyongyang, while not embracing the idea, proposed inter-parliamentary talks between the two sides, but the conditions it set for those talks made them unacceptable to Seoul. North Korea did not ignore these overtures completely, and in December 1988 high-level talks occurred between the prime minister of South Korea and the premier of the North; there were further talks in 1989, but these led nowhere.

Turning Inward

Kim Il Sung and his son responded to the unfavourable turn in North Korea's geopolitical situation by retreating into an extreme ultranationalism that insulated it from the 'collapse of communism'. Kim Il Sung had always been part of the wave of modern nationalism that took hold of many Koreans in the early part of the century. His aim was to restore the unity and full sovereignty of his country lost by the selfish, backward feudal elite and undermined by the foreign imperialists who exploited the country's weakness. His revolution was a nationalist project; socialism, communism and *Juche* were instruments to achieve it. Yet his intense, fierce nationalism was tempered somewhat by the internationalism of Marxism-Leninism. With the effective replacement of Marxism-Leninism with *Juche* as the ideological basis of society, the nationalist character of his regime became less constrained.

Kim maintained an ambivalent attitude towards his country's traditional culture. He disparaged the 'feudal' Confucian society of old Korea. Yet he was proud of his heritage, too. In the 1950s a People's Classics Research Institute translated the many-volume *Richo sillok* (Veritable Records of the Yi Dynasty) into Hangeul so that it could be more readily accessible.[5] Except for a brief wave of text burning in 1967, Kim did not, like Mao, carry out a wilful destruction of the country's heritage, although in the turmoil of the Korean War and the country's rapid modernization much of its physical remains were lost. Korean curved roofs topped some buildings, and girls were encouraged to learn the *gayageum*, a traditional Korean zither. Women wore the traditional *hanbok* on holidays and even at political rallies. In the 1960s the *Rodong Sinmun*, which represented Kim's views, complained when Soviet history gave too little credit to the country's ancient achievements and short-changed its antiquity.

Kim's pride in his cultural heritage became more pronounced in his later years, coupled with a shift towards a more strident racial-ethnic nationalism. This began modestly with the revival of some pre-modern traditions. In 1989 the government reinstituted the traditional holidays of Chuseok that had ceased to be celebrated after 1948, the Korean autumn thanksgiving festival and the Lunar New Year celebration. These had always been the two most important holidays of the year and had remained so in the South. It also reintroduced the celebration of Hansik, a festival that takes place 105 days after the winter solstice, and Dano, the fifth day of the fifth lunar year, two traditional festivals that were no longer observed south of the DMZ.

In August 1991, in a speech published in the *Rodong Sinmun*, Kim Il Sung praised 'genuine nationalism', which he stated differed from 'bourgeois nationalism'. He went on to declare, 'Our nation that has the same blood relation and the same language, and [which] has developed the great national culture is a highly patriotic, independent nation.'[6] The media began repeating Kim's quote that 'Our people have a long history of five thousand years and are an intelligent people who possess a glorious culture.'[7] North Korean histories had continually pushed back the dates for early Korean states.[8] Now they were being pushed back far earlier. Kim complained that archaeologists had failed to discover the true early origins of Korean civilization. Almost immediately they did so, finding evidence of an ancient Daedonggang civilization that pre-dated even the earliest known urban society in China. Korea was not, as historians had long believed, a later offshoot of Chinese civilization but was a totally independent, urban, state-level society, older than China, as old as Egypt. Shortly afterwards, his archaeologists made a more amazing discovery: the tomb of Dangun, the mythical founder of the first Korean state. According to tradition, he was born in 2333 BCE. South Korea, which had its own tendency towards racial nationalism, honoured Dangun as a symbol of the nation's uniqueness and homogeneity; his birth on 3 October was a national holiday. However, most textbooks and professional historians treated him as a myth. In the

DPRK too, Dangun was officially regarded, somewhat disparagingly, as a feudal myth. This changed when North Korea announced, on the eve of National Foundation Day in 1993, that its archaeologists had excavated the bones of Dangun and his wife as well as a gilded bronze crown and some ornaments. These remains were stated to be 5,011 years old. Few South Korean archaeologists or other scholars outside North Korea took these claims seriously, generally assuming the findings were most likely fabricated.[9]

All these amazing discoveries made at Kim's command were more than a mere burst of nationalist pride: they served a real purpose. They indirectly linked the Kim dynasty to the ancient progenitor of the Korean people. Official mythology had it that Kim Jong Il was born on Baekdusan on the China–North Korea border, a sacred spot and considered the birthplace of Dangun. The regime was implying that it was the successor to the founder of the Korean nation and upholder of the national spirit. By the late 1990s Dangun's name was frequently asserted as a symbol of the Korean nation. The third of October became 'the nation's day', with memorial services to 'King Dangun'. Kim Jong Il in public statements urged the Korean people to follow the 'spirit of Dangun'. Kim Il Sung was called 'a great sage of Dan'gun's nation born of heaven, and [the] sun of a reunified country'.[10]

Kim was always at heart an ultranationalist with a xenophobic streak. North Korea rarely acknowledged the foreign assistance it received, there were no streets or place names in honour of foreigners and all credit for liberation was given to Korean partisans. But in the early 1990s North Korean official histories presented an increasingly xenophobic racial-nationalist interpretation of the past. Textbooks portrayed Korea's history as the story of the constant struggle of a racially distinct, virtuous people against outside invaders. This change in tone was reflected in the choice of language in state propaganda. For example, the term *inmin* (people), normally used in socialist rhetoric and embedded in the name Democratic People's

Republic of Korea, became less often used, replaced by the more nationalistic and ethnic-racial tinged *minjok*.

Kim's propaganda organs went even further in exalting the racial distinctness and antiquity of the Korean race. His archaeologists made another even more remarkable discovery when, in the early 1990s, an early human labelled *Pithecanthropus* was unearthed. Dating back 1 million years, this hominid was declared the ancestor of all Koreans. Thus, it turned out, Koreans were descended from a distinct line of early humans. It was claimed that the Daedong basin where Pyongyang was located was both 'the cradle of mankind' and the home of a unique branch of the human race. 'Scientific evidence', one publication declared, 'supports the claim that there is a distinctive Korean race and that the foundation of the first state of the Korean nation by Dan'gun was a historic event, which laid the groundwork for the formation of the Korean nation.'[11] Kim's regime exceeded even the extremes of National Socialism in its effort to establish a biological basis for its national identity. To be fair, Kim's regime did not claim any kind of racial superiority, only racial purity and a separate, distinct bloodline that set them apart from other nations. This purity and uniqueness needed protection from contamination from foreigners. North Korean propaganda increasingly focused on the vulnerability of the Korean race, its need for unity in the face of foreign aggressors and the indispensable role of its brilliant leadership as its protectors. Koreans in pictures were also depicted as looking physically different, generally better looking than the foreigners.[12]

It is not clear how much of this reflected Kim's beliefs. Hunted down by the Japanese, bombed by the Americans and imprisoned as a young man by both the Chinese and the Soviets, he certainly had reason to distrust foreigners. But there was a practical purpose to all this, as the international socialist movement to which he belonged appeared to be crumbling and his own situation became more precarious: he needed a narrative that would justify and sustain the regime. An emotional appeal to the latent fear of foreigners, to racism and the image of a small country surrounded by hostile or untrustworthy powers all served to give a meaning to his rule. It explained the hardships that the country was suffering and rallied the people around him. Kim might have rigidly stuck to older development models, but he proved flexible and pragmatic in constructing narratives to insulate his country from the winds of change.

Facing Economic Crisis

The most severe setback for North Korea that came with its loss of international standing and allies was to its economy.[13] The loss of subsidized oil was especially traumatic. Pyongyang did not have the foreign exchange to pay for imported oil, and it was no longer receiving cheap, below-market-value oil from Russia. China provided some, but not enough. In a meeting with Deng Xiaoping in 1992, the Chinese leader made it clear that Beijing was too busy with its own reconstruction to offer more help.[14] Blackouts, always common, became so frequent in the DPRK that they had a crippling effect. Tractors and trucks stood idle, homes went through winter with little or no heat and shortages of fertilizers hindered agriculture. Severe energy shortages, along with ageing equipment, led to a decline in industrial output. The loss of Soviet aid came at a bad time, when most sectors of the economy were already in trouble. Agriculture was threatened by flooding from deforestation, food shortages worsened, and hunger and malnutrition were serious problems. North Korea's economic problems in the early 1990s were reaching a crisis point.

In 1992, on the occasion of his eightieth birthday, Kim invited representatives of other communist parties to join him. Thirty came. They were mostly from tiny, powerless parties such those of Jordan, Malta and Cyprus. The Chinese Communist Party did not come, nor did many of the other remaining larger parties. The gathering proved a dramatic display of his regime's isolation. Nonetheless, Kim took the opportunity to affirm that the KWP would not follow the path of reform of China, would not open the country to foreign investment or market forces. Instead it would adhere to 'our style of socialism' (*urisik sahoejuui*). In an interview with the *Washington Times* on 18 April 1992, Kim emphatically stated that North Korea was not going to emulate Chinese reforms:

> On detailed method of socialist construction, each country should develop a method reflecting their own situation because [the] environment for socialist construction varies in accordance with each country's size and level of development. We acknowledge that the Chinese policy of economic construction reflects the Chinese situation and register strong support [for it].[15]

He was careful not to offend his last remaining ally. In 1993, for example, Kim told a visiting delegation from Beijing that China's economic reforms were a 'tremendous success'.[16] But he made it clear that his government was sticking to the old ways – and so it did. During the early 1990s Kim's regime carried out the old mass-mobilization campaigns, such as the Three Revolutions Team Movement, the Cheollima Movement and the Taean Work System, to spur economic production.

Turning Over Responsibility to Jong Il

While the country was enduring these crises, Kim Il Sung began to accelerate the slow process of turning the power over to his son. Or it might be more accurate to say that Jong Il was busy further consolidating his power. By 1990 Jong Il was running the day-to-day administration of the country. Most party and cabinet officials reported directly to him. The one area in which the elder Kim retained the reins of power was in the military; it is not clear why. Some have speculated that the military was slow to accept his son as his successor owing to his lack of military credentials. Jong Il had never served in the military and had little experience working with it. His forays into military affairs, such as the tree-cutting incident in 1976 or terrorist attacks like the bombing of Flight 858 in 1987, did not go well. Rather than burnish his martial credentials, these attacks signalled recklessness. The tree-cutting incident forced his father into a rare public apology, and his terrorist attacks to sabotage the Olympics were ineffective and damaged the DPRK's reputation. Along with his generals, Kim himself may also have worried about his son's lack of military competence.

Over time this state of affairs changed, however. Jong Il had developed a military reporting system that enabled him to keep an eye on his military officers. And on 24 December 1991, at the nineteenth party plenum of the Sixth Congress of Korean Workers' Party, he was named Supreme Commander of the Korean People's Armed Forces. On 20 April 1992, Kim Jong Il was promoted to Marshal (*wonsu*), one week after his father became a Great Marshal (*daewonsu*, sometimes translated as generalissimo). Jong Il now had direct command over the military, with only his father able to countermand his decisions. The glorification of Jong Il continued, and his fiftieth birthday on 16 February 1992 was celebrated as a national holiday. State propaganda organs focused more on Kim Il Sung's 'brilliant' son. When Kim's 81st birthday was celebrated in 1993, the speeches in his honour centred around his 'remarkable foresight' in arranging for his succession. In late 1993 various organizations held rallies pledging loyalty to Kim Jong Il and emphasizing the need for a 'single-minded unity' around him.[17]

In 1992 Kim Il Sung, after publishing the first volume of his autobiography *With the Century*, stated that he now had the time to write: since 'a large part of my work is done by [KWP] Secretary for Organizational Affairs Kim Jong Il, I have been able to find some time.'[18] The process of handing over power appeared to go smoothly, with few major shake-ups in the leadership. Those few changes that did take place, such as the promotion to position number seven in the party hierarchy of Kim Il Sung's younger brother Kim Yeongju, after seventeen years of absence from the public eye, suggested continuity rather than any new departures for the regime.

Taking Back Some Responsibility

Kim, a person who had always taken a hands-on approach to governing, who had constantly travelled through his nation to oversee progress, had become more isolated in his last years. This was in part a product of old age, which made constant travel difficult, as well as his failing eyesight. He also had an eager son who enabled his isolation by carrying out most of the daily administration and screening the information that his father received. Underlings tended to report only good news, and Kim's less frequent on-the-spot inspections were increasingly stage-managed to avoid him encountering anything that might disturb him. Much of his time was spent on writing his memoirs. His separation from reality is reflected in the tone of these, where he writes that the 'revolution [is] progressing triumphantly and our country [is] prospering, with all the people singing its praises.'[19]

The 1990 harvest was a poor one, a result of adverse weather, lack of petroleum to power irrigation pumps and tractors, and the cumulative effect of years of agricultural mismanagement. But Kim was not informed about just how bad the situation was. Worried officials invited representatives of the World Food Program (WFP) to come to Korea to help provide food aid. In early 1991 an assessment team of four technical officers from the WFP arrived in Pyongyang to determine the country's needs. Rather strangely, they were told everything was fine, the harvest had produced an ample 10 million tons of grain and there was no malnutrition; nor was any explanation given for why they were invited. They left puzzled. What they did not know was that Kim had found out about their presence and was furious. He demanded to know why they were invited without his being informed, and why, if the harvest was good, they were needed at all.[20]

Hwang Jang-yeop, the party ideologist who defected to South Korea in 1997 and who is an invaluable source on the inner workings of the DPRK regime, recounts a story from the early 1990s. During a meeting of the Korean Workers' Party Central Committee that Kim was chairing, he criticized the minister of electric power for failing to provide a reliable supply of electricity. He complained that while watching a film, the electricity went out. As was customary when addressed by their Great Leader, the minister stood up erectly and replied, 'Currently there is not enough electric power to meet the requirement of the factories. Because of the heavy load in transmission to the factories, the voltage of electricity supplied to Pyongyang tends to drop.' Kim Il Sung responded, 'Then why can't you adjust the power supply transmitted to factories and allocate more to Pyongyang?' The minister explained, 'This would stop operation in a lot of factories.' Kim cut him off and ordered, 'I don't care if all the factories in the country stop production, just send enough electricity to Pyongyang.'[21]

But in 1992 Kim began to take a renewed interest in the details of administration. Most likely this was the result of the economic situation becoming so grave that it was impossible to shelter him from it. According to another defector, Kang Myong-do, in April that year Kim Il Sung was commenting to those around him that he saw only two smokestacks from power plants that actually had smoke coming out. He enquired why and was told that no coal was coming from the coal mines that fuelled the plants, because the workers had stopped receiving their rations.[22] Around this time Kim received a report from a trusted official, Kang Songsan, who was serving as the party secretary of North Hamgyeong, his home province. Kang was from a good revolutionary family and a graduate of Mangyeongdae Revolutionary School. He served as premier from 1984 to 1986. He gave Kim a frank report on the severe food and fuel shortages in this the coldest region of the country. This had always been a poor, remote area to which many untrustworthy members of the hostile class had been exiled. But Kim was shocked at the report Kang provided and decided to go and see for himself.[23] What he saw verified what the governor Kang had told him. He awarded the official with the Order of Kim Il Sung and reappointed him as premier.

Whether or not this was the turning point, at this time in 1992 Kim started to take a more active role in the management of the state. His growing awareness of just how bad economic conditions were is clear at the beginning of the following year when for the first time he referred to the economic failures in public. There were reports that he regretted turning over so much of the administration to his son, but of course he never stated this publicly, and none of these reports can be confirmed.[24]

On 1 January 1994 Kim presented his annual New Year's address. He began in the usual celebratory manner: 'Today we are ringing out 1993 a glorious year marked by heroic struggles and great exploits.' But this address was a little different, with reference to the troubles the country was facing. He told his people, 'The imperialists and reactionaries worked with greater malevolence than ever before to isolate and stifle our republic and crush our socialist cause.' He went on to praise the 1987–93 Seven-Year Plan under which 'we made great strides in all fields of socialist construction, despite enormous obstacles caused by unexpected international events.' 'Socialist Korea' was 'advancing triumphantly despite upheavals in the international arena.' He warned the people that the 'external and internal situation is tense.' And while continuing to praise the country's achievements, he warned his citizens of great challenges resulting from the international situation and that they faced an 'arduous struggle' ahead.

These hints at problems and the need of the people to prepare for hard times was an unusual if indirect and understated admission that things were not going entirely well.[25] It was a sign that he could no longer ignore the problems that almost all North Koreans were facing. But it was far short of capturing the reality of a collapsing economy, severe food shortages and widespread hunger, schools that had no fuel to heat classrooms, frequent blackouts and factories not operating because of a lack of energy and materials.

The Nuclear Crisis

As Kim became fully aware of the gravity of the economic situation he also became involved in a nuclear crisis. Foreign policy and military affairs were areas in which he had retained an active interest, even as he had turned over much of the everyday administrative management to his son. Under his direction North Korea developed a formidable weapons industry. Although it was never self-sufficient in military hardware, it did produce an impressive array of tanks, artillery, small arms and military vehicles. Besides conventional weapons, the DPRK also worked on developing biological, chemical and nuclear weapons and a missile delivery system. These were probably always an important part of Kim's military development plans, but his regime became more reliant on them as the country's economic and geopolitical position became less favourable. These weapons of mass destruction were of great concern to South Korea, the international community and, especially, the United States.

From the 1970s the Second Economic Committee, which supervised the arms industry of the DPRK, constructed and operated chemical weapons factories that produced mustard gas, sarin and other chemical agents.[26] It also developed biological weapons, including, it was believed, anthrax, botulism, cholera, haemorrhagic fever, the plague (*Yersinia pestis*), yellow fever and smallpox.[27] Seoul and Washington were aware of and alarmed by this work on biological and chemical weapons. While the DPRK joined the Biological and Toxin Weapons Convention in 1987, it remained one of only five countries that did not sign the 1993 Chemical Weapons Convention.[28]

Kim's focus was on developing nuclear weapons. As early as the 1960s he asked both Moscow and Beijing for assistance in this; both refused, although the Soviets supplied a small research reactor. Both allies also refused his request to help him with missile technology. Neither wanted Kim, with his history of provocative actions, to have either atomic weapons or a delivery system. Nonetheless, he remained persistent. He had good reason. At the same time his rival Park Chung Hee was secretly working on developing a nuclear weapon and missiles. When the USA found out they forced him to shut down the project. But the government of his successor surreptitiously began another programme to develop nuclear weapons, which again Washington forced him to shut down. Whether Kim knew about this or not is unclear, but he certainly probably suspected it. Meanwhile, of course, the USA stationed nuclear weapons and missiles in the South.

Kim began to focus more on nuclear weapons development in the 1980s, building a facility for reprocessing fuel into weapons-grade material. His scientists and engineers also began testing chemical high explosives for detonating a bomb. Under Soviet pressure Pyongyang signed the Nuclear Non-Proliferation Treaty (NPT) in 1985, but not the safeguards agreements.[29] When satellite photos in 1990 revealed a new structure that appeared to be capable of separating plutonium from nuclear fuel rods, American, South Korean and Japanese officials became alarmed. Under international pressure, including from China and Russia, Kim signed a nuclear safeguards agreement with the International Atomic Energy Agency (IAEA) in January 1992, opening up his nuclear facilities to inspection. North Korea played to the South Korean concern over nuclear weapons by working out a Joint Declaration in December 1991 not to test, manufacture, produce, receive, possess, store, deploy or use nuclear weapons.[30] This followed an easing of tensions. But despite the Joint Declaration, it was soon apparent that North Korea was continuing to work on nuclear weapons development. Kim insisted the programme was designed to develop nuclear power to deal with the country's energy shortage. That might not have been entirely false; he was hoping to develop nuclear power. But his prime motivation, it is clear from his actions, was to develop a nuclear weapon. This was not unreasonable from his point of view: he needed to compensate for his country's economic weakness and loss of Soviet support and a rising South Korea. And he genuinely feared a possible U.S. intervention, a fear reinforced by the Gulf War of 1990, which both showcased America's new advanced weapons – which they might be supplying to South Korea – and the willingness to use them against an adversary.

Kim's strategy was to stall and buy time to develop nuclear weapons. His officials, while promising to abide by international inspectors, gave incomplete reports of its facilities and made it difficult for the IAEA to carry out its duties. Then, in February 1993, North Korea announced its intention to withdraw from the NPT in June of that year.[31] The United Nations Security Council then passed a resolution calling for the DPRK to reconsider its withdrawal.

Kim's decision to close his country's nuclear facilities to outside inspectors created a full-blown crisis. The Clinton administration announced that if North Korea reprocessed plutonium, it would be crossing a 'red line' that could result in military action. In fact the USA took the crisis so seriously that a military contingency plan was presented to President Clinton in December 1993, known as USFK OpPlan 502716. Tensions were eased a bit when Kim's negotiators agreed to let the IAEA officials inspect the nuclear facilities on 16 February 1994, and the Clinton administration in response suspended Team Spirit, the annual joint military exercise. Still, the decision so concerned the Americans that they seriously considered a military strike on the DPRK's main reprocessing facility in Yongbyon, northeast of Pyongyang. In May 1994 an emergency meeting of policymakers in Washington began to weigh America's options. One of these was a possible military strike to destroy the facilities in Yongbyon. That the Clinton administration was giving serious consideration to such a move, even though it could result in a retaliation by the DPRK, which possessed several thousand long artillery pieces and rocket launchers that could inflict devastating damage on Seoul, indicates how serious the crisis had become.[32] Conflict on the peninsula could bring about tens of thousands of American and hundreds of thousands of South Korean casualties.

Two high-ranking U.S. senators, Sam Nunn and Richard Lugar, offered to fly to Pyongyang and meet with Kim, but he turned their offer down.[33] Kim himself gave mixed signals, telling a *Washington Times* reporter that the nuclear reactor might not be needed. His trusted negotiator Kang Sok Ju stated on 3 June that Pyongyang was prepared to dismantle the nuclear processor. The next day Selig Harrison of the Carnegie Endowment for International Peace arrived and met with Kang and other officials. He discussed freezing further development of the reprocessing plant and the rest of the nuclear programme in exchange for a light-water reactor that could generate electricity without producing material that could be weaponized. Kim met him on 9 June. When Selig presented his proposal, to his surprise Kim did not seem to have heard of it. The North Korean leader turned to Kang Sok Ju, who was present, and talked to him for five minutes in Korean, which Selig did not understand and which was not translated. Kim then said, 'This is a good idea. We can definitely accept it if the United States really makes a firm commitment that we can trust.' At the meeting Kim stated, as he had before, that he had no intention of developing nuclear weapons: 'What would be the point of making one or two nuclear weapons when you have ten thousand plus delivery systems we don't have? We would be a laughing stock. We want nuclear power for electricity.'[34] While Kim's interest in nuclear weapons was never in doubt, it is possible he sincerely considered this proposal given its attractiveness to the regime.

Kim had invited Jimmy Carter to North Korea in 1991, 1992 and 1993, but each time the U.S. State Department had persuaded or pressured him not to go. Kim had always wanted direct talks with the USA, but American policy was that there could be no separate negotiations with the DPRK without ROK participation. Carter, Kim remembered, had been in favour of the withdrawal of U.S. forces from the South. He remained a promising conduit to Washington. This time the Clinton administration reluctantly okayed Carter's visit to Pyongyang, but he was doing so as a private citizen.

Carter arrived in Seoul on 13 June 1994, where he was greeted with less than enthusiasm by Kim Young Sam and his administration that came to power in 1993. After Kim ignored the 1991 agreement with the ROK that the Korean Peninsula would be nuclear-free, the leadership in Seoul was very sceptical of any further promises. They had concluded, correctly, that Kim was determined to develop nuclear weapons. Two days later, on 15 June, Carter crossed the DMZ with his wife Rosalynn and was driven to Pyongyang. Kim warmly greeted them; his two-decade-long effort to directly deal with U.S. leaders had come to fruition. While Carter was not an official, he was an influential ex-president well connected to the Washington decision-makers. This was good enough for Kim. Like Selig, Carter found Kim very much in charge. While he listened to his advisers, he did not hesitate to make on-the-spot decisions. Carter was there to confirm the U.S. offer to build light-water nuclear reactors in return for the North Koreans shutting down the nuclear programme. He knew Kim was open to this idea, but at the last minute the Clinton administration instructed him to include a new condition: that the North Koreans not only remove the fuel rods in their reactor but not place new ones in it. Carter was unhappy with this new demand, which would make his negotiations harder, but to his surprise Kim readily accepted it.

Kim invited Carter and Rosalynn to a cruise aboard his yacht on the Daedong river. The two couples, Carter and his wife and Kim and his wife Kim Seongae, continued their conversation as they sailed. At one point Carter brought up concerns about missing American servicepeople from the Korean War and suggested that as a goodwill gesture a joint USA–DPRK effort be made to recover their remains. Kim was non-committal, but Seongae suggested it was fine. 'Okay, it's done, it's done,' Kim responded.[35] Then, while seated at a small table in the cabin, Carter presented a request from South Korean president Kim Young Sam that a summit between them be arranged. Kim agreed, responding that both sides were at fault for not having done this.

On 18 June Carter returned to Seoul, where at a press conference he explained that Kim had agreed to freeze his nuclear programme in return for U.S. help in nuclear power technology and for official assurances that neither the United States nor any other outside forces would attack North Korea.[36] Carter might have been acting as a private person, and there was some annoyance at his private diplomacy, but the Clinton administration accepted the terms, and negotiations began that led to what was known as the Agreed Framework signed in October 1994. This was a legally non-binding agreement between the United States and the DPRK, not a treaty, since the USA had no official relations with North Korea and would not negotiate formal treaties with that country until the Korean War officially ended. North Korea agreed to remain a party to the Nuclear Non-Proliferation Treaty and to its terms for international inspection. This meant it agreed to place its 5-megawatt nuclear reactor and the two larger reactors it was constructing under IAEA inspection. North Korea also agreed it would take steps to implement the Joint Declaration of the Denuclearization of the Korean Peninsula, which it had made with the ROK at the end of 1991. All its spent nuclear fuel stocks would be stored and eventually disposed of and not reprocessed. Thus its capacity to produce weapons-grade plutonium would be eliminated, and its existing plutonium would be removed from harm's way. Since North Korea's nuclear reactors were ostensibly for the purpose of generating electric power, in return for shutting them down, two 1,000-megawatt light-water reactors were to be built as gifts by the USA and other outside parties. These would supply electricity but be incapable of producing weapons-grade material.[37]

It is not known why Kim accepted his southern counterpart's offer of a summit. He had invited Kim Young Sam's predecessor, Roh Tae Woo, to his eightieth birthday, but it is not clear how serious this was. His real goal might have been to use the summit as a way of accomplishing what he had long sought: the eventual withdrawal of the Americans from the South. Or perhaps he genuinely saw the need to improve relations before he passed away. For whatever reason he fully embraced the idea of welcoming the South Korean president.

Kim Il Sung's Last Days

Kim's meeting with Carter seemed to invigorate him. For the following three weeks he was busy preparing for the meeting with South Korean president Kim Young Sam. He made two on-the-spot visits to cooperative farms, continuing to show his concern for the problems of food production. He met many foreign visitors, far more than usual.[38] On 6 July he held a meeting with about two dozen officials and a senior economic adviser. He told them that his priorities were 'Agriculture first, light industry first and foreign trade first', repeating what he had stated in his New Year's address. He listed a set of targets: 850,000 tons of fertilizer, 12 million tons of cement, the completion of one hundred ships, improvements on the railways and more emphasis on metal industries. He explained that the light-water nuclear reactors would take too long, so to deal with the energy shortages, more power plants burning heavy fuel oil needed to be constructed.[39] Considering the sad shape of the North Korean economy, none of these goals was very realistic. But they at least showed that Kim's priorities were dealing with energy shortages, food scarcity, improving living standards and increasing international trade; that he was aware of the problems facing the state, if not how to solve them.

His focus, however, was on the upcoming visit by the South Korean president, which he seemed to be genuinely excited about. It is not clear how realistic his expectations were. He dusted off his old idea of a confederation of the two Koreas under a single name but with two separate systems. It was for him a halfway house to reunification. Did he still maintain expectations or hope that once the two Koreas were more open to each other, his system would prevail? If so, it was a fantasy by 1994. Or the proposal may have been tactical, just an effort to gain trade, aid and other advantages from the South while waiting for a time when fortunes favoured the DPRK. Kim Young Sam had indicated he was only interested in smaller, confidence-building steps, starting with reuniting divided families. Although a former democratic dissident and opponent of the military regime, he shared the military's distrust and contempt towards Kim's regime. But he did have a surprise gift for his northern counterpart: an offer of 500,000 tons of rice, an amount far exceeding the 100,000 to 200,000 tons that northern officials had requested through ROK businessmen.[40]

Kim personally supervised the preparations for the coming visit. He decided to take the ROK president to his beloved mansion at Mount Myohyang with its magnificent views. It was where he had recently taken the Japanese lawmaker Shin Kanemaru. On 7 July he was driven up to his palace, stopping for an on-the-spot inspection at a collective farm on the way. It was an extremely hot day. His handlers probably worried about his physical exertion when temperatures were reaching 38 degrees Celsius (100°F). Arriving at the palace, he carried out a personal inspection, looking at the guestrooms where Kim Young Sam and his hundred-member entourage, accompanied by eighty South Korean journalists, would stay, checking the bathrooms and ordering his staff to have the refrigerators well stocked with fresh spring water. Then, after dinner, when he had complained of being tired, he suddenly collapsed, suffering a massive heart attack. It was a bad place for a medical emergency, since the road to Myohyang was unpaved and slow-going. A medical helicopter was delayed by bad weather that night so that doctors and health staff were unable to arrive swiftly. Kim Il Sung was pronounced dead at 2 a.m. on 8 July 1994.[41]

The Death of Kim Il Sung

At noon on 9 July 1994, millions of North Koreans, having been told there would be an important announcement, gathered around TV sets. They watched as the tearful newsreader Chong Hong-kyu, wearing a black suit and tie, announced, 'Our Great Leader has left our side.' In a voice throbbing with emotion, he stated, 'Our country is enveloped in the deepest sorrow in the five-thousand-year history of the Korean nation.'

The news came as a shock, both to North Koreans and to outsiders. Kim had seemed so healthy and vigorous in the days and weeks before, even to those foreigners who had encountered him in person at this time. Such encounters were rare enough that each report is an important hint. In June 1992 an American Korean expert, William J. Taylor from the Center of Strategic and International Studies in Washington, DC, attended a luncheon with him and reported, 'He walks and moves vigorously for age 80. His handshake is firm. When I left, he shook hands and pulled me toward him, his arm muscles are in good tone. His eyes are clear and his eye contact firm and compelling. Most important . . . his mind is quick and crystal clear.'[42] Carter, during his June 1994 visit, found Kim vigorous and alert.[43] He had a tumour on the back of his neck, but this had been examined by East German doctors in the 1970s who pronounced it benign.

In fact Kim may not have been as healthy as he appeared in public and to select visitors. He had trouble with his eyesight and had slowed down his activities in the early 1990s – although this would be expected of a person his age. He was known to have hardening of the arteries. A South Korean official who was among his luncheon guests in February 1992 found him dribbling his food and slurring his speech. A cameraman from the American news broadcaster CNN attending his eightieth birthday celebrations in April 1994 noticed how carefully stage-managed his public appearance was. Tiny lights near the ceiling turned as Kim got up to speak, giving him a healthy, rosy colour.[44] His own son later died of a stroke, suggesting a family history of cardiovascular trouble. So it should not be surprising that the 82-year-old leader, taking up a newly vigorous schedule, should have died of a heart attack.

Nonetheless, rumours circulated around South Korea that Kim had died after an argument with his son Jong Il. In fact among the elite in the North, rumours spread that his death was deliberately caused by Kim Jong Il, impatient to assume full power.[45] According to some of these his son opposed the meeting with the South Korean president, fearing the consequences of opening up the country too much or becoming economically dependent on the rival regime. One defector with connections to elite families later reported that such rumours were common among them.[46] Reports of the Great Leader's death being connected with a dispute with his son also appeared in accounts from non-elite refugees from the North, so they appear to have been widespread.[47] There were accounts of varying credibility that a power struggle was going on.[48] According to one, Kim had been turning to his son Kim Pyongil. Pyongil had certain qualities that Jong Il lacked: he was outgoing and charming, not quiet and reserved, a handsome man who looked like a leader. A widow of the former Japanese prime minister who stopped over and met with Kim before his death reported that he told her his good health was thanks to Kim Pyongil: 'He's been helping me lately.'[49]

There might be some truth to these rumours, but more probably they simply reflect the fact that his son was not liked or respected among the elite like his father was. Kim did seem disturbed by Jong Il's stewardship of the state and did step in after 1992 for a more active role. However, there is no evidence that there was a sharp dispute between them over the agreements he had made with Jimmy Carter. After his death Jong Il continued with their implementation without much interruption. And while the visit with Kim Young Sam never took place, six years later Jong Il welcomed his successor, South Korean president Kim Dae Jung, to Pyongyang. Nor is it likely that after more than two decades of careful preparation, Kim was suddenly going to abandon his eldest son for a younger one as his successor.

The Eternal President

The announcement of Kim Il Sung's death was the beginning of a national outburst of public grief on a scale and intensity never seen before. Authorities declared a ten-day national mourning. On 19 July the public funeral took place after a two-day delay. A black limousine carried Kim Il Sung's body in a closed coffin of shiny black enamel decorated with silver filigree. It sat atop a thick bed of flowers on the roof. It was followed by a procession of black limousines carrying giant portraits of the late Great Leader, as well as army bands and goose-stepping soldiers. Hundreds of thousands of mourners lined the streets, many falling to their knees, some flailing their arms in the air, most in tears.

Accompanying the body of Kim Il Sung was his son and successor Kim Jong Il. Next was General O Jinu, one of Kim Il Sung's surviving Manchurian comrades. Kim's younger brother Kim Yeongju was there, but not his widow Kim Seongae or her sons.

There would be no reminder of that branch of the family, no one to challenge the notion that Jong Il was his successor. The limousine took two turns around Kim Il Sung Square, drove past Kim Il Sung University, past the 30-metre-tall (100 ft) gold statue of Kim and through the great triumphal arch built to commemorate his sixtieth birthday. His body was laid to rest at his former residence at the Kumsusan Palace, which now became a mausoleum.[50]

In 1998 his son proclaimed Kim Il Sung the 'Eternal President'. Three decades after his death he remains the President, his birthday is still the most important national holiday and his birth in 1912 remains year one of the 'Juche calendar', adopted in 1997. His face is still ubiquitous, his thought authoritative and his grandson Kim Jong Un rules the DPRK with absolute authority. That Kim Il Sung still dominates North Korea a generation after his death, that the political system he shaped remains intact, that he is still held in such reverence that only he can be referred to by the exulted term Great Leader (*widaehan suryeongnim*) and that a direct descendant of his rules is truly remarkable. No dictator in modern times has been so successful in arranging his succession and perpetuating his rule beyond his death.

Kim Il Sung's death brought the end of a remarkable half-century of rule. Few people succeeded in shaping a society to the extent that he did. His impact on North Korea can hardly be exaggerated. His rule had been exceptionally long, the longest of any modern dictator (broken only by Fidel Castro a few months before he stepped down in 2006). Kim ruled a decade longer than Lenin and Stalin combined, and nearly twice as long as Mao Zedong. He was both the founder of the state and its only ruler. When he died he was for the vast majority of North Koreans the only ruler they had ever known.

Yet Kim Il Sung was, by his own measurements for success, a failure. He left behind a country that was poor, hungry and isolated. The last years of his rule saw the country move from stagnation to economic decline, from one setback to another. For decades he portrayed the DPRK as the vanguard of progress for the entire Korean nation, North and South. By 1994, however, the North Korean regime no longer had much to offer Koreans outside its borders. Observers abroad were now waiting for the collapse of North Korea, and its absorption by the South was seen as likely if not inevitable. Kim Il Sung's goal was to create a unified, prosperous, strong, independent and progressive nation. He left behind a country that was divided, a division that he had hardened rather than undermined. And far from making North Korea an example of progress and prosperity, he left it the poorest of industrial nations, an international pariah whose people suffered from widespread malnutrition.

References

1 EXILED YOUTH

1 These are also rendered Paekche and Koguryo, respectively, in English.
2 Kim Il Sung, *With the Century*, vol. I (Pyongyang, 1993), p. 3.
3 Ki-baik Lee, *A New History of Korea*, trans. Edward W. Wagner and Edward J. Shultz (Cambridge, MA, 1984), p. 266.
4 Korean Friendship Association, 'Ardent Patriot Kim Ung U', *KFAUSA Newsletter*, https://kfausa.org/ardent-patriot-kim-ung-u, 24 June 2014.
5 Kim Il Sung, *With the Century*, vol. I, p. 9.
6 Ibid., p. 5.
7 Ibid., pp. 6–7.
8 Wada Haruki, *Kim Il Sŏng-gwa Manju chŏnchaeng* [Kim Il Sung and the Manchurian War] (Seoul, 1992), p. 26.
9 Kim Il Sung, *With the Century*, vol. I, p. 8.
10 Ibid., p. 17.
11 Ibid., pp. 7–8.
12 Yong-ho Choe, 'Christian Background in the Early Life of Kim Il-Song', *Asian Survey*, XXVI/10 (1986), p. 1085.
13 Kim Il Sung, *With the Century*, vol. I, p. 12.
14 Dae-Sook Suh, *Kim Il Sung: The North Korean Leader* (New York, 1988), p. 5.
15 Kim Il Sung, *With the Century*, vol. I, p. 12.
16 See Kang Myongdo testimony compiled by Tae Won-ki, in the twelve-part series in *Joongang Ilbo*, starting 12 April 1995 (see Bradley Martin, *Under the Loving Care of the Fatherly Leader* (New York, 2006), p. 500).
17 Kim Il Sung, *With the Century*, vol. II (Pyongyang, 1993), pp. 445–6.
18 Ibid., vol. I, pp. 32–3.
19 Ibid., pp. 12, 37–8.
20 Charles K. Armstrong, *The North Korean Revolution, 1945–1950* (Ithaca, NY, 2003), p. 18.
21 Owen Lattimore, *Manchuria: Cradle of Conflict* (New York, 1932), pp. 224–5.
22 Ibid., p. 239.
23 Ibid., p. 241.
24 Alyssa Park, *Sovereignty Experiments: Korean Migrants and the Building of Borders in Northeast Asia, 1860–1945* (Ithaca, NY, 2019).
25 Ibid., p. 79.

26 Seomin Kim, *Ginseng and Borderland: Territorial Boundaries and Political Relations between Qing China and Chosŏn Korea, 1636–1912* (Oakland, CA, 2017), pp. 157–8.
27 Kim Il Sung, *With the Century*, vol. I, p. 64.
28 Ibid., p. 66.
29 Jae-Cheon Lim, *Leader Symbols and Personality Cult in North Korea: The Leader State* (London, 2015), p. 57.
30 Wada, *Kim Il Sŏng-gwa Manju chŏnchaeng*, p. 30.
31 Kim Il Sung, *With the Century*, vol. I, p. 90.
32 Ibid., p. 82.
33 'The 1,000-Ri Journey of National Liberation', *Korea Today*, 306 (March 1982), p. 37.
34 Kim Il Sung, *With the Century*, vol. I, p. 75.
35 Ibid., pp. 134, 150, 171.
36 Ibid., p. 73.
37 Ibid., p. 90.
38 Ibid., pp. 213, 219.
39 Suh, *Kim Il Sung*, pp. 7–8.
40 Kim Il Sung, *With the Century*, vol. I, p. 173.
41 Wada, *Kim Il Sŏng-gwa Manju chŏnchaeng*, p. 34.
42 Kim Il Sung, *With the Century*, vol. I, p. 259.
43 Wada, *Kim Il Sŏng-gwa Manju chŏnchaeng*, pp. 41–2.
44 Sydney Seiler, *Kim Il-song, 1941–1948: The Creation of a Legend, the Building of a Regime* (Lanham, MD, 1994), p. 66.
45 Fyodor Tertitskiy, 'The Personal File of Jin Richeng (Kim Il-sung): New Information on the Early Years of the First Ruler of North Korea', *Acta Koreana*, XXII/1 (2019), pp. 111–28.
46 Kim Il Sung, *With the Century*, vol. I, p. 10.
47 Choe, 'Christian Background in the Early Life of Kim Il-Song', pp. 1082–91.
48 Kim Il Sung, *With the Century*, vol. I, p. 103.
49 Ibid., p. 102.
50 Ibid., pp. 102–3.
51 Ibid., p. 238.
52 Ibid., vol. II, p. 190.
53 Choe, 'Christian Background in the Early Life of Kim Il-Song', p. 1089.
54 Ibid., pp. 1089–90.
55 Fyodor Tertitskiy, *Kim Ilseong Jeon'gi* [A Biography of Kim Il Sung] (Paju, 2022), p. 29.
56 Ibid., p. 30.

2 THE GUERILLA FIGHTER

1 Andrei Lankov, *From Stalin to Kim Il Sung: The Formation of North Korea, 1945–1960* (New Brunswick, NJ, 2002), p. 53, n. 7.
2 Chong-Sik Lee, *The Korean Workers' Party: A Short History* (Stanford, CA, 1978), pp. 19–20.

3 Ibid., pp. 20–29.
4 Gi-Wook Shin, *Peasant Protest and Social Change in Colonial Korea* (Seattle, WA, 2014), pp. 75–91.
5 Nam Koon Woo, *The North Korean Communist Leadership, 1945–1965: A Study of Factionalism and Political Consolidation* (Tuscaloosa, AL, 1974), p. 45; Zhihua Shen and Danhui Li, *After Leaning to One Side: China and Its Allies in the Cold War* (Stanford, CA, 2011), pp. 52–3.
6 Anthony Coogan, 'Northeast China and the Origins of the Anti-Japanese United Front', *Modern China*, XX/3 (1994), pp. 283–314.
7 Wada Haruki, *Kim Il Sŏng-gwa Manju chŏnchaeng* [Kim Il Sung and the Manchurian War] (Seoul, 1992), p. 109.
8 Fyodor Tertitskiy, *Kim Ilseong Jeon'gi* [A Biography of Kim Il Sung] (Paju, 2022), p. 33.
9 Hongkoo Han, 'Colonial Origins of Juche: The Minsaengdan Incident of the 1930s and the Birth of the North Korea–China Relationship', in *Origins of North Korea's Juche*, ed. Jae-Jung Suh (Lanham, MD, 2012), pp. 37–63.
10 Wada, *Kim Il Sŏng-gwa Manju chŏnchaeng*, pp. 41–2.
11 Party History Institute, *Brief History of the Revolutionary Activities of Comrade Kim Il Sung* (Pyongyang, 1969), p. 42.
12 Charles K. Armstrong, *The North Korean Revolution, 1945–1950* (Ithaca, NY, 2003), pp. 33–45.
13 Ibid., p. 35.
14 Jae-Cheon Lim, *Leader Symbols and Personality Cult in North Korea* (London, 2015), p. 62.
15 Armstrong, *The North Korean Revolution*, pp. 33–4.
16 Yi Yong-sang, *Sam Saek ŭi Kunbok* [Three Colors of a Military Uniform] (Seoul, 1994), p. 259.
17 Tertitskiy, *Kim Ilseong Jeon'gi*, pp. 34–5.
18 Kim Il Sung, *With the Century*, vol. IV (Pyongyang, 1993), p. 53.
19 Ibid., p. 23.
20 Armstrong, *The North Korean Revolution*, p. 22; Kim Sŏngho, *1930 Minsaengdan sagŏn yŏn'gu* [The Minsaengdan Incident in Yanbian in the 1930s] (Seoul, 1999).
21 Kim Hakjoon, *Dynasty: The Hereditary Succession Politics of North Korea* (Stanford, CA, 2015), pp. 32–3.
22 Han, 'Colonial Origins of Juche'.
23 Armstrong, *The North Korean Revolution*, p. 29.
24 Kim Il Sung, *With the Century*, vol. IV, p. 27.
25 Ibid., p. 30.
26 Ibid., pp. 303–30.
27 *Hangil ppaljjisan ch'angaja dŭl ŭi hoesanggi* [Recollections of the Participants in the Anti-Japanese Armed Struggle] (Pyongyang, 1959–69); see Suzy Kim, *Everyday Life in the North Korean Revolution, 1945–1950* (Ithaca, NY, 2013), p. 270, n. 101.
28 Armstrong, *The North Korean Revolution*, p. 23.

29 Wada, *Kim Il Sŏng-gwa Manju chŏnchaeng*, pp. 158–9.
30 Lankov, *From Stalin to Kim Il Sung*, p. 53; Dae-Sook Suh, *Kim Il Sung: The North Korean Leader* (New York, 1988), p. 36.
31 Kim Il Sung, *With the Century*, vol. VII (Pyongyang, 1993), p. 167.
32 *Korea Today*, 173 (January 1971), p. 8.
33 Kim Il Sung, *With the Century*, vol. VI, p. 169.
34 Suh, *Kim Il Sung*, p. 35.
35 Ibid., p. 37.
36 Wada, *Kim Il Sŏng-gwa Manju chŏnchaeng*, p. 161.
37 Suh, *Kim Il Sung*, pp. 35–7.
38 Robert Scalapino and Chong-Sik Lee, *Communism in Korea* (Berkeley, CA, 1972), p. 202.
39 Kim Il Sung, *With the Century*, vol. VII, p. 124.
40 Ibid., p. 132.
41 Kim Kwang-un, *Pukhan Chŏngch'i yŏn'gu* [Studies of North Korean Political History], vol. I (Seoul, 2003), pp. 106–7.
42 Wada, *Kim Il Sŏng-gwa Manju chŏnchaeng*, p. 172.
43 Kim Hakjoon, *Dynasty*, p. 34.
44 Suh, *Kim Il Sung*, p. 37.
45 Tertitskiy, *Kim Ilseong Jeon'gi*, p. 43.
46 Fyodor Tertitskiy, 'The Personal File of Jin Richeng (Kim Il-sung): New Information on the Early Years of the First Ruler of North Korea', *Acta Koreana*, XXII/1 (2019), pp. 111–28.
47 Lankov, *From Stalin to Kim Il Sung*, p. 54.
48 Ibid., pp. 54–5.
49 Charles Armstrong, 'Centering the Periphery: Manchurian Exile(s) and the North Korean State', *Korean Studies*, XIX (1995), pp. 1–16.
50 Fyodor Tertitskiy, unpublished manuscript.
51 Lankov, *From Stalin to Kim Il Sung*, pp. 56–7.
52 Tertitskiy, *Kim Ilseong Jeon'gi*, p. 59.
53 Ibid., pp. 61–2.
54 Ibid., p. 63.

3 THE CHOSEN ONE

1 Kim Kwang-un, *Pukhan Chŏngch'i yŏn'gu* [Studies of North Korean Political History], vol. I (Seoul, 2003), p. 95.
2 Jungsoo Lee, *The Partition of Korea After World War II: A Global History* (New York, 2006), pp. 40–42.
3 Charles Armstrong, *The North Korean Revolution* (Ithaca, NY, 2003), p. 41.
4 Andrei Lankov, *From Stalin to Kim Il Sung: The Formation of North Korea, 1945–1960* (New Brunswick, NJ, 2002), p. 3.
5 Kim Sŏng-bo, *Pukhan ŭi yŏksa*, vol. I: *Kŏn'guk kwa inminjujuŭi ŭi kyŏnghyŏm* [North Korean History, vol. I: Establishment and Experience of the People's Democracy] (Seoul, 2011), p. 31.
6 Armstrong, *The North Korean Revolution*, p. 55.

7 Dae-Sook Suh, *Kim Il Sung: The North Korean Leader* (New York, 1988), p. 127.
8 Lankov, *From Stalin to Kim Il Sung*, p. 17.
9 Armstrong, *The North Korean Revolution*, p. 58.
10 Suh, *Kim Il Sung*, p. 61.
11 Kim Kwang-un, *Pukhan Chŏngch'i yŏn'gu*, vol. I, pp. 116–21.
12 Ibid., p. 121.
13 Fyodor Tertitskiy, *Kim Ilseong Jeon'gi* [A Biography of Kim Il Sung] (Paju, 2022), p. 78.
14 Lankov, *From Stalin to Kim Il Sung*, p. 18.
15 Estimates of the number of those attending varies considerably.
16 Lankov, *From Stalin to Kim Il Sung*, pp. 19–20; Tertitskiy, *Kim Ilseong Jeon'gi*, pp. 94–5.
17 Tertitskiy, *Kim Ilseong Jeon'gi*, p. 4.
18 Fyodor Tertitskiy, 'Will the Real Kim Il Sung Please Stand Up?', *NK News*, www.nknews.org, 18 July 2022.
19 Lankov, *From Stalin to Kim Il Sung*, p. 7.
20 Tertitskiy, *Kim Ilseong Jeon'gi*, p. 84.
21 Lankov, *From Stalin to Kim Il Sung*, pp. 18–19.
22 Ibid., p. 18, n. 33.
23 Kim Kwang-un, *Pukhan Chŏngch'i yŏn'gu*, vol. I, p. 152.
24 Suh, *Kim Il Sung*, p. 70.
25 Shin Jongdae, 'North Korean State-Making: Process and Characteristics', in *The Routledge Handbook of Modern Korean History*, ed. Michael Seth (London, 2016), pp. 197–210.
26 Suh, *Kim Il Sung*, p. 71.
27 Fyodor Tertitskiy, *Kim Ilseong Jeon'gi*, p. 103.
28 Ibid., pp. 86–7.
29 Erik Van Ree, *Socialism in One Zone: Stalin's Policy in Korea, 1945–1947* (Oxford, 1989), p. 59.
30 Armstrong, *The North Korean Revolution*, p. 59.
31 Suh, *Kim Il Sung*, p. 69.
32 Kim Kwang-un, *Pukhan Chŏngch'i yŏn'gu*, vol. I, p. 372.
33 Hwang Chang-yŏp, *Na nŭn yŏk-sa ŭi chilli rŭl poatta* [I Saw the Truth of History] (Seoul, 1999).
34 Armstrong, *The North Korean Revolution*, p. 134.
35 Jae-Cheon Lim, *Leader Symbols and Personality Cult in North Korea* (London, 2015), p. 79.
36 Armstrong, *The North Korean Revolution*, p. 223.
37 Ibid., p. 228.
38 Kim Hakjoon, *Dynasty: The Hereditary Succession Politics of North Korea* (Stanford, CA, 2015), p. 42; Armstrong, *The North Korean Revolution*, p. 226.
39 Armstrong, *The North Korean Revolution*, p. 171.
40 Lankov, *From Stalin to Kim Il Sung*, pp. 34–6.

41 Suh, *Kim Il Sung*, p. 102.
42 Kim Kwang-un, *Pukhan Chŏngch'i yŏn'gu*, vol. I, p. 577.
43 Lankov, *From Stalin to Kim Il Sung*, pp. 37–8.
44 Owen Miller, 'North Korea's Hidden History', *International Socialism*, 109 (2006), pp. 153–66.
45 Kim Seong-bo [Kim Sŏng-bo], 'The Decision-Making Process and Implementation of the North Korean Land Reform', in *Landlords, Peasants, and Intellectuals in Modern Korea*, ed. Pang Kie-Chung and Michael D. Shin (Ithaca, NY, 2005), pp. 207–41.
46 Kim Sŏng-bo, *Pukhan ŭi yŏksa*, vol. I, pp. 232–4.
47 Armstrong, *The North Korean Revolution*, p. 91.
48 Suzy Kim, *Everyday Life in the North Korean Revolution, 1945–1950* (Ithaca, NY, 2013), p. 119.
49 Armstrong, *The North Korean Revolution*, p. 148.
50 Kim, *Everyday Life in the North Korean Revolution*, pp. 221–2.
51 Sŏ Tongman, *Puk chosŏn sahoejuui ch'eje sŏngnipsa, 1945–1961* [History of the Establishment of the North Korean Socialist System, 1945–1961] (Seoul, 1998).
52 Much of the work of Charles Armstrong has been discredited by incidents of plagiarism, but his original studies of the Soviet occupation still remain useful.
53 Armstrong, *The North Korean Revolution*, p. 220.
54 Chŏng Ch'ang-hyŏn, *Kyŏt'esŏ pon Kim Chŏng-il* [Kim Jong Il as Seen by an Entourage] (Seoul, 2000), p. 72.
55 Tertitskiy, *Kim Ilseong Jeon'gi*, p. 107.

4 FAILED REUNIFICATION

1 Wada Haruki, *The Korean War: An International History* (Lanham, MD, 2014), p. 3.
2 Kathryn Weathersby, 'Korea, 1945–50, To Attack, or Not to Attack? Stalin, Kim Il Sung, and the Prelude to War', *Cold War International History Project Bulletin*, 5 (Spring 1995), pp. 1–9.
3 Ibid., p. 8.
4 Ibid., p. 9.
5 Erik Van Ree, *Socialism in One Zone: Stalin's Policy in Korea, 1945–1947* (Oxford, 1989), p. 180.
6 Wada, *The Korean War*, p. 31.
7 Shen Zhihua and Danhui Li, *After Leaning to One Side: China and Its Allies in the Cold War* (Stanford, CA, 2011), p. 25.
8 Kim Kwang-un, *Pukhan Chŏngch'i yŏn'gu* [Studies of North Korean Political History], vol. I (Seoul, 2003), p. 577.
9 Wada, *The Korean War*, pp. 39–40.
10 Ibid., p. 35.
11 Dae-Sook Suh, *Kim Il Sung: The North Korean Leader* (New York, 1988), p. 121.

12 Chŏng Ch'ang-hyŏn, *Kyŏt'esŏ pon Kim Chŏng-il* [Kim Jong Il as Seen by an Entourage] (Seoul, 2000), p. 78.
13 Fyodor Tertitskiy, *Kim Ilseong Jeon'gi* [A Biography of Kim Il Sung] (Paju, 2022), p. 98.
14 Ibid., pp. 132–3.
15 'Telegram from Stalin to Shtykov', 30 January 1950, Wilson Center Digital Archive, Washington, DC, https://digitalarchive.wilsoncenter.org, accessed 5 March 2025.
16 'Ciphered Telegram, Shtykov to Comrade Stalin', 31 January 1950, Wilson Center Digital Archive, Washington, DC, https://digitalarchive.wilsoncenter.org, accessed 5 March 2025.
17 Adrian Buzo, *The Guerilla Dynasty: Politics and Leadership in the DPRK, 1945–1994* (Sydney, 1999), p. 77.
18 Weathersby, 'Korea, 1945–50, To Attack, or Not to Attack?', pp. 1–9.
19 Ibid., pp. 7–8.
20 Chen Jian, *China's Road to the Korean War: The Making of the Sino-American Confrontation* (New York, 1994), p. 112.
21 Shen and Li, *After Leaning to One Side*, pp. 24, 32.
22 'Telegram from Shtykov to Vyshinsky', 30 May 1950, Wilson Center Digital Archive, Washington, DC, https://digitalarchive.wilsoncenter.org, accessed 5 March 2025.
23 Andrei Lankov, *From Stalin to Kim Il Sung: The Formation of North Korea, 1945–1960* (New Brunswick, NJ, 2002), p. 61.
24 Tertitskiy, *Kim Ilseong Jeon'gi*, p. 142.
25 Callum A. MacDonald, 'So Terrible a "Liberation": The UN Occupation of North Korea', *Bulletin of Concerned Asian Scholars*, XXIII/2 (1991), pp. 6–7, 17.
26 Wada, *The Korean War*, p. 100.
27 Ibid., p. 105.
28 Ibid., pp. 107–8.
29 Ibid., p. 108.
30 Shu Guang Zhang, *Mao's Military Romanticism: China and the Korean War, 1950–1953* (Lawrence, KS, 1995), p. 73.
31 Wada, *The Korean War*, pp. 112–14.
32 'Ciphered Telegram from DPRK leader Kim Il Sung and South Korean Communist Leader Pak Heon-yeong to Stalin (via Shtykov)', 29 September 1950, Wilson Center Digital Archive, Washington, DC, https://digitalarchive.wilsoncenter.org, accessed 5 March 2025.
33 Tertitskiy, *Kim Ilseong Jeon'gi*, p. 146.
34 Chen, *China's Road to the Korean War*, pp. 161–3.
35 Ibid., pp. 172–3.
36 Ibid., p. 188.
37 Alexandre Mansourov, 'Stalin, Mao, Kim and China's Decision to Enter the Korean War, September 16–October 15, 1950', *Cold War International History Project*, 6–7 (Winter 1995), pp. 94–107.

38 Chen, *China's Road to the Korean War*, p. 161.
39 Ibid., p. 162.
40 Wada, *The Korean War*, p. 127.
41 Kang Chŏng-gu, 'Han'guk chŏnchaeng kwa pukhan sahoechuŭi kŏnsŏl [The Korean War and the Construction of North Korean Society]', in *Han'guk chŏnchaeng kwa nampukhan sahoe ŭi kuchojŏk pyŏnhwa* [The Korean War and Structural Change in North and South Korean Society], ed. Son Ho-ch'ŏl et al. (Seoul, 1991), p. 170.
42 Suh, *Kim Il Sung*, p. 122.
43 Zhang, *Mao's Military Romanticism*, p. 121.
44 Ibid., p. 132.
45 Ibid.
46 Ibid., pp. 57–8.
47 Shen and Li, *After Leaning to One Side*, pp. 79–80.
48 Kathryn Weathersby, 'From the Russian Archives: New Findings on the Korean War', *Cold War International History Project Bulletin*, 3 (Fall 1993), p. 16.
49 Suh, *Kim Il Sung*, p. 138.
50 Wada, *The Korean War*, pp. 182–3.
51 Shen and Li, *After Leaning to One Side*, p. 91.
52 Kathryn Weathersby, 'New Russian Documents on the Korean War, Introduction and Translations', *Cold War International History Project Bulletin*, 6–7 (Winter 1995–6), p. 77.
53 Wada, *The Korean War*, pp. 281–2.
54 Kang Chŏng-gu, 'Han'guk chŏnchaeng kwa pukhan sahoechuŭi kŏnsŏl', p. 174.
55 Conrad Crane, *American Airpower Strategy in Korea, 1950–1953* (Lawrence, KS, 2000), pp. 168–71.

5 CONSOLIDATION OF POWER, 1953–61

1 Andrei Lankov, *From Stalin to Kim Il Sung: The Formation of North Korea, 1945–1960* (New Brunswick, NJ, 2002), p. 62.
2 Wada Haruki, *The Korean War: An International History* (Lanham, MD, 2014), p. 205.
3 Lankov, *From Stalin to Kim Il Sung*, pp. 125–53.
4 Wada, *The Korean War*, p. 223.
5 Sŏ Tongman, *Puk chosŏn yŏn'gu* [Studies on North Korea] (Paju, 2010), p. 126.
6 Lankov, *From Stalin to Kim Il Sung*, pp. 92–3.
7 Nam Koon Woo, 'The Purge of the Southern Communists in North Korea: A Retrospective View', *Asian Forum*, V/1 (1973), pp. 43–54; Dae-Sook Suh, *Kim Il Sung: The North Korean Leader* (New York, 1988), p. 360.
8 Kim Sŏng-bo, *Pukhan ŭi yŏksa*, vol. 1: *Kŏn'guk kwa inminjujuŭi ŭi kyŏnghyŏm* [North Korean History, vol. 1: Establishment and Experience of the People's Democracy] (Seoul, 2011), pp. 154–5.

9 Lankov, *From Stalin to Kim Il Sung*, pp. 96–7.
10 Suh, *Kim Il Sung*, pp. 132–4.
11 Chin O. Chung, *Pyŏngyang between Peking and Moscow: North Korea's Involvement in the Sino-Soviet Dispute, 1958–1975* (Tuscaloosa, AL, 1978), p. 23.
12 Hwang Chang-yŏp, *Na nŭn yŏk-sa ŭi chilli rŭl poatta* [I Saw the Truth of History] (Seoul, 1999), p. 26.
13 Bazázs Szalontai, *Kim Il Sung in the Khrushchev Era: Soviet–DPRK Relations and the Roots of North Korean Despotism, 1953–1964* (Stanford, CA, 2006), p. 43.
14 Suh, *Kim Il Sung*, p. 40.
15 George Ginsburgs, 'Soviet Development Grants and Aid to North Korea, 1945–1980', *Asia Pacific Community*, 18 (Fall 1982), pp. 42–63.
16 Joel Kotlin and Charles Armstrong, 'A Socialist Regional Order in Northeast Asia after World War II', in *Korea at the Center: Dynamics of Regionalism in Northeast Asia*, ed. Charles K. Armstrong et al. (Armonk, NY, 2006), p. 121.
17 Sŏng Hye-rang, *Tŭngnamu chip: Sŏng Hye-rang Chasŏjŏn* [Wisteria House: The Autobiography of Song Hye-rang] (Seoul, 2000), p. 258.
18 Andrei Lankov, *Crisis in North Korea: The Failure of De-Stalinization, 1956* (Honolulu, HI, 2005), p. 179.
19 Fyodor Tertitskiy, *Kim Ilseong Jeon'gi* [A Biography of Kim Il Sung], (Paju, 2022), p. 171.
20 Zhihua Shen and Danhui Li, *After Leaning to One Side: China and Its Allies in the Cold War* (Stanford, CA, 2011), p 71.
21 Robert Scalapino and Chong-sik Lee, *Communism in Korea* (Berkeley, CA, 1972), pp. 497–503.
22 Szalontai, *Kim Il Sung in the Khrushchev Era*, pp. 72–3.
23 Sheila Miyoshi Jager, *Brothers at War: The Unending Conflict in Korea* (New York, 2013), p. 360.
24 Lankov, *Crisis in North Korea*, pp. 62–3: Sŏ Tongman, *Puk chosŏn yŏn'gu*, pp. 130–35.
25 Lankov, *From Stalin to Kim Il Sung*, p. 57.
26 Ibid., pp. 57–8.
27 Tertitskiy, *Kim Ilseong Jeon'gi*, pp. 185–6.
28 'Report by N. T. Fedorenko on a Meeting with DPRK Ambassador to the USSR Ri Sang-jo', 30 May 1956, Wilson Center Digital Archive, Washington, DC, https://digitalarchive.wilsoncenter.org, accessed 5 March 2025; James Person, '"We Need Help from Outside": The North Korean Opposition Movement of 1956', Cold War International History Project Working Paper 52 (August 2006), pp. 2–85, available at www.wilsoncenter.org.
29 Person, '"We Need Help from Outside"'.
30 Lankov, *From Stalin to Kim Il Sung*, p. 166.
31 'Notes from a Conversation between the 1st Secretary of the PRL Embassy in the DPRK with Comrade Pimenov, 1st Secretary of the Embassy of

the USSR, on 15. X.1957', 16 October 1957, Wilson Center Digital Archive, Washington, DC, https://digitalarchive.wilsoncenter.org, accessed 5 March 2025.

32 Tertitskiy, *Kim Ilseong Jeon'gi*, p. 198.

33 Hwang, *Na nŭn yŏk-sa ŭi chilli rŭl poatta*, p. 109.

34 Szalontai, *Kim Il Sung in the Khrushchev Era*, p. 102.

35 Andrei Lankov, 'Kim Takes Control: The "Great Purge" in North Korea, 1956–1960', *Korean Studies*, XXVI/1 (2002), pp. 92–3.

36 'Notes from a Conversation between the 1st Secretary of the PRL Embassy in the DPRK and Comrade Samsonov, 1st Secretary of the Embassy of the USSR on 20.XII.1956', 24 December 1956, Wilson Center Digital Archive, Washington, DC, https://digitalarchive.wilsoncenter.org, accessed 5 March 2025.

37 Szalontai, *Kim Il Sung in the Khrushchev Era*, p. 114.

38 Suh, *Kim Il Sung*, p. 521.

39 Nam, 'The Purge of the Southern Communists in North Korea', pp. 113–24.

40 Lankov, *Crisis in North Korea*, p. 181.

41 Ibid., pp. 181–3; Andrei Lankov, *North of the DMZ: Essays on Daily Life in North Korea* (Jefferson, NC, 2007), p. 68.

42 Lankov, *Crisis in North Korea*, p. 180.

43 Lankov, *North of the DMZ*, p. 67.

44 Suh, *Kim Il Sung*, p. 174.

45 Jae-Cheon Lim, *Leader Symbols and Personality Cult in North Korea* (London, 2015), p. 65.

46 Lankov, *Crisis in North Korea*, p. 205.

47 Lim, *Leader Symbols and Personality Cult in North Korea*, p. 22.

48 Heonik Kwon and Byung-ho Chung, *North Korea: Beyond Charismatic Politics* (Lanham, MD, 2012), p. 16.

49 Hwang, *Na nŭn yŏk-sa ŭi chilli rŭl poatta*, pp. 102–3.

50 Lankov, *North of the DMZ*, p. 279.

51 Lankov, *Crisis in North Korea*, p. 217.

52 Kim Sŏng-bo, *Pukhan ŭi yŏksa*, vol. I, p. 212.

53 Robert Scalapino, 'Korea: The Politics of Change', *Asian Survey*, III/1 (January 1963), pp. 31–40, 63.

54 'Kangson, Home of the Chollima', *Korea Today*, 241 (September 1976), pp. 25–32; Joan Robinson, 'Korean Miracle', *Monthly Review*, XVI/9 (January 1965), pp. 541–9.

55 Chung, *Pyŏngyang between Peking and Moscow*, p. 33, n. 169.

56 Ilpyong J. Kim, *Historical Dictionary of North Korea* (Lanham, MD, 2003), p. 24.

57 Bon-Hak Koo, *Political Economy of Self-Reliance: Juche and Economic Development in North Korea, 1961–1990* (Seoul, 1992), p. 85.

58 Yim Sang-chŏl, *Pukhan nongŏp* [North Korean Agriculture] (Seoul, 2000), p. 35.

59 Hy-Sang Lee, *North Korea: A Strange Socialist Fortress* (Westport, CT, 2001), p. 65.
60 Chung, *Pyŏngyang between Peking and Moscow*, p. 170, n. 42.
61 'Chongsan-ri: A Historic Village', *Korea Today*, 221 (January 1975), pp. 46–48; Suh, *Kim Il Sung*, p. 167.
62 Chung, *Pyŏngyang between Peking and Moscow*, p. 36.
63 Mun Woong Lee, *Rural North Korea under Communism: A Study of Sociocultural Change* (Houston, TX, 1976), p. 100.
64 Yong Soon Kim, 'Language Reform as a Political Symbol in North Korea', *Stanford Journal of East Asian Affairs*, CXLII/3 (1980), pp. 216–35.
65 Chung, *Pyŏngyang between Peking and Moscow*, p. 33.
66 Ibid., p. 38.
67 Jager, *Brothers at War*, p. 360.
68 Tertitskiy, *Kim Ilseong Jeon'gi*, p. 164.
69 Chŏng Ch'ang-hyŏn, *Kyŏt'esŏ pon Kim Chŏng-il* [Kim Jong Il as Seen by an Entourage] (Seoul, 2000), p. 77.
70 Ibid., p. 78.
71 Ibid., pp. 78–9. Other sources believe they married in 1953 or that they were already married when they moved back to Pyongyang.
72 Lankov, *Crisis in North Korea*, pp. 70–71.
73 Nam, 'The Purge of the Southern Communists in North Korea', pp. 121–2; Lankov, *Crisis in North Korea*, p. 208.
74 Suh, *Kim Il Sung*, pp. 171–2.
75 Jae-Cheon Lim, *Kim Jong Il's Leadership of North Korea* (London, 2009), pp. 91–2.

6 DIPLOMAT, MILITANT, GREAT THINKER

1 Byung Chul Koh, *The Foreign Policy Systems of North and South Korea* (Berkeley, CA, 1984), p. 276.
2 Kim Hakjoon, *Dynasty: The Hereditary Succession Politics of North Korea* (Stanford, CA, 2015), p. 60.
3 Monikka Han, '1960 nyŏntae Pukhan-ŭi kyŏngche kukpang pyŏngchin nosŏn-ŭi ch'aet'aek-kwa taenam chŏngch'aek' [North Korea's Choice of the Simultaneous Economic-Military Strengthening Strategy and Its Policy towards South Korea]', *Yŏksa-wa hyŏnsil* [History and Reality], 50 (2003), pp. 133–64.
4 Dae-Sook Suh, *Kim Il Sung: The North Korean Leader* (New York, 1988), p. 215.
5 Hy-Sang Lee, *North Korea: A Strange Socialist Fortress* (Westport, CT, 2001), p. 54.
6 Sung-joo Han, 'North Korea's Security Policy and Military Strategy', in *North Korea Today*, ed. Robert A. Scalapino and Jun-Yop Kim (Berkeley, CA, 1983), pp. 144–63, 155.
7 Ibid., p. 51.

8 Joseph S. Chung, 'Economic Planning in North Korea', in *North Korea Today*, ed. Scalapino and Kim, pp. 164–88, 180.
9 Suh, *Kim Il Sung*, p. 178.
10 Chin O. Chung, *Pyŏngyang between Peking and Moscow: North Korea's Involvement in the Sino-Soviet Dispute, 1958–1975* (Tuscaloosa, AL, 1978), pp. 65–6.
11 Ibid., p. 86.
12 Ibid., p. 88.
13 Suh, *Kim Il Sung*, pp. 182–3.
14 Chung, *Pyŏngyang between Peking and Moscow*, pp. 88–90.
15 Bernd Schaefer, 'North Korean "Adventurism" and China's Long Shadow, 1966–1972', Cold War International History Project Working Paper 44 (October 2004), pp. 5, 9, available at www.wilsoncenter.org.
16 Suh, *Kim Il Sung*, pp. 192–3.
17 Sheila Miyoshi Jager, *Brothers at War: The Unending Conflict in Korea* (New York, 2013), p. 376.
18 Suh, *Kim Il Sung*, p. 221.
19 Jae-Cheon Lim, *Kim Jong Il's Leadership of North Korea* (London, 2009), pp. 38–9.
20 Ibid., p. 39.
21 Ibid., pp. 38–9.
22 Chŏng Ch'ang-yŏng, *Kyŏt esŏ pon Kim Chŏng-il* [Close Be Kim Jong Il] (Seoul, 2000), pp. 99–100.
23 Lim, *Kim Jong Il's Leadership of North Korea*, p. 42.
24 Sŏng Hye-rang, *Tŭngnamu chip: Sŏng Hye-rang Chasŏjŏn* [Wisteria House: The Autobiography of Song Hye-rang] (Seoul, 2000), pp. 312–17.
25 Lim, *Kim Jong Il's Leadership of North Korea*, p. 39.
26 Robert Collins, *Marked for Life: Songbun, North Korea's Social Classification System* (Washington, DC, 2012), available at www.hrnk.org.
27 Ibid.; Andrei Lankov, *North of the DMZ: Essays on Daily Life in North Korea* (Jefferson, NC, 2007), pp. 68–9.
28 Lankov, *North of the DMZ*, p. 31.
29 Lim, *Kim Jong Il's Leadership of North Korea*, p. 40.
30 Jae-Cheon Lim, *Leader Symbols and Personality Cult in North Korea* (London, 2015), p. 25.
31 Kim Hakjoon, *Dynasty*, p. 55.
32 Ibid., pp. 62, 64.
33 Lim, *Kim Jong Il's Leadership of North Korea*, p. 39.
34 Hwang, *Na nŭn yŏk-sa ŭi chilli rŭl poatta*, p. 115.
35 'What Are the "Ten Principles"?', *Daily NK*, www.dailynk.com, 9 August 2013.
36 Lim, *Kim Jong Il's Leadership of North Korea*, p. 72.
37 Koh, *The Foreign Policy Systems of North and South Korea*, pp. 123–4.
38 Kim Sŏng-bo, *Pukhan ŭi yŏksa*, vol. 1: *Kŏn'guk kwa inminjujuŭi ŭi kyŏnghyŏm* [North Korean History, vol. 1: Establishment and Experience of the People's Democracy] (Seoul, 2011), pp. 154–5.

39 Suh, *Kim Il Sung*, pp. 234–6.
40 Andrei Lankov, 'The Demise of Non-Communist Parties in North Korea (1945–1960)', *Journal of Cold War Studies*, III/1 (Winter 2001), pp. 103–25.
41 Mitchell Lerner, '"Mostly Propaganda in Nature": Kim Il Sung, the Juche Ideology and the Second Korean War', North Korea International Documentation Project Working Paper 3 (December 2010), available at www.wilsoncenter.org.
42 Suh, *Kim Il Sung*, p. 230.
43 Lim, *Kim Jong Il's Leadership of North Korea*, pp. 48–51.
44 Suh, *Kim Il Sung*, p. 230.
45 Fyodor Tertitskiy, *Kim Ilseong Jeon'gi* [A Biography of Kim Il Sung] (Paju, 2022), p. 222.
46 Han, '1960 nyŏntae Pukhan-ŭi kyŏngche kukpang pyŏngchin nosŏn-ŭi ch'aet'aek-kwa taenam chŏngch'aek', pp. 142–3.
47 Schaefer, 'North Korean "Adventurism" and China's Long Shadow', pp. 12–13.
48 Narushige Michishita, 'Calculated Adventurism: North Korea's Military-Diplomatic Campaigns', *Korean Journal of Defense Analysis*, XVI/2 (Fall 2004), pp. 188–97.
49 Soon Sung Cho, 'North and South Korea: Stepped-Up Aggression and the Search for New Security', *Asian Survey*, IX/1 (January 1969), pp. 29–32.
50 'Telegram from Pyongyang to Bucharest, TOP SECRET, No. 76.051, Urgent', 26 January 1968, Wilson Center Digital Archive, Washington, DC, https://digitalarchive.wilsoncenter.org, accessed 5 March 2025.
51 Kim Hakjoon, *Dynasty*, pp. 74–5.
52 Ibid., p. 75.
53 Lerner, '"Mostly Propaganda in Nature"'.

7 THE SUN KING

1 Robert Scalapino and Chong-sik Lee, *Communism in Korea* (Berkeley, CA, 1972), p. 662.
2 Fyodor Tertitskiy, *Kim Ilseong Jeon'gi* [A Biography of Kim Il Sung] (Paju, 2022) p. 276.
3 Scalapino and Lee, *Communism in Korea*, pp. 662–3.
4 Dae-Sook Suh, *Kim Il Sung: The North Korean Leader* (New York, 1988), p. 244.
5 Ibid., p. 245.
6 Scalapino and Lee, *Communism in Korea*, pp. 664–5.
7 Ibid., p. 665.
8 Ibid., p. 666.
9 Narushige Michishita, 'Calculated Adventurism: North Korea's Military-Diplomatic Campaigns', *Korean Journal of Defense Analysis*, XVI/2 (Fall 2004), pp. 188–97.
10 Suh, *Kim Il Sung*, p. 254.

11 Kim Hae-wŏn, *Pukhan ŭi Nambukkhan chŏngch'i hyŏpsang yŏn'gu* [Research on North Korea's Political Negotiations with South Korea] (Seoul, 2012), p. 71.
12 Robert R. Simmons, 'North Korea: Year of the Thaw', *Asian Survey*, XII/1 (January 1972), pp. 25–31.
13 Kim Hae-wŏn, *Pukhan ŭi Nambukkhan chŏngch'i hyŏpsang yŏn'gu*, pp. 71–2.
14 Suh, *Kim Il Sung*, p. 256.
15 'Memorandum, Hungarian Foreign Ministry', 16 February 1976, Wilson Center Digital Archive, Washington, DC, https://digitalarchive.wilsoncenter.org, accessed 5 March 2025.
16 Chong-sik Lee, 'The Evolution of North–South Korean Relations', in *North Korea in a Regional and Global Context*, ed. Robert A. Scalapino and Hongkoo Lee (Berkeley, CA, 1986), pp. 115–32.
17 Byung Chul Koh, *The Foreign Policy Systems of North and South Korea* (Berkeley, CA, 1984), p. 286.
18 Yongho Kim, *North Korean Foreign Policy: Security Dilemma and Succession* (Lanham, MD, 2011), p. 102.
19 Koh, *The Foreign Policy Systems of North and South Korea*, p. 288.
20 Andrei Lankov, *North of the DMZ: Essays on Daily Life in North Korea* (Jefferson, NC, 2007), p. 7.
21 Kim Sŏng-bo, *Pukhan ŭi yŏksa*, vol. II: *Chuch'e Sasang kwa yuilch'eje* [North Korean History, vol. II: Juche and the Monolithic Ideological System] (Seoul, 2011), p. 75.
22 Jae-Cheon Lim, *Kim Jong Il's Leadership of North Korea* (London, 2009), p. 63.
23 Christopher Hale, 'Multifunctional Juche: A Study of the Changing Dynamic between Juche and the State Constitution in North Korea', *Korea Journal*, XLII/3 (September 2002), pp. 283–308.
24 Allan Bouc, 'A Visit to North Korea', *New York Times*, 14 June 1971.
25 Benedict S. David, 'Visitor to North Korea Describes Vast Building Drive', *New York Times*, 10 August 1971.
26 Harrison Salisbury, *To Peking and Beyond: A Report on the New Asia* (New York, 1973), p. 200.
27 John H. Lee, 'By Any Standards Industry Is Powerful', *New York Times*, 4 June 1972.
28 Selig S. Harrison, *Korean Endgame: A Strategy for Reunification and U.S. Disengagement* (Princeton, NJ, 2002), p. 27.
29 Benjamin R. Young, *Guns, Guerillas, and the Great Leader: North Korea and the Third World* (Stanford, CA, 2019), p. 27.
30 Ibid., p. 75.
31 'Great Juche Idea Is Widespread among World People', *Korea Today*, 277 (September 1979), pp. 45–52.
32 Chŏng Ch'ang-hyŏn, *Kyŏt'esŏ pon Kim Chŏng-il* [Kim Jong Il as Seen by an Entourage] (Seoul, 2000), p. 115.

33 Kim Hakjoon, *Dynasty: The Hereditary Succession Politics of North Korea* (Stanford, CA, 2015), p. 77.
34 Lim, *Kim Jong Il's Leadership of North Korea*, p. 53.
35 Chŏng, *Kyŏt'esŏ pon Kim Chŏng-il*, p. 100.
36 Ibid., pp. 110–11.
37 Ibid., p. 111.
38 Ibid., pp. 111–12.
39 Lim, *Kim Jong Il's Leadership of North Korea*, p. 23.
40 Kim Hakjoon, *Dynasty*, p. 67.
41 Lim, *Kim Jong Il's Leadership of North Korea*, pp. 36–7.
42 Ibid., p. 42.
43 Alzo David-West, 'Nationalist Allegory in North Korea: The Revolutionary Opera "Sea of Blood"', *North Korean Review*, II/2 (2006), pp. 75–87.
44 Lim, *Kim Jong Il's Leadership of North Korea*, p. 70.
45 Kim Hakjoon, *Dynasty*, pp. 80–81; Lim, *Kim Jong Il's Leadership of North Korea*, p. 68.
46 Takashi Sakai, 'The Power Base of Kim Jong Il: Focusing on Its Formation Process', in *North Korea: Ideology, Politics, Economy*, ed. Han S. Park (Englewood Cliffs, NJ, 1996), pp. 105–22.
47 'Komdok: A Great Leap Ten Years', *Korea Today*, 346 (July 1985), p. 29.
48 Daniel Tudor and James Pearson, *North Korea Confidential: Private Markets, Fashion Trends, Prison Camps, Dissenters and Defectors* (Tokyo, 2015), p. 93.
49 Lim, *Kim Jong Il's Leadership of North Korea*, p. 54.
50 Ibid., p. 82.
51 Chŏng, *Kyŏt'esŏ pon Kim Chŏng-il*, pp. 201–2; Lim, *Kim Jong Il's Leadership of North Korea*, pp. 82–3.
52 Chŏng, *Kyŏt'esŏ pon Kim Chŏng-il*, p. 203.
53 Morgan E. Clippinger, 'Kim Jong Il in the North Korean Mass Media: A Study of Semi-Esoteric Communication', *Asian Survey*, XXI/3 (March 1981), pp. 289–309.
54 Ilpyong J. Kim, *Historical Dictionary of North Korea* (Lanham, MD, 2003), p. 114.
55 Author conversation with North Korean refugee, Seoul, May 2013.
56 This is confirmed by the author's experience meeting North Korean academics in the 1990s.
57 Lankov, *North of the DMZ*, p. 47.
58 Ibid., p. 35.
59 Ibid., pp. 207–8.
60 Mun Woong Lee, *Rural North Korea under Communism: A Study of Sociocultural Change* (Houston, TX, 1976), p. 54.
61 Lankov, *North of the DMZ*, pp. 173–4; Ralph Hassig and Kongdan Oh, *The Hidden People of North Korea: Everyday Life in the Hermit Kingdom* (Lanham, MD, 2009), p. 128.
62 Lankov, *North of the DMZ*, p. 181.

63 Ibid., pp. 170–71; Lim, *Kim Jong Il's Leadership of North Korea*, p. 73.
64 There is a large literature on the North Korean 'gulag'. One example is David Hawk, *The Hidden Gulag: The Lives and Voices of 'Those Who Are Sent to the Mountains'*, 2nd edn (Washington, DC, 2012).
65 Tertitskiy, *Kim Ilseong Jeon'gi*, p. 276.

8 STABILITY AND STAGNATION

1 Jae-Cheon Lim, *Kim Jong Il's Leadership of North Korea* (London, 2009), p. 83.
2 Ibid., p. 84.
3 Ibid., pp. 83–4.
4 Adrian Buzo, *The Guerilla Dynasty: Politics and Leadership in the DPRK, 1945–1994* (Sydney, 1999), p. 109.
5 Hwang Chang-yŏp, *Na nŭn yŏk-sa ŭi chilli rŭl poatta* [I Saw the Truth of History] (Seoul, 1999), pp. 115–16.
6 Bradley Martin, *Under the Loving Care of the Fatherly Leader* (New York, 2006), p. 156.
7 B. C. Koh, 'North Korea: Old Goals and New Realities', *Asian Survey*, XIV/1 (January 1974), pp. 36–42.
8 Sŏng Hye-rang, *Tŭngnamu chip: Sŏng Hye-rang Chasŏjŏn* [Wisteria House: The Autobiography of Song Hye-rang] (Seoul, 2000), pp. 471–3.
9 Jae-Cheon Lim, *Leader Symbols and Personality Cult in North Korea* (London, 2015), p. 39.
10 Sŏng, *Tŭngnamu chip*, p. 474.
11 Kim Hakjoon, 'The Hereditary Succession from Kim Jong-il to Kim Jong-un: Its Background, Present Situation, and Future', in *Troubled Transition: North Korea's Politics, Economy, and External Relations*, ed. Sang-hun Choe, Gi-Wook Shin and David Straub (Stanford, CA, 2013), pp. 229–59.
12 Lim, *Kim Jong Il's Leadership of North Korea*, p. 84.
13 Byung-Yeon Kim, Suk Jin and Keun Lee, 'Assessing the Economic Performance of North Korea, 1954–1989: Estimates and Growth Accounting Analysis', *Journal of Comparative Economics*, XXXV/3 (2007), pp. 564–82.
14 Young C. Kim, 'The Democratic People's Republic of Korea in 1975', *Asian Survey*, XVI/1 (January 1976), pp. 82–94.
15 Byung Chul Koh, 'The Impact of the Chinese Model on North Korea', *Asian Survey*, XVIII/6 (1978), pp. 626–43.
16 Young Whan Kihl, 'North Korea in 1983: Transforming "The Hermit Kingdom"', *Asian Survey*, XXIV/1 (January 1984), pp. 100–111.
17 Hy-Sang Lee, *North Korea: A Strange Socialist Fortress* (Westport, CT, 2001), pp. 138–9.
18 Andrei Lankov, *North of the DMZ: Essays on Daily Life in North Korea* (Jefferson, NC, 2007), pp. 84–7.
19 Yim Sang-chŏl, *Pukhan nongŏp* [North Korean Agriculture] (Seoul, 2000), pp. 24–35.

20 Tessa Morris-Suzuki, *Exodus to North Korea: Shadow from Japan's Cold War* (Lanham, MD, 2007), pp. 190–92, 235–6.
21 Kim Pyong-il, *Historical Dictionary of North Korea* (Lanham, MD, 2003), pp. 106–7.
22 Buzo, *The Guerilla Dynasty*, pp. 109–10.
23 Kim Pyong-il, *Historical Dictionary of North Korea*, pp. 50–51.
24 Young Whan Kihl, 'North Korea in 1984: "The Hermit Kingdom" Turns Outward!', *Asian Survey*, XXV/1 (January 1985), pp. 65–79.
25 Nadia Brazhanova, *Koro e sŏn Pukhan kyŏngje* [North Korean Economy at a Crossroads], trans. Yang Chun-yong (Seoul, 1992), p. 96.
26 Ibid., p. 97.
27 Adrian Buzo, *Politics and Leadership in North Korea: The Guerilla Dynasty*, 2nd revd edn (London, 2018), pp. 76–7.
28 Ibid., pp. 122, 140.
29 Koh, 'The Impact of the Chinese Model on North Korea', pp. 626–43.
30 Buzo, *Politics and Leadership in North Korea*, p. 77.
31 Paul Fischer, *A Kim Jong Il Production: The Extraordinary True Story of a Kidnapped Filmmaker, His Star Actress, and a Young Dictator's Rise to Power* (New York, 2015).
32 Martin, *Under the Loving Care of the Fatherly Leader*, p. 339.
33 Ibid., pp. 339–40.
34 'Miserable Aspects of South Korea', *Korea Today*, 348 (October 1985), pp. 42–5.
35 Buzo, *The Guerilla Dynasty*, pp. 123–4.
36 'South Korea – Danger Spot for the Olympiad', *Korea Today*, 357 (June 1986), p. 49.
37 Buzo, *The Guerilla Dynasty*, p. 150.
38 Byung Chul Koh, *The Foreign Policy Systems of North and South Korea* (Berkeley, CA, 1984), p. 224.
39 Dae-Sook Suh, *Kim Il Sung: The North Korean Leader* (New York, 1988), p. 288.
40 Martin, *Under the Loving Care of the Fatherly Leader*, p. 197.
41 Fyodor Tertitskiy, *Kim Ilseong Jeon'gi* [A Biography of Kim Il Sung] (Paju, 2022), p. 305.
42 Martin, *Under the Loving Care of the Fatherly Leader*, p. 195.
43 Ibid., p. 198.
44 Ibid., p. 199 (interview with Kim Young-song).
45 Ibid., p. 201.

9 FADING DREAM, FAILING STATE

1 Adrian Buzo, *The Guerilla Dynasty: Politics and Leadership in the DPRK, 1945–1994* (London, 2018), p. 188.
2 Ibid., p. 224.
3 Benjamin R. Young, *Guns, Guerillas, and the Great Leader: North Korea and the Third World* (Stanford, CA, 2019), p. 148.

4 Buzo, *The Guerilla Dynasty*, p. 178.
5 Kim Sŏng-bo, *Pukhan ŭi yŏksa*, vol. I: *Kŏn'guk kwa inminjujuŭi ŭi kyŏnghyŏm* [North Korean History, vol. I: Establishment and Experience of the People's Democracy] (Seoul, 2011), p. 258.
6 Jin Woong Kang, 'Historical Changes in North Korean Nationalism', *North Korean Review*, III/1 (2007), pp. 86–104.
7 John Jorganson, 'Tan'gun and the Legitimization of a Threatened Dynasty: North Korea's Rediscovery of Tan'gun', *Korea Observer*, XXVII/2 (1996), pp. 273–306.
8 Yong-ho Ch'oe, 'Reinterpreting Traditional History in North Korea', *Journal of Asian Studies*, XL/3 (May 1981), pp. 503–23.
9 *Korea Newsreview*, 16 October 1993, pp. 30–31.
10 Korean Central News Agency, 1 March 2000, BBC Worldwide Monitoring.
11 'Pyongyang: Capital of the Korean Nation', *Korea Today*, 2 (1995), p. 45.
12 Sung Minkyu, 'The Biopolitic of North Korea: Political Crisis, the Body and Visual Power', *Seoul Journal of Korean Studies*, XXVIII/2 (December 2015), pp. 231–57.
13 Buzo, *The Guerilla Dynasty*, pp. 214–15.
14 Chen Jian, 'Limits of the "Lips and Teeth" Alliance: An Historical Review of Chinese-North Korean Relations', in *Uneasy Allies: Fifty Years of China-North Korea Relations*, Woodrow Wilson International Center for Scholars, Asia Program Special Report No. 115 (September 2003).
15 Yongho Kim, *North Korean Foreign Policy: Security Dilemma and Succession* (Lanham, MD, 2011), p. 86.
16 John Merrill, 'North Korea in 1993: In the Eye of the Storm', *Asian Survey*, XXXIV/1 (January 1994), pp. 10–18.
17 Ibid., p. 18.
18 Buzo, *The Guerilla Dynasty*, p. 209.
19 Kim Il Sung, *With the Century*, vol. III (Pyongyang, 1993), pp. 421–2, cited in Bradley Martin, *Under the Loving Care of the Fatherly Leader* (New York, 2006), p. 500.
20 This is based on Natsios' interview with a North Korean defector; Andrew S. Natsios, *The Great North Korean Famine* (Washington, DC, 2001), p. 166.
21 Annie Eun Jung Kim, 'Thoughts on Hwang Jang-yup's Memoirs', *Daily NK*, www.dailynk.com, 11 July 2023.
22 See Kang Myongdo testimony compiled by Tae Won-ki, in the twelve-part series in *Joongang Ilbo*, starting 12 April 1995 (see Martin, *Under the Loving Care of the Fatherly Leader*, p. 500).
23 Natsios, *The Great North Korean Famine*, pp. 167–9.
24 One of these is from Oh Yung-nam, a former captain in the State Security from a prominent family who defected to the South; Martin, *Under the Loving Care of the Fatherly Leader*, p. 506.
25 Kim Il Sung, 'New Year's Address', 1 January 1994, available at www.marxists.org.

26 Joseph S. Bermudez, *The Armed Forces of North Korea* (London, 2001), pp. 222–31.
27 Ibid., pp. 231–3.
28 Victor Cha, *The Impossible State: North Korea, Past and Future* (New York, 2012), p. 233.
29 Ibid., pp. 249–50.
30 Kim Hae-wŏn, *Pukhan ŭi Nambukkhan chŏngch'i hyŏpsang yŏn'gu* [Research on North Korea's Political Negotiations with South Korea] (Seoul, 2012), pp. 130–35.
31 Hy-Sang Lee, *North Korea: A Strange Socialist Fortress* (Westport, CT, 2001), pp. 182–3.
32 Ibid., pp. 183–4.
33 Donald Oberdorfer, *The Two Koreas: A Contemporary History* (New York, 1998), p. 317.
34 Ibid., p. 322.
35 Ibid., pp. 332–3.
36 Martin, *Under the Loving Care of the Fatherly Leader*, pp. 496–7.
37 Arms Control Organization, 'The U.S.–North Korean Agreed Framework at a Glance', www.armscontrol.org, accessed 14 January 2017.
38 Oberdorfer, *The Two Koreas*, p. 338.
39 Ibid., p. 339.
40 Ibid.
41 Much of this is based on what North Korean officials told American journalist Julie Moon, see Oberdorfer, *The Two Koreas*, pp. 339–40.
42 Ibid., p. 341.
43 Ibid., p. 333.
44 Ibid., p. 340.
45 Fujimoto Kenji, *Kim Chŏng-il ŭi yorisa* [Cook of Kim Jong Il], trans. Sin Hyŏn-do (Seoul, 2003), p. 233.
46 Martin, *Under the Loving Care of the Fatherly Leader*, p. 507.
47 For an example, see Yeonmi Park, *In Order to Live: A North Korean Girl's Journey to Freedom* (New York, 2016).
48 Fujimoto, *Kim Chŏng-il ŭi yorisa*, p. 233.
49 Martin, *Under the Loving Care of the Fatherly Leader*, p. 507.
50 T. R. Reed, 'Tumultuous Funeral for North Korean', *Washington Post*, 19 July 1994.

Bibliography

Bermudez, Joseph S., *The Armed Forces of North Korea* (London, 2001)

Buzo, Adrian, *Politics and Leadership in North Korea: The Guerilla Dynasty*, 2nd revd edn (London, 2018)

Cha, Victor, *The Impossible State: North Korea, Past and Future* (New York, 2012)

Chen, Jian, *China's Road to the Korean War: The Making of the Sino-American Confrontation* (New York, 1994)

Choe, Yong-ho, 'Christian Background in the Early Life of Kim Il-Song', *Asian Survey*, XXVI/10 (1986), pp. 1082–91

Chung, Chin O., *Pyŏngyang between Peking and Moscow: North Korea's Involvement in the Sino-Soviet Dispute, 1958–1975* (Tuscaloosa, AL, 1978)

Collins, Robert, *Marked for Life: Songbun, North Korea's Social Classification System* (Washington, DC, 2015), available at www.hrunk.org

Fischer, Paul, *A Kim Jong Il Production: The Extraordinary True Story of a Kidnapped Filmmaker, His Star Actress, and a Young Dictator's Rise to Power* (New York, 2015)

Han, Hongkoo, 'Colonial Origins of Juche: The Minsaengdan Incident of the 1930s and the Birth of the North Korea–China Relationship', in *Origins of North Korea's Juche*, ed. Jae-Jung Suh (Lanham, MD, 2012), pp. 37–63

Hassig, Ralph, and Kongdan Oh, *The Hidden People of North Korea: Everyday Life in the Hermit Kingdom* (Lanham, MD, 2009)

Hawk, David R., *The Hidden Gulag: The Lives and Voices of 'Those Who are Sent to the Mountains'*, 2nd edn (Washington, DC, 2012)

Jager, Sheila Miyoshi, *Brothers at War: The Unending Conflict in Korea* (New York, 2013)

Kim, Hakjoon, *Dynasty: The Hereditary Succession Politics of North Korea* (Stanford, CA, 2015)

Kim Il Sung, *With the Century*, 8 vols (Pyongyang, 1993–4)

Kim, Suzy, *Everyday Life in the North Korean Revolution, 1945–1950* (Ithaca, NY, 2013)

Kim, Yongho, *North Korean Foreign Policy: Security Dilemma and Succession* (Lanham, MD, 2011)

Koh, Byung Chul, *The Foreign Policy Systems of North and South Korea* (Berkeley, CA, 1984)

Kwon, Heonik, and Byung-ho Chung, *North Korea: Beyond Charismatic Politics* (Lanham, MD, 2012)
Lankov, Andrei, *Crisis in North Korea: The Failure of De-Stalinization, 1956* (Honolulu, HI, 2005)
—, 'Kim Takes Control: The "Great Purge" in North Korea, 1956–1960', *Korean Studies*, XVI/1 (2002), pp. 92–3
—, *North of the DMZ: Essays on Daily Life in North Korea* (Jefferson, NC, 2007)
Lee, Chong-sik, *The Korean Workers' Party: A Short History* (Stanford, CA, 1978)
Lee, Hy-Sang, *North Korea: A Strange Socialist Fortress* (Westport, CT, 2001)
Lee, Jungsoo, *The Partition of Korea after World War II: A Global History* (New York, 2006)
Lee, Mun Woong, *Rural North Korea under Communism: A Study of Sociocultural Change* (Houston, TX, 1976)
Lim, Jae-Cheon, *Leader Symbols and Personality Cult in North Korea* (London, 2015)
—, *Power and the Elite in North Korea: Paektu and Kanbu* (London, 2024)
Martin, Bradley, *Under the Loving Care of the Fatherly Leader* (New York, 2006)
Nam, Koon Woo, *The North Korean Communist Leadership, 1945–1965: A Study of Factionalism and Political Consolidation* (Tuscaloosa, AL, 1974)
Natsios, Andrew S., *The Great North Korean Famine* (Washington, DC, 2001)
Oberdorfer, Donald, *The Two Koreas: A Contemporary History* (New York, 1998)
Party History Institute, *Brief History of the Revolutionary Activities of Comrade Kim Il Sung* (Pyongyang, 1969)
Ree, Erik Van, *Socialism in One Zone: Stalin's Policy in Korea, 1945–1947* (Oxford, 1989)
Salisbury, Harrison, *To Peking and Beyond: A Report on the New Asia* (New York, 1973)
Scalapino, Robert, and Chong-sik Lee, *Communism in Korea* (Berkeley, CA, 1972)
Seiler, Sydney, *Kim Il-song, 1941–1948: The Creation of a Legend, the Building of a Regime* (Lanham, MD, 1994)
Shen, Zhihua, and Danhui Li, *After Leaning to One Side: China and Its Allies in the Cold War* (Stanford, CA, 2011)
Suh, Dae-Sook, *Kim Il Sung: The North Korean Leader* (New York, 1988)
Szalontai, Balázs, *Kim Il Sung in the Khrushchev Era: Soviet–DPRK Relations and the Roots of North Korean Despotism, 1953–1964* (Stanford, CA, 2006)
Tertitskiy, Fyodor, 'The Personal File of Jin Richeng (Kim Il-sung): New Information on the Early Years of the First Ruler of North Korea', *Acta Koreana*, XXII/1 (2019), pp. 111–28
—, 'Will the Real Kim Il Sung Please Stand Up?', NK *News*, www.nknews.org, 18 July 2022
Wada, Haruki, *The Korean War: An International History* (Lanham, MD, 2014)

Weathersby, Kathryn, 'From the Russian Archives: New Findings on the Korean War, *Cold War International History Project Bulletin*, 3 (Fall, 1993), pp. 16–26

—, 'Korea, 1945–50, To Attack, or Not to Attack? Stalin, Kim Il Sung, and the Prelude to War', *Cold War International History Project Bulletin*, 5 (Spring 1995), pp. 1–9

Young, Benjamin R., *Guns, Guerillas, and the Great Leader: North Korea and the Third World* (Stanford, CA, 2019)

Zhang, Shu Guang, *Mao's Military Romanticism: China and the Korean War, 1950–1953* (Lawrence, KS, 1995)

Index